SPLIT

SPLIT

A Double Memoir

LYDIA KNIGHT

JAMES FAN

WITH STEELE CAMPBELL

GOOD
MEDICINE
PRESS

Split: A Double Memoir

For permissions, contact goodmedicinepress@gmail.com

Published by Good Medicine Press
Santa Fe, NM 87506
https://goodmedicinepress.com

ISBN: 978-1-967446-02-5
First Edition: Aug 2025
Library of Congress Control Number: 2025945147

Cover design by Kels Quinn & Steele Campbell
Ghostwritten by Steele Campbell

This is a work of nonfiction. While all attempts have been made to verify the information provided, the author does not assume any responsibility for errors, omissions, or contrary interpretation of the subject matter herein. Names, including the authors', have been changed for privacy.

Printed in the United States of America

To every woman discovering her truth.

*"The green hills cannot forever block the river;
it will flow east in the end."*

-Xin Qiji
Song Dynasty Poet

My Father

We had to keep running. My mom said he could be anywhere. He could hide triggers or send others to trigger us. Once triggered, we couldn't know what we would do. Our other selves would come out, split from our daily selves in mindless obedience. Then the worst would happen—even worse than what had already happened. And what happened was already too much. I can't remember it all. My mom said that part of the brainwashing was I would forget all the horrible things. And thank goodness. Or rather, thank God.

It was because of God we escaped when we did. We prayed to thank Him every day and again at night. We could receive answers and protection from the Lord. His was the good that would win against all evil, even evil as widespread as the cult.

God knew about the cult and knew we were running from them. If we listened carefully, we would know what to do. When I was small, I did not know how to listen to God yet, but my mom did. She would work with God to keep us safe. My mom assured us of this whenever we were scared, which was often. She also told us we should be scared.

We were running from The Fly. That's what we called him. Just like a house fly, he could be very still and stalk about unnoticed. Then, when the room became quiet, he would buzz, making himself known while remaining impossible to catch. This would be fine if he were just a house fly. But this man wanted to hurt us. To take us away. We had to watch for any signs he might be around. We had to stay alert.

We were scared now that we knew what we ran from. I don't remember if we were scared when we first left. Before my mom knew he was dangerous, we lived with The Fly. I called him Daddy. Victor, two years younger than me, didn't call him anything. He wasn't yet born when we left. And he never spoke when we visited The Fly. Victor didn't want any of his words to be used as tools in The Fly's mouth.

I remember leaving his house but not the house itself. I must've pushed it from my memory along with the horrible things that happened there. This was a way my body kept me safe. I did not want to remember. The memories could trigger me, then I would be helpless against the cult. Then I would leave my mom forever. I remember a fence around The Fly's house in Los Angeles. I think the fence was brown and always had many cars parked alongside the front. The house could be any color. I don't try to recall which. The only clear memory I have is leaving the house and looking back upon it. Then we went to live with G-ma.

I never referred to him as my dad, or father, or even by his first name. It was always The Fly. My mom used to live with him. So did I. When she met him, she couldn't have known what he truly was or how he would use her to get to us. My mom helped me remember the things I could not. She told me the stories that I had forgotten. She said it was important I knew these things so I would know what to look out for and the horrors we escaped.

My mom was very careful to keep us safe. Danger could be anywhere, and she was always watchful. Once, after we had been staying with G-ma and Grandpa Tom in the Hollywood Hills, The Fly came for us. G-ma told us to stay inside while she went out to talk to him. He threatened her, but she stood strong for us. She would not let him take us away. God knows what would have happened. Maybe God doesn't know that. But Satan surely does.

The Fly yelled and screamed at G-ma to let him have us, but she wouldn't. She wouldn't even let my mom outside for fear of her safety. When G-ma came back inside, The Fly took a rock from the pond and broke the large pane of glass on the door. It split and splintered and bowed in and out every time he pounded, demanding to be let in. It was a miracle it could hold him back. The door held strong solely thanks to the angels of the Lord. We were scared The Fly would come in and take us away for good. G-ma got her gun and called the police. She guarded us until they came and The Fly left.

As soon as he left the angels let go, and the glass in the door shattered to the floor. We were safe once again. After that, G-ma would not tell him if we were home whenever he called for us. She refused to let him know anything more about us.

He could be suddenly dangerous. At times, he might seem kind and caring. This was a false face he wore. My mom told us to be wary. He was a master of deception and knew when and where we would be vulnerable.

G-ma even told us how once, when my mom and Victor and I were out, that The Fly came looking for her. Not for us, but for her. He knocked on the door. G-ma knew it was him. She didn't answer. She thought he had come unannounced to find us and take us away when our guard would be down. No one knew to expect him. He knocked again. G-ma waited in silence. He knocked harder. G-ma thought that if she stayed motionless, he would think we were not home and leave.

He called G-ma's name. "Angela, Angela." Then she was scared. She didn't know why he was looking for her or how he knew she was home by herself. She stayed still and hoped he would go away. She thought The Fly had been with Grandpa Tom just before that. Now she worried what had happened to her husband. He could be dead and she would be next. The Fly knocked on the window and called her name again. She didn't want to move for fear she would make a noise. She couldn't call the police because then he would know she was there alone. She told us how scared she was. She thought she would never see us again.

G-ma worried that The Fly had already found us. For all she knew, Grandpa Tom could be hurt or worse. So could we. She shook with fear. She could be the next victim. She didn't know what The Fly was capable of or who else he had with him. As part of the cult, others would join him for their evil deeds. They would revel in hurting someone who knew what they did in dark places.

We had to first run to G-ma's house in the Hollywood Hills and then out of state entirely. Even though the court had told my mom to stay in Los Angeles, she had to keep us safe. She said she followed a higher law: God's law. She was given children to care for and protect. If she listened to God, she could do just that. Only He could not lead us astray.

We escaped. Not many people had ever escaped the cult. But we did. We were sure, or at least my mom was—which was good enough for us—that the cult knew we had escaped. And they kept looking. So we kept running.

我的父親

My Father

I have many appreciations.

I lived a simple life. A good life. As kids we only worried about food. That is all. As long as we had food enough for our family and had one another, we had everything. We had a house by the riverbank, a well inside the house, very deep, and Father traded for the rice and oil we need. Mama cooked for us. Very good food. We ate together as family. Very simple.

The street in front of the house was so full of people always. There were kids my age to play with, and there were older kids who wore the school uniform and played at games which didn't include me. My third sister, Xinyi, said I cannot play with them until I dress in school uniform. And she told me I cannot go to school if I don't know my characters. I didn't know them all, but I could read better than Mama. I trusted Xinyi to tell me the truth—she had her uniform for two years already and brought home good marks.

Father's friends would come to sit in the courtyard beside the house. Some would stay for days. They would drink, argue, smoke, and tease me and my sisters. And they laughed. Always laughing. They seemed very happy to be there, like me. Mama was the only one who was not happy. She did not like them staying around, and, at night, I could hear her yelling at Father. He would not yell back, but he did not change.

Father could do everything so good, but he did not do. He would sit with his friends, and they would drink rice wine my father brought out in small wooden barrels. He would say life was better when the Japanese soldiers had gone and Chiang Kai-shek's soldiers came from the mainland. They took down all the signs in Japanese. All things now were in Mandarin. "The way it should be," Father says. "This is better. More simple." He says this, but the Japanese soldiers are not the ones that put him in jail or took the land away.

They put him in jail for making rice wine. He said it was because he sold wine to the wrong soldiers, not for making it. "Everybody likes to drink," he said. But Mama didn't drink. She said drinking makes devils of men where they cannot be trusted. None of us kids would drink. Father drank enough for all of us. He was true to his word. He would rather do than talk. And rather drink than do. He was very smart. I knew he is smart because I came from him and I am very smart. Plus, he could do anything he wanted to do, but he didn't want. I wanted, but yet I could not do.

Father always did what he wanted. He was born last after six brothers and six sisters, and if he did not find food for himself, there would've been none left at the table for him. He learned how to cook and how to find food. He also learned he liked to drink wine. So, he learned to make wine. He spent more time with his wine than he did at home. But I loved him more than home, so I would go with him when he hiked past the army camp and up the hill to his hidden still.

His wine was always very good, even when he was young and could not be seen in public drinking. He loved his wine and loved to drink it with others. Good for him that everyone else loved to drink his wine too. It was the best wine around. Even the Japanese soldiers knew this. This is why they left his still alone. They never put him in jail, but they did not leave him alone.

Before I was born, there were Japanese soldiers always at the house, sitting and drinking with Father. Mama didn't like this, but at least they were not causing trouble. Father assured her they would keep all of us safe. That was part true. There was no place to buy any wine anywhere, so Father's business grew. Pretty soon there were more soldiers at the house. Men my father didn't know would come to buy wine from him. Some would stay, some would take their bottles and leave with their friends, leaving Father with a handful of money. He would never count it in front of them. That was rude. Mama counted it as soon as she could and put it away in a place she thought was hidden from Father.

The Japanese soldiers took what they wanted for their own. They had land, houses they never used, and so much money. They liked Father. He was always generous and welcoming. And he had rice wine. They liked it, so they appreciated him. The soldiers would greet him in the street and bow. He was very popular with them and seen as successful. But they all left.

When the Japanese soldiers left Taiwan, they could only take their uniforms and their guns. They also took as much rice wine as they could because it was better here. They could not take their houses and land. They did not take their signs, their new roads, or army camp. These they left for the new government. Their land and houses they gave away. They could not own anything in Taiwan, so many gave the deeds to land and houses across the city to Father. He bowed very deep and pushed bladders of rice wine into their hands. Mama was in tears when she saw the deeds pile up in the little house. Father had turned down living on Mama's family land because he didn't want to be seen all the time drinking. Instead, they lived in the small house where my first and second sisters and first brother were born. Now they could move to any house they wanted. They had so many to choose.

These new houses came with one condition: that Father continue to make rice wine and send it to Japan. The soldiers knew what they wanted from him. And they knew he would agree. To them, everyone in Taiwan always agrees. Disagreeing was against the law. So was making the rice wine, and selling the rice wine, and drinking the rice wine. But breaking one law could land you in prison, while breaking the other could gift you friends and fortune. Father always prided himself in knowing which laws he could break and which he had to follow. Mama told him to follow all the rules, that nothing was worth the risk of punishment. The soldiers could take anything, even family, she told him. But Father would not give up his drinking. He figured a way to have what he wanted and keep his freedom.

Before Chiang Kai-shek arrived from China with his gold and his thousands of soldiers, Father did very well. He would make rice wine and stack the barrels in an empty storeroom, then carry them at night to the flat ships bound for Japan. He covered the barrels with mint leaves so the alcohol could not be smelled, and he wrote 'Tea Leaves' in Mandarin and Japanese on the barrel. This worked very well, and Father often talked about expanding his business. He could turn one of the unused storefronts he now owned into a commercial still. He would make us rich, he dreamed while dipping his ladle into a fresh barrel. Mama dreamed of wearing fancy clothes and having more than one room for my first and second sisters and my first brother.

Then one day, before I was born, Chiang Kai-shek's soldiers came to the house early in the morning to take Father away. He went without protest, handcuffed and looking straight ahead of him. Mama wept in the street and called after him. She yelled at the soldiers that they shouldn't do this—Father was Chinese and they were Chinese. She yelled that we are not the enemy. That we are loyal. They did not listen. They locked Father up in prison where he could not drink.

In prison they do not give the prisoners anything but water to drink, and they gave them no food.

Mama had to feed my father. She would pack up a lunch and walk to the jail so Father could eat. It was two hours walking, and Mama would go every day. She had to leave my first and second sisters and first brother and third sister, who was very small, with the neighbors and make the long journey alone. Her children were growing and constantly hungry. They did not see her for most of the day. Mama was tired and running out of money for food. At least there were no strange men at the house.

Mama was at peace for a while until soldiers came to the house. At first, she sent them away. They came back again and again. These soldiers were not like the others. They did not ask for rice wine, and they did not ask for Father. They knew Father was in jail and that he owned deeds to houses and land. Every time Mama told them to talk to Father, but they would come back the next day to talk to her. Mama could not read, and who knows what lies the soldiers told her. They had come to talk to her day after day for months, and Mama still walked to the jail everyday with food for Father, even though it was little more than rice and broth. The soldiers told her that without my father she could not live in any of the properties, and that unless she signed the papers, my father would never get out of jail. In order for him to ever come home, they told her, she would have to sign the deeds to them.

I think eventually Mama tired of saying No. My siblings would ask for more food, Father would ask if there was any news of getting him free, and the soldiers would ask for the houses and land.

She told everyone No, until she couldn't anymore. She signed the deeds and was able to tell each of them Yes. Finally.

Father was not happy the land and houses were gone. Mama felt that they had come to him because of drink and left him because of drink, so it was all the same. Father got his freedom; the soldiers took the land; and my family moved back to the house on the riverbank where we had enough food. Life was simple again. Then I was born.

My Brother

My brother and I met Susan through the Victims of Violent Crime program in California. She was our therapist, or counselor, or psychologist—she was someone my mom and grandmother had found for us to talk to. Susan knew about the cult and their kind of abuse. My mom and G-ma knew we needed someone who could understand. I never asked my mom if Susan was part of the cult herself. Not many outsiders knew how it worked. But apparently, Susan was safe. She said she was there to help, though to me she just asked questions. If you had asked Victor, she was simply there while he played.

Susan was also my mom's therapist. The routine never changed: my mom would go in for her session while Victor and I sat in folding chairs outside the office. When she finished, she'd take us both by the hands and lead us into Susan's office. Toys were on the floor and board games on the shelves. But before we could play, Victor had to build his egg. Every single time, he'd take all the couch cushions and construct an egg on the floor. He'd climb inside and pull the last piece shut, sitting quietly for a while. With a grand gesture, he'd pop out. Then we would play.

Susan would observe us, saying nothing. She would just watch, and we would play. Toward the end of our time, she would sit down on the floor beside us. We knew what came next. She'd peer over the tops of her glasses and say, "Oh, right now can I ask you a couple questions?"

Alright.

"Like you want to talk about... is there anything you want to talk about?"

"No, not really," I would say.

"Here, let me ask you some questions." She'd ready her pen on her clipboard and look straight at me. Victor never spoke to her, so she didn't ask him.

The questioning matched what G-ma would ask me at home. G-ma would sit at her vanity applying powder. It seemed she spent so much time in front of the ornate mirror and the row of shaped glass jars half-filled with creams. She'd pause while I watched and crouch down close to me. "Do you remember how they hurt you?"

I would try to remember. I was just a little kid, maybe four or five, staring up at G-ma's looming face. Nothing came to mind, which always disturbed me. Something so horrible had happened to me and I couldn't remember any of it. The cult had abused me, used me in their evil rituals and then erased my memories to protect themselves. I feared I was still under their control. Nothing could bring the memories back.

G-ma's questions would get more specific. "Did they hurt you with a stick?"

That sounded right, so I'd agree. G-ma would nod, mostly to herself, much like Susan.

"Do you remember what they hurt you with? Try." Susan asked, kneeling beside me.

"Um, a stick."

"Yes, Ok." She would nod. sometimes closing her eyes. "What color was it?"

"Red."

"Red because of blood?"

"Um, yes."

"Ok." Susan would look at her clipboard. No one ever questioned my answers or corrected me. "Good job," they'd say. "Thank you for telling me."

I assumed I must have the right answer. It seemed the adults already knew the answers. They knew everything about the cult, much more than me. They weren't asking to learn; they were asking to confirm I knew what they did.

When they nodded and said, "Yes, good," I trusted my response. I was remembering correctly. I kept talking, reassured. Whatever I couldn't remember from G-ma, I'd just guess. The first thing that popped into my head always felt right. I thought that was memory. Susan was there to confirm it.

Between Susan and my mom, they knew everything. We saw Susan for a long time. During appointments, we'd play and she'd ask some specifics. "I don't want to cause flashbacks, but can you try to remember what happened? Did you know you can have flashbacks of the abuse?"

"Yes." I always got that one right.

I told her that I was tied to a table. The table had a star on it, but it was upside down. Many men walked around in circles, pointing sharp things at me. They told me they would cut my eyes with knives. They told me they were going to eat my brother. They would possibly eat me too, but first were going to cut me open, and break my bones, then heal me so they could do it again. They said they locked my mom in a dark closet where she could hear me scream but couldn't see anything. They warned that one day my mom would try to kill me. I told Susan everything, but she already knew. And now she knew I knew.

"Did this happen?" She would ask. I would agree. "When that happened, what was that like? How bad was it?" She wanted all the worst details. I repeated what I'd heard, hoping my hearsay would excuse my missing memories. I couldn't remember the worst parts of it, the breaking bones and the rape. The cult had erased those memories. It made me sad when I couldn't remember because that meant the cult could still control part of my brain, I was still connected to them.

After answering Susan's questions, we got to pick any flavor fruit roll-up from the big drawer under her bookshelves. We never had them at home, so it was a thrill.

Susan helped keep us safe. She warned us about unexpected flashbacks. She explained how the cult programmed our brains through abuse. She told my mom I would have violent flashbacks on my wedding night. My first sexual experience would trigger memories of cult abuse, rape, and ritual torture. The cult had erased my memories, but my body remembered. That night could split my personality, maybe forever. Susan and my mom got along very well. Together they knew what to watch for and how to prevent the cult from splitting me to another personality. Then I wouldn't know what I'd do, or who I'd be. But I wouldn't be me.

Years later, in college, I wrote Susan a thank-you note expressing my gratitude. I had stayed safe all this time. Partly because of what she had known and what she helped me know too. Victor liked the strawberry fruit roll-ups best, and popping out of his egg. He also stayed safe.

二哥

Second Brother

By the time I was born we lived in the house by the riverbank and Father was making rice wine again. After jail he stopped for a while, but he missed the taste of his own, and the friends it brought him, and the money. Mama did not want him to make any more, or to drink any more, but Father did what he wanted to do. And when he brought the money home, Mama would hide it away and not say anything more about his drink. Then, when I could walk, I had a fourth sister, Ya-chi, and two years after that a second brother, Cheng.

I played in the courtyard with Ya-chi and all the kids from other houses and waited for my day when I could go to school. My second brother stayed with Mama all day, crawling behind her. When he crawled too far from the door, Mama called to me to bring him back to her. I could lift him, but Mama told me not to carry him, so I would say his name and he could crawl to me. Then I backed up closer to Mama and called again, then again. He was small, but very smart.

One time Cheng won a contest for being smart. All the mothers put their crawling babies at one end of a yard. They placed a board as tall as a sitting baby in the middle and the mothers called from the other side. Many of the babies crawled to the board but cannot cross. Only Cheng climbed the board to reach Mama. She was very proud of him. I wondered if I won the baby challenge, but Mama said I was too big for the game. My third sister, Xinyi, said I still was too small for her games. But I don't have to be big to appreciate how good life is.

Father stayed home a lot. He also drank a lot. My first brother said it is not much different having him home except Mama doesn't walk to the jail. It was nice to have him home. He was always happy and laughing. Everyone was happy to see him. They called him Mr. Nice Guy. When he was not at home drinking, he was either making more rice wine or helping another family.

Father understood the medicine hidden in wild plants and how to use it. Very useful. He was proud to support his friends, and many times when someone near killed a pig, or had extra eggs, they brought them to us and left them in Mama's hands. She offered to pay them though there never was much money. They would refuse and bow to her, saying they are grateful for Father. His good nature helped everyone else to have a good nature toward us.

His influence even spread up to the army camp up the hill. Over four thousand of Chiang Kai-shek's soldiers lived in the barracks up there. We could see their trucks going up the long road and through the gates. Sometimes a few of them walked by and Mama would get nervous. She refused to talk to them, and they only stopped in when Father was home. He would invite them to sit and give them rice wine to drink. They often drank, but did not usually sit. Father said that helping them will create better opportunities for all of us. Mama said that he must look after family first, and that no earthly success can ever justify a failure in the home. Mama couldn't read, but was very wise. Father would laugh and pat her hands. "Our home is Taiwan," he would say. "So large."

When soldiers I recognize came by, they would ask if I am old enough to go to school. "I am not yet old enough," I tell them. "But I am ready." I would salute to them, which made them laugh. They liked me, and I could appreciate them here. Just as I appreciated Father, always helping and happy. This was a good life. Everyone was at home, and everyone else was our friend. This was all we needed for happiness. With our family together, nothing could go wrong.

Many times it would rain for days. The water in the river turned brown and moved in waves like the ocean. Sometimes the ocean pushed back against the river and there was too much water every-where. Then the sun would come out, and Taiwan grew even stronger because of the rain. "It must rain if everything is to grow," Father says. So much rain, so much Taiwan. And everything always was green. Plants grew in the courtyard from between the tight stones.

The spring before I started elementary school was very wet. The rain was warm. My third sister Xinyi and I would lay on the stones in the courtyard and let the rain wash over us, or we would play where the water ran down the street like little streams. My fourth sister would play with us too. We would set leaves in a stream and watch them race down the road, goading them forward with sticks. My second brother, Cheng, would want to play. But he toddled slowly, and Mama did not like him to wander where she could not see.

Our house was small, and Father would leave supplies in the courtyard to not take up space for our family. He would have stacks of barrels to be filled or a wheelbarrow of leaves he had brought from the mountain. Once he left an empty bucket out at the end of the courtyard that maybe went forgotten or maybe we did not notice it there. It was Cheng who found it.

Mama was talking to many of the other ladies who lived near when Cheng discovered the bucket. It had filled with rain water. Perhaps Cheng splashed in it, watching his reflection ripple apart then piece back together in waves. Perhaps he was thirsty. No one can be sure. Mama found him toppled inside the bucket, only his legs visible. She screamed and the other women came running. They held him upside down and tried to shake the water from his lungs. Water dripped from him. They laid him on the warm stones and rubbed the blue from his cheeks. They rubbed his hands. But they could not rub the life back into him.

When Father came home, Mama sat in the courtyard with Cheng in her arms. She rubbed his head, smoothing his forehead and cheeks, and she wept. She did not see Father come. And Mama would not look at him when she did see.

Mama wanted to blame Father for leaving the bucket. She wanted to blame this too on Father's drink. It was no more Father's fault than the rain's. She could not blame Cheng. So she blamed herself. Father never blamed anyone.

Mama stayed inside and cried. She did not know what to do. She wailed that she had failed her family, her children. Many of her friends visited. Not many would she allow in. We would tell them she could not see them. It would be rude for her to say so. The few who she did see all said the same: that she could find peace from so much suffering in Buddha. Eventually she agreed with them. This would be her way for penance, her only way for rest, she said. When she made the decision to devote her life to the Buddhist Temple, not even Father could deny the light in her eyes.

When Mama went to Temple, she took my first sister, my second sister, and my fourth sister. My first and second sisters were donated to the temple. They would live there and work there for free, no pay. My fourth sister was too small to work and too small to be left behind, so she would go with Mama. They each packed up only a change of clothes and a bowl and left our home. Though there were four of us in the small house by the river, it felt empty without them there.

My father, first brother, Tsung-han, third sister, Xinyi, and I stayed in the house on the riverbank when Mama went to live at the Buddhist Temple on the mountain. It was hours and hours away and we did not see her or my other sisters. There were not many people who lived on the mountainside. Up there they had no school, so we stayed by the river. It was supposed to be the four of us together, but after Cheng drowned, it was mostly just three.

Father was never home. We could not find him at the still or at the neighbors'. The men who wanted rice wine stopped coming by. The soldiers too did not stop at our house anymore. Except one. One soldier who was high up in the army knew Father and knew what had happened. He would stop by and ask my brother if Father had been home recently. Some days he would leave a little package of rice or a fish for us to eat.

We did not have much to eat, but what we could find we would eat. Instead of school, Tsung-han and Xinyi and I would hunt for food. There is so much that can grow in the wild. We would pick guava, catch fish in the riverbank, and shoot birds with a slingshot. Tsung-han was a very good shot. What we killed we would eat. Sometimes the neighbors would offer us some vegetables when they had more than enough. Xinyi, who was only seven years old, would make a fire and cook what we could find. We ran wild along the hills and no neighbors said anything. They knew Mama had left, and if they knew where Father was, they did not say. Some days he would come home, bring food, sleep for a long time, then go off again.

One day when Tsung-han and I were hunting for birds we discovered endless food. Our life was going to be so good—even better. At the army camp up the hill they fed all the soldiers. The soldiers ate behind the gates. We were not allowed inside the gates. Neither was the trash truck that came every week to empty their bin. They had built the bin half inside and half outside the tall walls with tops of sharp wire. This way the trash collector could take it away without going inside. It was the half outside we discovered. There was a heavy metal door we had to slide to one side. Inside were piles of uneaten food. We had the burnt rings of rice when someone left it on the pot too long, piles of steamed vegetables the soldiers did not finish, and all kinds of fruit that was only a little bruised. Still perfectly good. And much better than being hungry. Tsung-han would load the front of my shirt full and we would scamper down the hill. We were very well fed, and kept Xinyi fed as well.

Sometimes Father would stop by home and bring rice and oil. He would never eat the food. He would sleep, and then be gone again. We never knew where to find him. One time the heavy rains came and the sky was dark for days. The river grew sharp waves and turned brown with mud. Then the waves of the river started to move backward. The sea was pushing back against the river and all the water had no place to go. Many of our neighbors left their homes. But we had no place to go without Father. We could not find him, so we had to wait.

We knew all this water was not just the sea. It was a typhoon. When the water began jumping out of the riverbed and onto the street in front of the house, we ran inside and sat upon the highest bed in the darkness. Father did not come then. Soon the waves splashed in the courtyard, and we could hear the sounds of water in Mama's kitchen outside. Father still did not come. Then we heard a knock at the door.

The door opened before we could reach it, and a soldier stood in the grey-green light with the storm clouds behind him. It was the officer who brought us food. He did not ask us where Father was. He did not ask us anything. "Come," he told us. We followed him into the rain and wind. I held Xinyi's hand and we left our house by the riverbank.

The officer took us inside the army camp and showed us to a bed. The winds were strong and the rain cut through the windows made of paper. We sat in the dark and wondered if we would ever see Father again. The typhoon raged all night and not one of us slept. We huddled on the bed together, quiet and scared. No one mentioned Father, though we all thought of him. We knew he wouldn't leave us. Not for good. He wouldn't fail his family. Family was the most important thing. More important than food or a house on the riverbank or a temple or even a typhoon.

Late the next day, after the storm had clashed against the mountain and retreated, the officer sent us home with full bellies and little sacks of food. On the walk down to the riverbank we saw trees had split or had been blown down. There were houses without roofs, great sections of walls missing. Branches were everywhere. However, our house by the riverbank still stood. The courtyard had been filled with water and it washed away everything we had left outside. Pieces were missing from the roof tiles, and the door laid on the ground in front like a welcome mat. On the top step before the door sat Father. He was dry. And alive. He ran to us, picked each of us up, and held us. He said to us then, that there was not any sense in a family that was not together. We should all be one.

We should be together to care for each other. To love each other. He said we would leave our house on the riverbank and join my mother by the Buddhist Temple. We would be a family once again. The storm had not left much of anything, so we did not have to pack. It was not sad to leave. We soon would be all together. As a family, we left the riverbank for a new home.

Finding Space

Growing up, where I lived was the experience of extremes. We lived either in luxury as unwelcome guests or in stark poverty by ourselves. The choice wasn't mine—I followed my mom, though it seemed even she had limited control. Greater forces governed our lives: the courts, the cult, The Fly, money, the Lord. When we had to move, Mom would cite one of these powers as if they were the ultimate authority we must obey. It wasn't her fault. She was under the same pressures we were.

After escaping The Fly, we fled to G-ma's house in the Hollywood Hills. This was luxury. G-ma had always been fancy. During Grandpa Tom's time as a foreign diplomat, she hosted very important dinners with very important people. She would recount lengthy stories of their conversations and how they complimented her. She would say their names, then pause and more loudly say, "You might not know who they are, but they are VERY important." G-ma and Grandpa had lived throughout Africa and South America in places with long, important names filled with equally important people. G-ma never ran out of stories.

The house in the Hollywood Hills, as G-ma would always say as though there were another nearby, was extravagant. The heavy wooden door had a frosted glass panel in the center which let the light in but none of the shapes. Inside stood two stone lions guarding a great hall. The parlor housed couches we couldn't sit on. The dining table we never used was long and beautiful with a little carved ring near the edge I would trace with my fingers. Eight place settings usually sat upon the polished wood.

When guests visited, G-ma would rearrange the table settings, set out name cards, and bring in help to host. The visitors would talk loudly first in the parlor, their voices carrying through the house, before moving to that grand table for dinner and laughter. My mom, brother, and I would stay unseen in the back of the house, eating off plates balanced on chairs while sitting on the kitchen floor. Sometimes I would slink along the cold walls, hidden from view, to eavesdrop on the grown-ups, but when Mom noticed me, I would come back with her, waiting for either the guests to leave or for sleep.

That grand table and its laughter belonged to guests and Grandpa Tom alone. Even when no one was visiting, we ate in the kitchen, sometimes standing over the stove eating straight from the pans. Then we could go back to being invisible.

We stayed in the guest room, though we weren't guests. G-ma told everyone we were visiting but she did not tell them for how long. The one bed in the room went to Mom. My brother and I slept in sleeping bags on the floor. On rare occasions I would sleep on top of the bed but never in it. We would roll our sleeping bags on top of the quilt and snuggle in. We had to keep the room ready for real guests, so we could not dirty the sheets or rumple the covers.

This didn't prevent the mess.

G-ma did not like a mess. Her house was supposed to be kept quiet with everything in its exact place and no clutter in sight. Still, she'd apologize to every visitor: "Oh, I didn't have time to clean everything up, you know how life gets." This was not true. She had time and did clean. She did not want to give the impression that she had cleaned, rather that this was as messy as the house became. Guests never saw the guest room.

My mom kept her own space cluttered to keep G-ma away. That's what she said. G-ma had always hated messes, so my mom learned to be messy. There was always stuff on the floor, stuff everywhere we stayed. There would be papers on the floor, wrappers left where things were opened, and clothes piled wherever they fell.

Sometimes G-ma would look into the room and scowl at the debris strewn everywhere. Other times she would spit at it in a really exaggerated way so we could not deny her displeasure.

This defensive mess kept G-ma out, but we still lived there. We'd make our beds on top of all the chaos, our sleeping bags unfurled over the papers and clothes as extra cushioning and sleep. Each morning we'd roll up our sleeping bags to avoid adding to the clutter. Unless we forgot. Then we would pull our sleeping bags from under the day's debris and lay them again on top.

We were always there. I wasn't in school yet, and Victor was just a toddler. My mom didn't work and neither did G-ma, so the four of us would be in that house for days without leaving. We weren't allowed to go in the living room. We weren't allowed to touch anything that wasn't ours. G-ma monitored the entire house constantly. The guest room felt like Mom's territory, and the outside belonged to the cult. They didn't own it, but danger lurked among other people—the cult could be anywhere. We might be discovered. I had to stay inside between Mom's world and G-ma's, though I wanted so badly my own space. I dreamed of privacy, of something that belonged just to me.

There was a space in the guest room closet—a sliver of empty space between the dresser and wall, unused and unfilled. Without asking, I claimed it as mine. I would line up my treasures there in neat rows. Shiny rocks I'd collected lined the front. Behind them sat my precious blue lizard I loved so dear. Small and plastic, with the teeth and toes flattening into wisps I would pull while holding it. It had come in a pack of two, but the blue one was mine. Afraid of losing it to the mess, I made it the central guest in my tiny sanctuary. It had a home and so did I. I had a tiny corner no one else wanted. It was mine. There I was not in anyone's way. There, I belonged.

Before I started second grade, we made our escape. All of us together. Mom announced that the endless parade of courts, doctors, and psychiatrists had finally ended. Now we could leave for good—for the best, she said. We moved north to the small town of Beaver, Utah. G-ma relocated too, finding an apartment in St. George and working with a real estate agent to see homes in the area. I thought we were finally free, that The Fly and the cult could never find us this far away. But that hope was too soon. We still needed to hide.

We packed everything from G-ma's house and Mom's storage unit, making the long drive to a single-wide trailer in Beaver. I could barely contain my excitement—I would finally have my own room. I was finally going to have a bed. It was a fold out cot where I could lay my sleeping bag, but at least I wouldn't have to sleep on the floor anymore.

The boxes that filled one side of my room didn't bother me. My mom had grown up all over the world, cared for by nannies while Grandpa Tom worked and G-ma entertained. She had things from everywhere she kept safe in storage until we found our own home. We didn't unpack them in the trailer because we were just renting. This was temporary. We might need to leave again.

I started at a new school with a new name to protect us from the cult. Mom gave Victor and me her previous surname, removing The Fly's name from hers. Other cult members could track us through his name. Then he could find us. But here, far away from him, we felt safe. I had space, a room, and a new identity.

I thought everything was perfect despite our poverty. We'd traded cramped luxury for our own home with little else. We were always on food stamps. Though sometimes we'd run out of food and there would be nothing to do except wait for more stamps. Food stamps only came in once a month. We would stock up. The cupboards and fridge had something on every shelf, and we ate well. It was a time of plenty—another extreme.

Soon the cupboards would start to empty. I'd eat canned peaches and drink the syrup like juice. Or I would sit with my mom and brother on the couch and eat fruit cocktail from the can with a fork. My mom didn't cook every day. She saved proper cooking for special occasions. When hunger struck, she would always offer the same solution: a tortilla with butter. She lived off them, and so did we. A plain flour tortilla, dabbed with butter, rolled into a pinwheel and microwaved for ten seconds. It was warm and kept the hunger from hurting but never satisfied me.

When food ran low, we sometimes visited the Bishop's Storehouse, where the Mormon Church distributed farmers' surplus to those in need. As devout members with little means, we qualified perfectly. But this resource wasn't always available, though I never understood why. I assumed those greater forces had decided for us again. I trusted Mom, who trusted the Lord. We would be provided for.

Sometimes the Lord would provide for us by allowing us to get resourceful. One time the cupboards emptied completely—no fruit cans, no tortillas. In the fridge was nothing but condiments. There wasn't even any milk, not even milk which Mom consumed by the gallon. I searched behind the pans in the lower cabinets. There discovered a large container of sauerkraut and an enormous can of green beans. It was heavy and unopened. I could not lift it from the bottom shelf, but I announced its existence to my mom with pride. We would eat.

That night we had green beans, just plain. The next day we had green beans with mayonnaise. The next was green beans with salt and ketchup. We tried every condiment to try to change the taste of those beans. After a week of nothing but beans I sat crying at the table. I wanted something else. I tried to eat the sauerkraut, but it only paired with more beans. I dreaded coming home from school to those beans. My classmates brought fancy lunches of string cheese, sandwiches cut into triangles, and apples with peanut butter. I thought it was so fancy. I dreamt what it would be like to be rich and have fruit and peanut butter simultaneously.

I ate school lunch while fantasizing about Mom shopping that day. I dreamed of coming home to find milk for her, macaroni and cheese for Victor and me, maybe even a cookie she had bought for us just because. My hunger distracted me from lessons. I wanted so much to eat a warm dinner with different foods like the other kids did. But when I went home for dinner it was green beans without dessert. I didn't know what else to do. I cried. I prayed. And when I hurt from hunger I cried and prayed harder.

It wasn't long before we went back to G-ma's.

安全

Safety

On the mountain I had very good childhood. There was so much to eat. Father built us a house, a strong house that could withstand a typhoon. We all stayed together. Me and Mama and Father. There was also my first brother, my third sister, and my little sister. My first and second sisters lived at Buddhist Temple. We saw them sometimes when we went to school which was built right next to the temple, on the right if you were looking at the big, red doors, on the left from inside.

When we first came to the mountainside, we did not have a home and the whole family could not live at the Temple on the hill. I didn't care; we were together, and there was so much food. I do not think that the land had been cultivated for a thousand million years. Whatever was planted would grow: squash, cucumber, and the mushroom. Father grew so many mushrooms. Even without that we could eat. There were always wild vegetables under the large trees. Wild bamboo was good for eating when small and good for making things when taller. We would cut them down to make toys and little boats to float down the river. Besides that, my first brother and I would hunt. We could catch and eat birds, sometimes snakes, and the large rats who did not seem afraid of us. These were not the same rats that scurried through our home when we lived down by the riverside among the paved streets and small houses of everyone else. Up here they were wild, like the wild pigs, and large. They would stand up on their two back legs and look at us, perhaps as curious to see us as we were to see them. This made them easy to catch and they provided us with a lot of meat. Mama and Father did not eat any of these wild things. There were enough vegetables and wild fruit to keep them full.

Mama and Father only ate meat on the first and fifteenth of the month after we went to Temple. We would cook meat or fish or chicken to offer to the gods. Mama would light some incense and lay the offering before Quan Yin, the goddess she said would look after us children and heal her heart from sadness. We would kneel behind her and chant the Om Mani Padme Hum softly and bow when she bowed. Father did not come to Temple, and soon my first brother stopped coming as well. Mama said nothing about their absence. When walking back from Temple she would tell us that Quan Yin was the way out of negativity and would keep us happy and safe if we trusted in her. I did not trust in Quan Yin, but I trusted in Mama, so I followed her to Temple and back. When we returned, we would eat the offering, now blessed, and Mama would thank the gods for our happiness. Father would continue whatever project he was working on, or sit with friends who brought wine up the mountain to drink with him.

When I came with Father to the mountainside, we did not have a home and we did not have a school. The Temple allowed us to eat there with Mama and my first and second and fourth sister. But we did not stay. Land was different up here than it was next to the riverbank. Down there all the land was divided by the government. First the Chinese owned it all and would give it in deeds to the people. Then the Japanese said it was theirs and made the people pay taxes to them for their own land. Then Chiang Kai-shek's army said it belonged to the people who had the deeds. The people bartered and traded and scammed and forged so they could have the land they wanted. Up here no one knew who owned the land. Mama's family had owned some at one point, but now no one was sure. There were not many people. The ones who were here were all spread out and knew there was more than enough land and space for someone new. They were very kind.

One of our first days on the mountain, we hiked up to the waterfall and higher up the mountain, where we could see over the hillside to the Pacific Ocean. The ground was covered in leaves from the typhoon and many trees were bare. The birds were slow, and we saw monkeys jumping among the branches where they watched us. Father looked at the land for a long time thinking. Then we followed the stream down the mountain until Father stopped. He had learned what he wanted to. Father looked back up the hill and walked into the woods. When he stopped, we knew it was for good. He turned around, placed his hand against a couple nearby trees. Then he smiled. This is where he built our house.

To build a house on the mountain meant you had to move a lot of dirt and cut down many trees. You could have as much land as you wanted if you cut down the trees. Father dug out behind the house and cut down the trees around it. From the trees he built the house, very strong, without using any nails. He built it stronger than a typhoon, he said. If we wanted more land to make more garden, we could cut down more trees. There was so much wood. We would have plenty to cook with and plenty to keep us warm.

We had so much wood, Father began to sell charcoal. He could make the best charcoal. He would dig a long pit and build a fire. Then he would lay a dried tree in the pit and cover it up with dirt. After a couple days he would dig up the tree and it would all be charcoal. This was very valuable to families who didn't live on the mountainside and couldn't make their own. Before we would dig up the tree, Father would put the large wash basin over where the tree was buried and Tsung-Han and I would fill it with water we brought from the stream. It would warm up and we could all take a bath in warm water. It was so good. So warm and safe. Then when the charcoal was dug out and stacked, we would carry it down the mountain to trade for rice and sesame oil. The trip to town and back would take six hours of walking. Sometimes we did this with 40 or 50 pounds on our backs. Often, one of the shopkeepers would feed us steamed buns. Everyone treated Father with kindness. The walk back up was always easier with full bellies and rice for Mama.

Other than the few things we brought up the hill from trading charcoal, the mountain provided all we needed. If we needed something else, Father would make it. If he couldn't make it, he would trade, but most things he could make. He liked to invent things. So did I. I took after him and would invent what I wanted to have.

Once I decided I wanted to fly, so I made wings from the thin bamboo growing in the thrushes and large leaves I could knock down with a long bamboo. It worked pretty good, but not perfect. Near the back of the house, I could climb up the mountain side and jump on the roof. Then I could crawl to the front of the house. When stretched, my wings felt huge and I could see the shadow on the ground beneath me, large and monstrous. Then I would fly. Not very long. Not very far. But for a moment.

More than I liked to fly, I liked to swim. The stream near the house went fast and clear, slowing down here or there where we could fish and swim. We went to the water almost every day. Mama said not to drink it, that the water should be boiled, but water this clear tasted so good.

Often, we would leave school to go to the water. The school was new and so was the teacher. When we were first on the mountainside, there was no school. The families worked together to build a school next to the Temple where my two sisters lived.

The government there said that if we would build the school, they would send a teacher. They sent a teacher and a caretaker. The teacher taught lessons to all of us children in the same room. The caretaker was to look after the school and to boil water for all the kids. He had been a soldier in Chiang Kai-shek's war on the mainland before coming here. We heard he had no family and lived in a little room down the hill near town. Sometimes we would see him at school and other times by the water. But he was always around.

One day at school, someone ran in to say the caretaker had fallen in the water. This was nothing to worry as everyone played in the water near the school where it pooled. This time, the messenger said, was different. We all ran to the water. The caretaker floated face down in the slow pools, drunk. I threw off my shirt and jumped in and swam to him. I was a very good swimmer and was never afraid. We dragged him back on the bank, wet, and motionless. We pushed on his chest until he coughed up water. Then he threw up the alcohol, opened his eyes to us then shut them again. Seeing that he would not die, we left him to dry in the sun. The teacher was not surprised when we told him. Later he held my shoulder and told me it was a brave and kind thing I did for the caretaker. That was the last it was mentioned.

Even though our classroom was new, the teacher often taught outside. We would sit on the hillside behind the Temple and do our lessons. Somedays he would take us into the woods and show us plants we could eat, how to harvest fruits, press leaves to get their oil, or to hunt. Sometimes, even, we would run around the hillside on our own, finding things to eat, hunting birds and rats, and playing games we had made up. Often when we were not in the classroom, we would go swimming.

The water above the Temple ran clear and fast. Down the hill it slowed down, though stayed so clear we could dig for clams without the water getting muddy. Where our stream poured into the larger one in the valley, there was a road. The stream ran under the road through a tube to the other side. Sometimes, for fun, we would duck under the surface and swim through the tube to the other side. It seemed like we could come back out into a different world. This was fun and only required bravery the first time. I knew the way very well and would often be the leader because I had no fear of the water. Inside the tube there was enough air to draw a full breath. There was not much space up there, but enough to suck in some mossy air and keep swimming.

After a large rainstorm, the teacher did not have class. There was no reason. Just no class. Everyone from school went down to the water. We took off our shirts and tied them into a net to catch some fish. After a while of no fish we decided to swim. The other kids followed me downstream to the road. The water ran fast and pulled us as quick as we could swim, slick as a fish in the current. With a deep breath I ducked under the surface and into the tube. The water pushed behind me. My fingers and feet brushed the moss-covered tube to keep me in the center so I would not scrape the cement.

Then I stopped. Not because I wanted to. There was something in the way. The water pushed against me. I pressed against a branch that had washed under and jammed. Leaves and weeds wrapped around the branch I could not swim past. I pressed my hands against it, but it was stuck and too large to swim past. I had been leading and knew the others would follow me under the road.

The water rushed fast past me, and I could not swim back out. My lungs began to hurt with the air I was holding. Up at the top I could not find space to breathe. I pressed my lips against the moss-slicked cement at the top of the tube. Water ran up my nose, but through the moss I could suck just enough air for one more breath. Then, spinning around, I pushed with the current and kicked the branch as hard as I could. It shuddered and slipped but still was stuck. Again, I kicked; again, it slid. I tried for another breath and could only get a sputtering of air. I could feel someone's hands behind me stuck in the current. I shut my eyes even tighter, bit down on nothing and kicked the top of the branch. A piece snapped around my foot and it all began to slide.

The current pulled me and the branches through the tube. I scraped against the tube trying to push faster. I could not hold my breath any longer. It pressed out of me in a great bubble as I kicked and kicked and pushed. No longer swimming, I fought the branches and weeds as the current dragged us to the open stream on the other side.

The first breath I could draw on the far side hurt. It hurt like being born, I imagined. I coughed water and paddled what was left of me to the bank. There I took air as fast as I could until my head swam and I felt dizzy. My body wheezed. Everyone who had followed me came through. Some were scared that the tube had been faster than before. No one knew how close we were to staying under, stuck. I did not tell them. It was not theirs to worry. We were out; we could breathe. My foot hurt and my lungs. But we all made it through.

We walked back where we had left our clothes. Some kids talked about how cool it was to swim so fast. They had never known such speed, I heard them say. Some talked how the tunnel seemed darker than other times. I didn't talk. I didn't mention how my foot was scraped and bleeding from the broken edge of the branch. I didn't tell anyone how we all almost died. We were safe. That is what mattered. And now we were going home.

The teacher did not care if we were at school, only if we showed up for the day. Then we would go and play. Sometimes we would catch fish with our clothes, or go hunting. Sometimes the teacher would go hunting with us and we would hunt the eagle and the other birds. But to us it was all play. School was play, and the river was play. Even at home was play. All the time.

Sometimes we would walk down the mountain to the town. Once Father gave Xinyi and me a dollar to buy some betelnuts for him. Usually, we could buy ten betelnuts for a dollar. This guy was very nice and gave us eleven. On the way back home, my third sister and I negotiated about the extra betelnut. If Father received an extra, it would just go to the same place as the other ten. He would eat it or give it to his friends when they came to sit under the trees outside the house. Xinyi decided we should eat it. Maybe it was my idea.

Xinyi bit through the leaf into the nut and gave me the rest. Already her lips were red. I chewed through the other half of the bitter, pepper nut. Xinyi scrunched her face and spit out blood red juice. I spit too and soon my lips and mouth were numb. I kept trying to spit it all out. We walked along the road leaving a trail of red spit.

Our bodies became warm and Xinyi sat down. We could not be found drunk on betelnuts on the road so we crawled behind a bush. We threw up and looked at each other in confusion. This was not fun. There was no reason we could see why Father and his friends would enjoy feeling this way. Still drunk, we could not go home. Our teeth were red, our heads hurt, and everyone would know. So we hid. We wanted just to be sober again. We hid behind the bush by the side of the road, and we slept.

When I woke up it was already dark, and my head still hurt. Up the road a lantern light glowed. I knew it was Father. He would come looking for us. Steps away from our bush shelter he paused and called our names. I wanted to call out. I wanted to go home. Xinyi put her finger across my lips. Looking at her and speaking my wishes to her finger, I watched the safety of Father's light pass by. Again, we were in the dark.

We walked home under the stars of Taiwan. The same I remember watching from our house by the riverbank. The same, I was told, that were there when Father was small. We got home late and went straight to bed. We tried to keep our mouths closed when explaining where we had been. "Out playing. But no problem. We were not lost." We spoke with our jaws clenched. This way no one could see our red stained teeth.

I slept, happy to be home, happy to be with family, and happy to have such a simple life. We had gotten drunk, but now were safe. We had nothing to worry about. First and second sister were still at the Temple, and my first brother was home for now, looking toward the day he could go to the big city.

We were all on the same hillside, all happy and safe, and all family. Mama had found what she wanted even though Father still drank. We didn't have any medical bills; we didn't have any car payment. We didn't pay taxes. At that time, we didn't know what were taxes. We only had to find food. We didn't have electricity bill; we didn't have phone bill. We had what we needed, and were all safe. A simple life. A good life.

Staying Safe

We escaped the cult again. It was a miracle from the Lord. My mom and G-ma were holy. The Lord spoke to them. He didn't speak to them like they spoke to me. He spoke to them in a still, small voice from inside. I was told if I remained pure and righteous before God, asking humble questions with a clean heart, He would speak to me too. Holiness required avoiding all impure thoughts, impure actions, impure wishes, or disobedience. We had to obey completely. Otherwise we'd lose His protection and could fall back into the hands of the cult.

My mom heard the commands of the Lord in the middle of the night. He told her the cult was close, that the kids needed to be kept safe. I remember her waking us up to tell us it was time to go. We packed up our essential clothes and stuffed belongings, library books, and trash from the floor into boxes and bags, and moved away from that cold trailer to go back to safety with G-ma. We were starting over again. We had to.

G-ma was living in an apartment in St. George while searching for her dream home. She was always looking for the perfect home. We would spend hours at the parade of homes where G-ma would coo over drapes and dining sets. My mom reminded us not to touch anything when we went in, so we pretended each house already belonged to G-ma.

At her apartment was an extra room down the hall. G-ma had prepared it for a guest with one bed in the center of the room and all the crafts she'd made at Relief Society, the church's division of women organized to look after the needs of members and to teach girls how to be proper ladies. Victor and I rolled out our sleeping bags on either side of the bed. When it became clear we were going to be there longer, we brought in bunk beds. I missed having my own room in the trailer, but the cult had found us there. We'd fled in such a rush, throwing everything into boxes and suitcases. Those boxes would stay stacked in a new storage unit until we found our own space again.

I don't know if G-ma expected us to stay so long when we first arrived. We would pack up to visit, then simply stay. There was never an official announcement like when we moved to the trailer. We all shared that tiny guest room as months and years went by and the trash piled up.

The guest room could barely fit our three beds, my mom's on one side facing our bunk beds. My mom would spend long days just lying in bed while garbage and clothes covered the floor. It would pile on top of everything, and we would step over and through the piles to get dressed and sleep. At night, bugs crawled across my face as I lay on the bottom bunk beneath Victor. They lived in the mess on the floor and would wander onto one of us if we were still. I'd wake up terrified and shake out my sleeping bag and pillow. Though sleep was difficult after that, there was nowhere else to go. Eventually I would get exhausted from waiting and watching to see if anything else crawled on my bed.

But even bugs weren't reason enough to leave. Only greater forces could make us move. Something like the Lord or the cult.

The cult was the ultimate force. They had infiltrated governments, businesses, show-biz, law enforcement, and projected their messages on children's television shows and in so many toys. We didn't have many toys as it was, but there were some we couldn't play with even at a friend's house. Their sinister messaging was everywhere. Most didn't even recognize how they were being influenced. The cult was throughout every part of the world, but still stayed so secret. This was part of their plan.

One way the cult kept everything secret is by programming so many splits in their followers and victims. They would torture you past endurance, and in that agony, program trigger words that they could use on you later. To survive the pain, your personality would split. The torture would stop once you split. That new personality remained buried inside, summoned by anyone who knew the right words. These separate personalities don't know what the other does or thinks. They keep secrets even from each other.

The Fly had countless splits. Mom would tell me about them. Having spent years in the cult enduring horrible abuse, he had split thousands of times. It was part of their ritual. They had tortured him and he continued splitting and splitting. He was loyal to the cult and highly ranked. I found these stories fascinating. Mom would tell long stories about all The Fly's different personalities she had witnessed.

Some splits spoke perfect English while others struggled. She described him working happily gardening as one personality, then entering the house completely different. He might suddenly cook expertly though his previous split hated cooking. That was his chef personality.

Some splits deeply loved her and thought she was so beautiful. Others couldn't care less about her. Then he would be very mean. some splits, many who were bound to the cult, tried to poison my mom. There was poison in her drinks, she told us. He even poisoned the food she would cook when she wasn't looking. It made him sick as well, but the cult healed him and gave him strength to not succumb to the poison. My mom had to always be wary. Danger was everywhere.

There were splits with every kind of talent imaginable. One was a cook, another a carpenter. There was a caring father and a dedicated worker. Some splits spoke Japanese, others English. One loved God deeply while another worshipped money. The splits varied in age too, from the elderly to children, with some who couldn't even speak. Some splits swore to protect my mom while another tried poisoning her. The Fly tried to hide these different personalities, but my mom could tell them apart, especially when she looked back on things and put it all together like a complex puzzle.

My mom never knew which personality she'd encounter from one moment to the next. The constant uncertainty left her on edge. Because there were so many different splits, even The Fly couldn't keep track of which personality was in control.

This fractured existence allowed him to commit terrible acts that his other splits would not remember. The cult exploited this, my mom explained. They could order someone to perform their torture. Later that person would genuinely swear their innocence—even passing lie detector tests. But my mom didn't need any machine to tell her the truth; she just knew.

If we had stayed with The Fly, the cult would have kidnapped us, trafficked us to China, and sold us into sex slavery for the rest of our lives. They would have maintained complete control, using our bodies in devil worship. We would have been trapped, tortured, and violated until we were killed.

Once recaptured, life as we knew it would end. Through rituals and torture, the cult would split our personalities and control us completely. We would have no choices and no goodness. We'd be forced to obey their every command, even if that meant hurting ourselves or those we loved.

The cult maintained order through absolute control. It wasn't just about knowing where you were or what you were doing. It wasn't just about the rituals like The Fly and his friends had done. The cult could control every aspect of you: your thoughts, your desires. Once they had you, they could make you do anything.

More time with the cult meant they could create many split personalities. If you were more split, you would be easier to control. We weren't certain if Victor had multiple personalities. He was so young when The Fly could get to him.

I had many personalities they had split me into. They just hadn't manifested yet. At any moment of stress or if I heard the right combinations of words, I could switch into another personality. We didn't know how many splits I had or just who I could suddenly become. My mom said we couldn't get too close to anyone, and could trust no one but her. She would watch me closely to make sure I wasn't split, often looking into my eyes and asking me personal questions after I returned home from a friend's house or school. I tried hard to know all the answers she would ask. I didn't want to be split and didn't know if I could tell. My mom was the only one who could be sure.

We escaped when I was still young. My mom said I was too young to remember all the torture. I wondered if forgetfulness was part of my programmed personality. I wondered which personality had stuck. I feared some of my thoughts and words weren't truly mine. I wanted so much to be holy for God, but maybe there were thoughts and selves the cult had planted, actions I did daily that came from them. God wouldn't speak to me with such wickedness inside.

I had to be very careful of what I heard or saw. I didn't know what might trigger a switch. It could be anything, and then I would lose control. The church also wanted us avoiding certain content. Anything that might contain violence, nudity, profane words, or references to the cult and their behaviors could endanger our souls. And having a tattered soul would be even worse than what the cult could do to our bodies.

Because I had been split, I must be careful to not ever be around anyone in the cult. If they spoke my trigger words, I'd be lost to them forever. They could switch me to a helpless infant personality with specific phrases. I would collapse, defenseless, while they resumed their torture, slavery, and control.

I was always so afraid of being triggered into one of my splits. I was so afraid I was already split.

In the last memory of seeing my father, he attempted to trigger and control me. My mom told us he would. We were sent into a cult house while my mom stayed outside and prayed for us. She said the court made her, and she had to trust we would be protected. As soon as we went inside The Fly tried to give Victor and me little boxes he wanted us to open. We were so scared, we refused. My mom said this was what saved us. The cult offers gifts, but what is inside are often body parts from other victims as threats or pictures of our own abuse to program us with those images. Then he offered us cookies to eat, but we knew they could be poisonous. Again we had been made strong enough to resist his attempts on our lives. When we refused, The Fly left and my mom came in, her face red and wet from praying so hard. It was then my mom knew not even the courts could protect us and we had to escape for good.

We didn't often see him at a house. Usually, we met at my mom's church, where someone with God's priesthood power could watch over us. The Fly would be powerless there. I remember even though safe people stood nearby in the room, we were still scared. So so scared.

One time at the church, we watched *Free Willy* while The Fly stood in the back of the room. It was a one hour visit the court mandated. My dad wasn't allowed to talk to us. He wasn't allowed to speak or touch us. We didn't look at him when he came in.

My brother and I shook with fear, crying because our father wanted to kill us. If he couldn't reclaim us for the cult, he would murder us. We were too afraid to talk to him. My brother and I grew hungry, and my mom was struggling to open this bag of snacks for us. She could not get it open immediately. The Fly stepped forward. "Oh, I have a knife. I can help open." He came close to us unfolding a small pocketknife. My mom quickly retreated, saying she could manage. We ate our snacks and finished the movie while The Fly lurked in back, waiting for another opportunity. I could never watch *Free Willy* again after that.

Afterward, my mom knelt down to our level. "Did you notice the trigger he tried to use? 'I have a knife.' That could have switched your personality to one of your splits." Some miracle had protected me from triggering that day. Those words could have transformed me into someone else, separating me from my family.

All of our fasting had paid off. We were so grateful. All our prayers and those praying for us had kept us safe. I had been lucky. If I ever saw my father again, I did not know I would be so lucky. That was too much to ask, even of the Lord.

I remember another time a few months prior when The Fly visited us at the church. My brother and I colored at a small folding table. Some papers fell. I'm not sure if I dropped them or Victor did. The Fly instinctively rose to help, reaching to return them. Everyone panicked. They made him back off. He handed the papers to one of the church leaders and went to the back of the room without a word. He stood there until the hour was up and they asked him to leave.

I remember feeling so sad for The Fly. This confused me. I knew he was evil, had raped us, and was trying to kill us. I wouldn't make eye contact or turn around at all. I was so scared. Still, I felt sad for him.

I don't know where that sadness came from. Perhaps I sensed his emotions. Or perhaps he wanted me to feel sad so I would be more easily triggered. I'm not sure. I never told my mom about this feeling. She would probably have known why, but I kept this to myself. Eventually the feeling passed, but for a while I felt profound sorrow.

秘密

Secrets

When I was smaller, I told everything. Truth happened and no one owned it. Like the rain in Taiwan—it was everyone's and no one's. It ran down the green mountains, bloomed in flowers and trees, and gathered in massive rivers that cleansed and fed. It was what we drank and bathed in. I didn't yet realize it could also drown and flood. And I didn't know when I was small that sometimes it is best not to get wet.

My third sister, Xinyi, made me promise not to tell about the betelnuts. It was the first secret I kept. She told me to keep it from everyone, though I knew that meant Mama. The truth would get us in trouble, but it would also make Mama afraid. She didn't want us to end up like Father, who would not change his ways. Any sign we were more like him than her, and Mama would take us to Temple and supplicate to the gods for our sake.

The gods did not listen. Mama wanted my first and second sisters to never marry and to stay at Temple where the gods could assure their happiness. They did not listen to Mama or the gods. Soon after my first brother left for mandated military service, my first sister left Temple to move to Taipei. My second sister also would not stay. Mama said Buddha was the only way, but all of us found another.

The only fate Mama saw for me there on the mountainside was to become like my Father, so she sent me live with my second uncle and go to a better school. My uncle lived north of us in Xincheng. He was a good man, and my life was very happy.

I was not sad to leave home. Perhaps if I were still small. But at that time, I knew more about truth, water, and what keeps a family together. I was growing up. I did not have many things besides my school uniform which was getting too tight, so I moved from home with nothing. I was welcomed warmly by my second uncle on Father's side. I had everything I needed.

My uncle grew many pineapples and cut trees for wood. I would help him work outside when I wasn't in school. My aunt and her son would sell the pineapples and wood to the people in Xincheng. We saw my grandmother often. It was a good life.

Even then my grandmother was old and healthy. She was 93 and had birthed twelve children. She ate everyday a bowl of lean meat and a cup of rice wine. She said it was all she needed. That and her family. She would ask about school and I would tell her. She said I should be proud to go to middle school. She said that many people can't to go to school because they are too poor and have to work, or because the war took their teachers away. Now there was no war and more schools, but still I felt very proud. When I told her this, she would give me a piece of money. I was her youngest son's youngest son, and my cousin said she spoiled me. My uncle told me to go spend the money grandmother gave me. To buy something I would enjoy.

The three years of middle school were much more serious than school on the mountainside. This school wasn't about hunting and playing in the water. Here we were told to work hard at school and in life if we wanted anything. I didn't mind the work at school or with my uncle, and I had all I wanted already. Still, I liked to learn.

I helped my uncle work on the land, and would help to sell the wood and pineapples. I worked hard and thought I was contributing to the family. My aunt had different ideas. I had lived there for more than a year when she told me that my mother was not sending them any money to take care of me. I read from my aunt that this was an injustice. I respected my uncle and did not want to be a burden to him. I concocted a plan.

I would run away. I knew just how to do it. Hualien was the next city to the north. A train left Hualien for Taipei early in the morning. I could leave under the night without anyone seeing me. I tied some clothes and the money I had saved from my grandmother in a shirt and waited for midnight. Everyone was sleeping when I left for the station. I didn't have any shoes and went everywhere barefoot, but I took my cousin's shoes for the long journey. The train station was almost two hours away. After an hour, when my eyes had settled into the low light of a clear night, I had to leave the shoes behind. My cousin had larger feet and I began to get blisters along my heels. Barefoot would be best. I walked the rest of the way and waited for the train.

Along the east coast of Taiwan, the train moves slowly. There are sharp bends in the tracks and hills where one can just walk alongside the train and step on. Even without shoes I had no problem hopping on the train for the big city. I counted out all my coins to the ticket master who put them in his pocket and told me to sit in one place and be quiet. I was happy for the rest. I found the slow click of the tracks relaxing. I was ready for adventure and life was good.

In Taipei everywhere there are papers advertising for work. Jobs of all kinds and places which help you find work. Just my luck, the first one I walked into said they had a job for me and I could start today. I wouldn't have to find a place to sleep that night, as my new employer would provide a bed and meals. I was excited. I was going to make it on my own, just like my plan. Soon a man on a motorcycle came to take me to my new home.

This man was a butcher. This meant I was now a butcher's assistant. The experience I had hunting on the mountainside was very useful. I knew how to skin and cut meat, and I was very careful with the sharp knives. Every day we would wake up at 3 am and drive the motorcycle to the market to buy half a pig. Sometimes we would buy two halves. I would pull the hair from the skin then cut the skin clean. We would cut the meat into portions and hang it up in the front window of the house. There was no storefront, and customers would stop to look in the windows and walk in the front door. Any customer could see into the house where we all lived. This was different from the storefronts when we lived by the river, but the big city was different in almost every way.

I would sit among the shanks and ribs until we had sold the last of the meat, about 1 or 2 pm, then I could eat lunch. After lunch I would take the boss' kids, two young boys, to the park or to walk with them. I would look after them until dinner, which was always late. Then after cleaning and getting the knives ready for the next half of pig, I would sleep. This was life in Taipei.

Soon I began to miss my family. I missed my uncle and my cousin. I missed Mama and Father. I even began to miss my aunt. In the city every day was the same. Up early, cut meat, sell meat, watch kids, clean. And when it was time for me to get paid the boss always had some reason I should wait. "Not yet," he would say. "You are young and in training."

I worked for more than a month and never received any money. I wanted to go home, but I had no money to pay the train fare. My boss would not let me leave the house. I had run away and become a slave. I didn't know if I would ever get back to my family. I remembered my family. I sat up at night thinking about them. I sold pork and dreamed about them. Down the street I would see them in the faces of distant strangers. I did not forget them, and knew they would not forget me. In the few things I had brought with me, I remembered I had my first sister's phone number where she lived in Taipei. When the two young boys were playing in the park, I snuck away to use someone's phone.

Shu-fen was happy to hear from me, but still angry. "Where have you been? Everybody has been looking for you. Mama has been to Temple every day. Father has been searching every night."

She did not spare my feelings or listen to my struggle. Despite this suffering I had caused, she said she would send help. My brother was in the military in Taipei, and she would call him. She wrote down all the details of where I was staying and instructed me to not leave. Only after that she asked if I was safe and had enough to eat.

That night my brother came to the house on a motorcycle he had borrowed. My boss was very confused when he knocked and was visibly upset as my brother kept talking. They stepped into the street to discuss. I do not know if they talked about the money I was owed. When they came back inside, my brother motioned to me to come with him. My boss looked straight ahead as I was allowed to leave. Only the two little boys said goodbye. I never received any pay, but at least I could go home.

I rode away on the motorcycle, just like how I had come. However, I did not stay in the city and start my new life. My brother said I had to go back home. I was glad for that. And I was very glad for him.

My brother arranged with two native Taiwanese truck drivers to take me back down the eastern road to Hualien. I sat in the middle while they hauled their load around the twists and turns. The road was very small, and the truck was big. They drove slowly and spoke to each other in their language. For hours I sat there and did not say a word. They did not ask questions. I said, "Thank you," when they dropped me off on the outside of town. From there it was still a long way to my uncle's home.

Outside my uncle's home the family stood. My first sister told them I would be coming back. Everyone was watching as I walked back barefoot and with less than I had left with. The first person to greet me was my uncle. He hugged me tight and asked why. "Why did you do such stupid things? I cannot believe you. Why did you leave? What was the problem that made you run away? I want to know." His stern questions were asked with love. He cared about me. He was mad, but it was because he was worried. I understood.

I did not say anything. I did not want to lie to my uncle who was a good man. I could not tell about my uncle's wife complaining they had no money from my mother and that I was a burden to the family. If I told him this, my uncle might be very upset with his wife. I did not want to bring trouble to his family. They had given so much to me.

I did not say this then. I did not ever tell my uncle or my brother or my sisters. Not to anybody. I could not dishonor my family by telling them this. It is for that reason that I ran away, that I became a slave and was sold to a family. This secret I had to keep. I had the truth, and I kept it to myself. It was not theirs to carry. Or to know. I was back. My uncle was happy. Family was back together again. That was enough.

Even though I understood now how to stay quiet, some of the time I did not know what to say to break that silence. In my head it had to be just right. Words could lead to great decisions, both for a great love or a great pain. So, until I knew what to say, I would stay shut. Not to utter a falsehood. I became so good at this, I sometimes forgot to speak.

After I had returned home to my uncle's house, many times he asked me why I had run away. He thought that someone had been mean to me. But no one had. Everyone was very nice. It was only his wife. And this I could not say. I did not want my words to be the space between them. So I stayed shut.

I returned to middle school, still without shoes, though now I understood the big city in the way that none of the other boys in class could. There were only boys in my class. All the girls were in a different class—maybe some of them understood. The last year of middle school I found one girl I thought would understand if she didn't already. I talked to her a couple times and asked her to meet me after school by the big trees. She agreed and said she was excited. I was excited too.

She sat in the shade in her uniform and waited for me. I could see her as I approached. She did not look around to know if I was coming. I held my books wrapped in a leather strap, tucked in my uniform shirt, and flexed my bare feet before I walked up to her. I said, "Hi," and looked at her. She said, "Hello," and looked back. Then I didn't speak. I did not know what to say. She looked at me and I stared back at her. We didn't say any words. For a half-hour. Instead of talking I thought about her. And she thought about me—I suppose. Then I said, "I have to go. I have to go right now. Can I see you again tomorrow?"

The second day we sat there again. After some time of silence, I asked questions about her favorite subject, what she liked in school. We sat together four or five times, but I never touched her hand. I didn't know what to say, or what to do. I knew I wanted to touch her hand, to show her somehow that I liked her. The right words were not there. Or, if they were there, I couldn't tell what they were from inbetween my thoughts.

Middle school ended, and I never spoke to her again. It was decided I should leave my uncle's house near Hualien. There were more opportunities in Tai-Tung City where my second sister lived with her husband. It was larger and near the sea. I was excited to go, and hoped I would find more friends, more things to do, more learning, and more words.

Can't Ever Tell

You can't ever tell who is part of the cult. Law enforcement could be involved. Church members could. Even the high-ranking members of the Mormon Church could be secret cult members.

The cult liked to turn everything on its head. This way, evil could seem like good. So even the best people, full of goodness, could be part of the cult. It would be the ultimate evil to look so good to everyone else while being so bad in secret. Then, it would be nearly impossible for anyone outside to know who was involved. This is exactly what the cult wanted.

By staying so well hidden, the cult could infiltrate anywhere in our world. The Book of Mormon, which we read nearly every day, told about satanic signs and tokens of communication. Those who knew had patterns and signals they could send to one another. They could communicate in public and keep organized. We were lucky my mom knew all about their secret codes and gestures so we could be on the lookout. We had to be.

The cult had certain holidays. Red and black were the colors of Satan, and on holidays members of the cult would wear these colors together or wear mostly red. We would go to church on these holidays and would know that whoever was wearing red that day was part of the cult. I would never wear red and black together. I still don't.

During the first hour of church service, my mom would lean over to us and say, "Ok, you see who is wearing red here?" A lot of people were wearing red. These were all cult members letting each other know. We were some of the only ones who had escaped the cult. So, we were in the know. But these people here didn't know that we were once part of it. None of those in red and black knew that we knew they were cult members.

We were running for our lives and hiding among the enemy. They were unaware, for now. We did not signal to them that we were apart from the cult. And we did not let them know we knew what they were up to. The cult was much bigger than us. It was all across the world in every religion and government. We weren't trying to fight it. We only wanted to stay safe. And that meant staying hidden.

Being able to tell who was part of the cult and who wasn't was important so we would know who to stay away from. By knowing their signs and tokens as they did, we would know how to keep ourselves safe. My mom prayed to know. Then she told us what God told her.

It was so important to be informed. The only way we could stay safe and avoid the pitfalls of the devil was to know where he and his minions were hiding. My mom would often ask us to detect what symbols of cult activity we could find around us. Then she would tell us the ones we didn't even know about. There were symbols on groceries in the stores. There were words and symbols in music and on television. So many common things we would see were actually signals from the cult. The more we knew, the more we could see how widespread the cult's influence was. Many things we saw every day and thought were harmless were actually filled with messages from the cult. Satan put these symbols into everyday things like clothing and toys so everyone would be influenced.

Basements were where cultish things happened. There they tortured people, held satanic rituals, and kept people for sex slavery. Any house with a basement could have a tie to the cult. Even churches that have basements could have cult activity within them.

There were so many symbols in our toys. It was important to the cult to get to children at a young age. The younger someone was the more they could split that person through torture. Plus, youth is so innocent, just like Jesus said, so it was an extra delight to Satan to corrupt that innocence and turn someone to their side. Cabbage Patch Kids were part of the cult, Star Wars of course, the Smurfs because they used magic, even My Little Pony and Care-Bears because the rainbows were building a bridge from Lucifer's world of mythology and anti-Jesus to our own. There was so much. We had to stay alert.

I was lucky we didn't have many toys at home so that I would be kept pure and clean for the Lord. Some of my friends had these toys, but I didn't want to play with them. Sometimes I would see them with their toys and I would be sad knowing they were being influenced by the devil. This also was why my mom would not show us any of the presents the Fly sent. He would send a package and my mom would keep us all safe by making sure it was thrown out without us knowing what was inside. We wouldn't want to be triggered by him or whatever the package contained. Even if the things in the package didn't trigger us, they were sure to have cult symbols in them to keep us under Satan's influence.

There were lots of cult members in very public places, like politicians and celebrities. My mom was constantly telling us what she found out. Weird Al Yankovic was in the cult. So was Pee Wee Herman and lots of people who are involved in kids' shows because it was opportunity for pedophiles. We would watch music videos and learn about all the visual cult symbols, like phone cords wrapped around people or certain hairstyles. Even certain make-up or symbols they would make with their hands.

One day while G-ma was sitting with us watching TV, my mom came in too. My mom pointed out every single symbolic thing and what it meant to the cult. So much of everything was cult messages.

G-ma never praised my mom ordinarily, but she was so impressed that she knew all the cult symbols and really had a sense for being able to see it.

"Oh Beth, you know your stuff so well. I mean you really understand how the cult works and all their symbols. That is so good." From then on, even G-ma acknowledged my mom's knowledge of the cult as authority. She knew my mom had a sense for seeing and understanding the evil hidden behind the good. I had known she knew this all along. I hoped I would learn the same sense. It would keep me free.

The cult was especially after us because we had escaped. The cult does not like anyone to escape. It challenges their power. Everywhere the cult seeks power to oppose the freedom God gave us. Because we were clever enough to escape, they would be more determined to make us return. They would send more symbols, a greater influence our way to confuse us and lead us away from God. I prayed every night I would stay pure. I would stay away from all things related to the cult, and they would never find me again. I gave thanks for my freedom. I gave thanks to the Lord that he had given my mom such wisdom. His strength and her wisdom would keep us safe from the cult's influence. It was such a large responsibility. The cult was everywhere.

For anything good in our lives, or anything good in general, the cult had an opposite dark side. In the Mormon Church, when you are eight you can be baptized for the Lord in water. They say a prayer over you and dip you under the water to create an eternal covenant with the Lord to always follow him. What the cult does is when you are eight, you are baptized in blood because that is a mockery of God's plan. And you get baptized for Satan instead of Jesus.

Everything was like this. An even split. If we had something good, the cult had something similar which was evil. We prayed to the Lord, they prayed to Satan. We offered our time and service to help others; the cult devoted their lives to hurting others. We took the sacrament of bread and water to cleanse our sins; the cult drank actual blood and reveled in the filth of their wrongdoings. We were promised a heavenly home if we remained pure and worthy. In the cult they were promised to be leaders and kings of Hell, but only if they helped raise Hell on this Earth.

This split was true for everything. Family, fun, play, even sex. Sex is supposed to be a good thing and ordained by God in marriage. The cult made a mockery of it. They would do all sorts of things, like sex outside of marriage, and anal sex, and gang-rape. That sort of stuff. And since sex was so holy and such a prized gift from God, it was something the cult made dirty and hurtful.

I was prostituted by my father to all of his friends. The Fly was a high-ranked leader and all his friends were in the cult together. My mom figured all this out after we had left. Had she known before, she would not have let it happen, she assured me. All she knew at the time was how terrified we were of my father even before we were verbal. When he would come home, we would cling to our mom and shake and cry because we did not want to be with him. Sometimes my mom left us at the house alone with The Fly before she knew what was happening. When she came back, she could tell we were totally different, that we had been traumatized. What she didn't know was happening she could not protect us from. She only found out later that while she was out, The Fly invited all his cult friends over and they would gang-rape my brother and me.

I did not remember this happening because the trauma was too great. The cult intended it that way. My lack of memory would keep them safe from the law and keep me under control. Then they could do it again and again without consequence. I was thankful for my mom for telling me so I could be aware of what had happened and we could stay protected. And I was thankful to the Lord for showing her the truth. I wore this truth like armor.

For a while I knew it had happened, but I did not understand how. As I put the pieces together, I realized I had been just a baby. So had Victor. I did not understand how someone could rape a baby.

My mom put it together for me one day. I told her I did not understand. She looked at me and without pause said, "Well, think of what hole you could rape on a baby."

That was the first idea of anal sex I ever had in my life. It was terrifying and horrible. Now I knew what had happened to me and my baby brother. Now I knew what kind of monster my dad had been. Now I knew that I was a victim, a survivor of sexual abuse.

This became part of my story and part of myself. I had a favorite color, a favorite food, and I was a sexual abuse victim. And I had escaped the cult, but we didn't tell people that.

When I was in third grade, Victor and I would play on the playground after school until my mom came to pick us up. Often, we were the only ones there. I remember once some other kid was there playing as well, a little girl, my age. I had never met her before. I introduced myself to her so we could play. It was only her and me and my brother.

"Hi," I said. "What's your name?"

"Sandee. What's yours?"

"My name is Ella and I was physically and sexually abused."

"Oh, what does that mean?"

I had to think about it. It was a fact that I knew, and something I lived with, but I now needed to describe it.

"It's like when an adult hurts a kid really badly, but like in a sexual way."

"Ok," she said. Then we played on the playground because we were little and now friends.

我的道路

My Path

I passed the test to get into Tai-Tung City high school. Mama thought it would be best for me to stay with my second sister, Yu-wen, and her husband and children. It was a great opportunity to go to high school. Not everybody could go to school. Many after middle school had to find work, or go home and help out with the work there because they didn't pass the test. But I knew the answers and knew I would go to high school. It was more friends, more freedom, and more learning. I wanted more.

I always liked to play in water. Ever since I was a baby. Growing up did not change my hobby. Lucky for me my high school was very close to the ocean. After school sometimes we would walk the fifteen minutes to the ocean and swim. Or I would go on the weekends when I wasn't helping Yu-wen. Often, I swam during school.

I made friends quickly in Tai-Tung City, ones that aligned their thoughts with mine. Either they felt the same way about school, the rules, and swimming, or they could sense my love and convictions and wanted some of the joy I had. It did not matter. When I wanted to go swimming, they came along.

Our high school was surrounded by wire. High wire fence all around except at the entrance where the school police sat. They weren't really the police, but we called them the police. They were guards with no guns. They would watch us come in the morning, walk the halls to make sure we were in class, and see us leave in the evening with our books. Their responsibility was to watch the students for safety and to watch what they were thinking. If the students were thinking about Communism, they could get in big trouble. They had many rules. Most school police were ex-army, soldiers from Chiang Kai-shek's forces who could not go back to China. They stayed in Taiwan without family and looked for work. They still acted like soldiers and, in some ways, expected us to be soldiers. But we were not soldiers. We were high school kids who loved to swim.

During the school day, everyone was required to take a nap. After morning classes, it was time for lunch and a nap before the afternoon classes. Together, it was two hours of break. Some kids would study in bed instead of sleeping, and the school police would yell at them to sleep. Many would feign sleep when they heard the school police coming, holding still while he peeked in and counted the students in the sleeping dorms. Then they would giggle when he left. It was always a joke. But we didn't pretend sleep for him. We escaped.

At first it was just me and a few friends, maybe three or four. We would wait until the school police had checked in on us once. Then with our blankets and pillows we would assemble a dummy under the sheets to look like we were still there in the dim light. One check into the hallway to make sure we weren't seen, and we would leave. We had cut a hole in the wire fence which was hard to see unless you knew it was there. I would lift the wire up for my friends to sneak through and they would hold it for me. Once we were out, we were free.

It did not take long to get to the ocean and the waves. We would strip down to our underwear to keep our uniforms dry. No one could know we had been to the sea. We could not go back to school in wet clothes and give away our secret. Then we would play in the water. This was much better than a nap. We would shake ourselves dry, wring the drops from our underwear, put our clothes on and run back to school. Back under the wires, into the sleeping dorm, disassemble the dummies, and be ready for the rest of the school day.

The teachers did not know. The school police did not know. My second sister did not know. And most important, my parents did not know. Mama would not like that we were breaking any rules. She never went to school and never learned to read, so to her, school was a privilege she wouldn't risk losing. It was important we had the chance she did not. And she sacrificed much so we could go. She would remind us of this, and to study hard.

Swimming was such happiness. We would sneak out and play in the water, then return for more learning. Soon others wanted to join, though we tried to keep our secret. My friend Liu wanted to come even though he was not a strong swimmer. Because we liked him around—he was so funny—we could not say no. He came, and just like us, loved the water, the adventure, and the freedom.

One day, I remember Liu laughing and playing in the waves. The waves were large and topped with white foam. When they crashed, they pushed us back up the beach then dragged the sand back under so strong you could hear the suck of water rushing back to sea before the next wave crashed on top. Liu ran at the waves and jumped into the foam, then was pushed back up the beach. Many of us did this. Then, he jumped into a wave which pulled instead of pushed and he ended up on the other side. We laughed from the shore. Liu had conquered the wave. We shouted his name as he bobbed past the foam.

We saw him, then we didn't. His head would pop above the water before the ebb pulled him under. We rushed toward him. Later, if asked, we could not tell whose idea it had been. We knew what had to be done. Together, an arm here, a grasp on a leg there, we dragged him back to shore. Liu's face had taken the color of the shallow water. Sand clung all over his face. His stomach heaved in short bursts, but he did not breathe. Someone pinched his nose and filled his lungs with air. Then I pushed his chest in. He was solid, and nothing moved. Again, we filled his lungs and pushed them empty. Liu sputtered out some of the sea. Push again. More sea. Push. Push. Then he coughed and coughed the sea from him. His breaths came in long heaves. We stood around Liu covered in sand and coughing. He smiled when he had caught his breath as though it had been a joke. Someone then did make a joke, and we laughed. The fragility of life now far away, the important thing became getting back to school.

We brushed the sand from us and dried off as best we could. Our uniforms clung to us where the sea held on, and we ran back to school. We snuck under the wire in time for class to begin. We hadn't been found out. Some of the students would look at Liu and mimic choking, and Liu would laugh. Already the memory of his near passing was past, now as harmless as the trouble we did not get in for sneaking out. Our leaving during nap time was a slow secret before that. However, the story of Liu spread like a giant wave.

We didn't sneak out for a while. Too many knew. We didn't go again until Liu brought it up. He wanted to return to the sea. He said it was like a lover, that no matter how he had been treated, he was bound. He had to return.

Liu's escape from death made him popular. It also made the illicit outing a legend. Many more wanted to come. So many dummies were made during nap time. Some people made a lousy dummy. There were fifteen or sixteen dummies in the nap room.

People move different when they do something wrong. The human body does not let the muscles move the same in truth as it does in deceit. Before, we moved with our heads high, confident in our freedom. We knew we were breaking the rules, but it was the rule itself, not us which was wrong. Now, many of the group carried their disobedience like a weight. Some would turn around to see if anyone noticed us. Still, we made it to the sea.

We always hid our clothes and shoes under the bushes. Showing the newcomers where to hide their clothes was not necessary. It was already part of the Tale of Liu. The sea was still the same as it had been before, but the story had made it different. For those new, the sea was monumental, made grand by the whispers of how Liu had survived. They had known how the sea felt before they stepped in it themselves and could not see it without the crash and pull of those words.

This thought did not stay with me long. We were soon all in the water. Many more people made it more fun. I was glad for the crowd. Until we got out.

Someone accused another of hiding their clothes. It would have been a great practical joke. Everyone thought it was a joke until no one could find their clothes. They had all been hidden, and now all were missing.

We did not know what to do. We could not return to school without clothes. Nor could we not return to school. Nearby hung wash on a line, dried and flapping in the wind. Someone watched the yard while another pulled clothes from the line and passed them around. Some had pants that were too large. Another had just a long shirt. Another wore a dress. Some of the clothes were too big for us. At least our nakedness was covered. No one had shoes. We pieced together shabby outfits and returned to school.

The school police waited at the fence over our escape hole. He held a bundle of our clothes in his arms. "Not through here," he said. "Go through the gates at front."

We begged for our clothes, but he stood unmovable, like a soldier. "Go around front," he repeated. At the front gate the principal waited for us. We could do nothing but accept our fate. We were marched into the auditorium at school and onto the stage, followed by the school police. The rest of our clothes were on the stage in a pile. We stood in various undress in front of all the students to admit to the rules we had broken.

The school police used a microphone to talk to all eight hundred students and tell everything we had done at the beach. They accused us of sneaking out, deception for leaving dummies in our bed, damaging property for the hole in the fence, and conspiracy. The only thing they didn't mention was the petty theft of the clothes we were wearing. We would have to return the clothes, they told us. Immediately. We took off the clothes we had taken from the lines and handed them to the school police. We could not reach for our own clothes until we had fully admitted to what we had done to the student body. We were humiliated, and our punishment had not yet begun. For months during nap time we would have to clean the school and school yard. Not only this. The school would write a letter home to our parents to tell them we had made a major mistake. Four major mistakes would get us kicked out of school.

Consequence set in. To me, leaving school to swim was not anything bad. I was not missing my studies, only the nap. I could get enough sleep at night. But to Mama it would mean disrespecting the school I was lucky to attend. To her it was risking my education and my future. I could handle any punishment at school, even the embarrassment of standing in front of all the students in my underwear. At home it would be far worse.

All that night I thought about Mama. I could not sleep. I could not pay attention at school the next day. As soon as I was released from school, I ran straight to the train station to catch the next departure north. I had to get home to the mountain before the mail. I worried Mama had the letter in her hand, waiting for me. Mama could not read, so she would either have Father read it to her when he came home, or she would take it to a neighbor. In the presence of another, my shame would be undeniable. When the train stopped, I ran. Still in my school uniform I ran up the mountain. Mama was home. So was Father. So was the mail.

Father said he had just brought it in but didn't have a chance to read it yet. I was expecting something, I told them, and filed through the letters. The letter from school was there, unopened. My parents did not have a telephone so a letter was the only way for school to contact them. Because I had the letter, they had only contacted me. I opened and read all the details the school had written. I kept these to myself as I already knew what had happened. I knew I wouldn't tell.

Cold

Just like that, we moved again. It always happened in the middle of the night. We would get a suspicious call and suddenly, we'd be packing up to leave. There was very little preparation. My mom would tell us we were moving, and we would help pack. G-ma would never leave. She just stayed there. We would throw everything we could into the car and leave my grandmother's house. After a while, we would come back to visit and stay for a year.

My mom would say the cult may have found us and we needed to leave. To pack, she'd pull her hair back into a ponytail, her face serious and focused. We gathered everything that was piled on the floor, tossing items into whatever box was closest. We separated some of the trash from what we wanted to keep, though some garbage ended up packed along with our clothes to be sorted later.

This time we moved to Cedar City. It wasn't as far from G-ma's as Beaver, but far enough for my mom. She was tired of living with her mother and would constantly complain about how mean and horrible G-ma was, how she hadn't been treated right, and how she knew what was best for us when G-ma didn't. She was happy to move.

Grandpa Tom helped my mom buy a little trailer in the far back of a trailer park. We had the smallest trailer. Everyone else had a double wide, but ours was a single wide. At least I would have my own room. So would Victor. His room was next to mine and doubled as storage for our stacks of boxes.

Our tiny single-wide soon filled with our stuff, our lives. It started feeling like home. We started a new school, not having said goodbye to anyone at old one, and were expected to fit in. Except we couldn't. Everyone we met had to be told of our history.

Before we started school, my mom would meet with the principal, who would call in our teachers for a discussion. She would explain the abuse we'd been through, how we'd survived, and warn them not to be alarmed if we were sad for no apparent reason. She explained we could be triggered and might need extra or less attention, that we might need more time on our assignments as we still processed our trauma. She told them not to make a special case for us unless we needed it, and then to make that special case seem entirely normal.

We were expected to blend into our school. It would make it harder for any cult members to recognize us if we didn't stand out. We were to act as though we'd always been there and there was nothing to be concerned about. It didn't help that my brother and I were the only Asian children at a school filled with white, Mormon kids.

My mom also had to tell the bishop of our new ward what we'd been through and why we needed protection. He couldn't enter our membership records into the church's database. He was not to admit to any inquiries that we were living there and attending church. No official record of our whereabouts could be kept, reported, or shared.

Even our friends' parents had to be told. For those who couldn't be trusted with the whole truth about the satanic cult at our heels, my mom used the term "security situation." Then she'd explain that we were in danger, and that being with us could be dangerous for anyone else. This left us alone most of the time, except for the mandatory visits from church leaders.

Home Teachers were assigned to come to our house once a month, though my mom usually met them outside. Visiting Teachers from the Relief Society also came by. My mom would usually cancel or just talk to them on the phone. It seemed like she didn't want to have people visit.

The trailer became more and more our own private space. Everywhere there were clothes and my brother's toys on the floor. My mom had her stack of library books she always meant to read, and we each had our own spots where we sat. Those stayed cleared, as did the trails back to our rooms, mostly. We didn't have much, but everything we had was spread out. It made our place seem full, comfortable, like our own secret world that no one on the outside would understand.

It was comfortable until winter came. Then the trailer was miserable. I could never get warm, and when I finally did, I couldn't stay warm. I wanted to stay at school longer because they had heaters. Before my mom picked us up, I would hold my hands over the blasting vents to absorb as much warmth as I could until I could come back again.

Our small trailer was cold all the time. One day, I'd had enough and turned the thermostat up. I pushed the little red indicator past where the heat clicked on, all the way up to 81 degrees. Finally, the trailer began to warm up. I was relieved. I was so tired of being cold. When my mom noticed, she was furious. She rarely got angry with me, but this time she was livid. She turned the thermostat down until the heater clicked off and the trailer seemed to shudder in the Utah winter. My mom told me that I could never touch the thermostat again, repeating it for emphasis. I didn't. There weren't many rules at our house outside of staying safe and hidden from the cult. The rules I was given, I made sure to follow exactly. I never touched the thermostat again.

Once again, the trailer became cold. My bedroom especially seemed drafty. I would sleep in my sleeping bag on the bed and curl up as small as I could, still wearing my warm clothes. This was the only way I could get comfortable enough to fall asleep. No matter what, I couldn't get rid of the draft in my room.

One sleepless night, I was huddled in my sleeping bag, sticking out only my mouth to breathe to try to stay warm but couldn't. I was so sick of the cold, I felt around to find where the air was coldest. Behind the bed, on the far edge of the trailer, the whole corner of the room had sunk down. I pulled my bed away from the wall and looked out the hole where the floor had given way. I could see the snow outside on the ground. I could see outside where there was supposed to be a floor. And there was snow! I didn't know what to do or how to fix it. All I wanted was for my room to be warmer. But the draft was coming from outside. I grabbed some garbage off the floor and stuffed it in the hole. At least then the wind couldn't come in. At least then I could sleep.

我自己

On My Own

I did not want to be a bad person. There were so many paths in this life. Most promised virtue, but none could guarantee. They each had their rules, but no number of rules could make a good person. There were so many rules. Every religion had rules, every home. Every business had rules, and every school.

Tai-Tung City High School did not allow smoking. Some students still smoked in the bathrooms or sometimes in our nap room. When a teacher or the school police came near, the students would hide their smoke and deny they had been smoking. During nap time one day the school police came in suddenly. Many of us were in bed, but a couple were sitting up smoking. The one with the cigarette tried to swallow the smoke he had inhaled. The school police asked students, "I smell smoke. Are you smoking?" Everyone denied. When the student who had been smoking tried to tell the police that there was no smoke there, he could not hold it all in, and some of the smoke began to come out with his words. Everyone else laughed.

For the rest of the day, four hours, that student had to stand in the doorway of the classroom and face everyone. He could not sit. He could not do the lesson. He was lucky he did not have to stand longer. The school police could give whatever punishment they wanted.

Living with my second sister, Yu-wen, only cast a shadow of Mama's rules. Yu-wen had left the Buddhist Temple and her religious practice behind. For Mama's sake she would say she was still Buddhist. She would attend ceremony when we were home on the mountain, but not in Tai-Tung City. Even though she was a good person, she did not attribute this to being raised in Buddhist Temple. She left the temple and its ways, but was still good. Mama's rules did not form any more virtue than those of the school police.

Under someone else's rule, there was no difference between rightness and consequences. And though I was studying to be a teacher, there was more instruction on life in the world than in the classroom. Some rare days I would choose to school myself in the world rather than the classroom. I would walk to a new place of the city in search for meaning and learning. One day I walked through Tai-Tung City to see a movie in the theater.

The banners for the movies hung with wet paste on the wall outside. A man in a sandwich board and clown make-up shouted lines from the movies to the passers-by. Two young men in white shirts walked past him and stopped behind me. "Excuse me," one said in accented Mandarin. "Could you help us find our way?" They were Americans and very polite.

They were sent by a church, they told me, and wanted to teach people about a gospel. They were not interested in going to the movies with me. After I gave them directions, they invited me to their church. We talked for a while that day. They asked about my life and gave me pamphlets about their mission. We shook hands, and they promised to talk to me again. Even though they did not join me for my movie, I decided I would join them for their church. It would be new for me, and I was eager to learn.

Their church was not in a temple like the Buddhists. They did not have any incense or altars. A few people gathered together and prayed. A couple of the missionaries spoke about Jesus and good-ness. This was more than what the Buddhists explained or school offered. After the service I told the young men I would see them the next week.

It was a mistake to tell Yu-wen about the missionaries. She did not seem to care, but she did tell Mama. Mama was convinced the only way was the Buddhist way. She did not want tragedy like she had known to visit me because I did not worship the gods which promised her peace. She forbade me to go to the church again and made my second sister promise to watch over me.

Yu-wen stayed busy. She had a job, three children, and a husband who was an officer in the military and often gone. She had me there too, though I was nearly grown. She could not watch me all the time. When she was not looking, I would leave without telling her so I could go to the church. They were always happy to see me. There they talked about how to live a good life. They said their gospel promised an eternal life of happiness. It promised that families could be together always. They had many rules they said were to keep our souls pure for the blessings of the Lord. Their vision of purity was the closest I had found to goodness. Mama did not agree.

Mama came to the city on the train and found the church I had been attending. She waited for me outside until service was over. We walked back to Yu-wen's house together. Mama was worried about me, but she did not understand. Still, I could not lie to her or ask Yu-wen to lie to her. Church had become important to me, and I was learning about the goodness within myself from these foreigners. Mama did not trust them, and made Yu-wen promise again to keep me away from their influence.

My search for goodness had brought chaos to my home and family. It would not be honorable for Yu-wen and Mama to be divided. I could not find goodness by causing disruption. I decided to find my own apartment, continue with my schooling, and continue my learning with these American missionaries.

I rented a room in a large house with many other boarders. It had been a hotel before being converted to a house. Upstairs there were fifteen rooms and a few more downstairs. It was a full and lively house. Many of the other boarders were older. They were very kind to me.

Yu-wen was sad to see me go. I took my few books, my knapsack of clothes, and a rice cooker. Without my sister's kitchen, the rice cooker was my only way to prepare food. I would cook rice and steam veggies and meat right in my room. Meals were simple. I ate directly from the rice cooker with my chopsticks while I read. The missionaries had given me books and I had my schoolwork as well. I spent my days at school and my evenings with the missionaries or at the movies. And I always found time to play in the water. It was a good life with many appreciations.

The missionaries gave me a Bible because I did not have one. Our home had never had a Bible or many books. Mama did not read, and Father preferred to drink. I knew there was more learning within books. It did not mean it was better learning but different than what I had known. This alone deserved contemplation. After all, there might be goodness that someone else has found. This is what I sought in the books the missionaries gave me. They shared a Bible with me and told me of its importance. They gave me another book which was to complement the Bible. This told of Jesus in America and the history of the early Americans. In their services, they taught mostly from this Book of Mormon.

They also taught that I could ask God to know of goodness and truth. This seemed like a better way than any ritual I had seen or book I had read. I could learn the truth and how to be good from the source of goodness. Still, the missionaries told me, it was important to study the Book of Mormon and follow what the church leaders said. I thought truth should be evident and available to everyone. However, I studied their books and found goodness and kindness.

The missionaries were very kind, very good people. I wish Mama could see that they were helping me be a good person. This way she should not worry for me, I felt. I decided to show her this church was teaching me how to be good, and I committed to following their teachings.

I did not go to church every week, and sometimes the missionaries would come to look for me. They had Yu-wen's address and would knock on her door. Most people in Taiwan at that time did not want to talk to Americans. I do not know why. Many people feared they were different and wanted to change Taiwan.

Yu-wen would not speak to the American missionaries. My brother-in-law would talk to them and tell them I did not live there anymore. When they asked where they could find me, my brother-in-law would lie. He told them he did not know where I was living, though he did. I could not hold this against him. He did not want any more strife between my mother and Yu-wen. He was protective of his family, that's all.

My whole family and even the other boarders were against me to go to church. Because I was raised next to the Buddhist Temple, everyone thought I would also be Buddhist. Most of them were, but being Buddhist did not guarantee them to be a good person. When I would study my Book of Mormon, some boarders would warn me against the American missionaries and their religion.

One day I was cooking rice and some vegetables in the rice cooker on the table next to my bed. My room was not very large, but I did not need much space. I rarely cooked meat as it was more expensive. I had gone outside to take in the evening while my dinner cooked. Apparently, the plug was very old, and I had been using it every day. It got too hot and started a fire.

My dinner did not burn, but the table next to the plug started to burn and smoke, and it almost caught my wooden bed on fire. Luckily for me there were many people living upstairs. One of them smelled the smoke, knocked on my door, then opened it and found the fire. They put it out while someone ran to find me.

I was very lucky my bed did not burn and the house did not burn because of me. I was very lucky that only the table burnt. Also, my rice cooker was burnt and unusable. I was thankful to God that nothing more was ruined. It was a close call.

However, some of the boarders told me that the fire was because I was believing in the wrong god. They said this was a reminder to stay Buddhist. But the fire started because of an old cord and too much electricity—not because of Buddha. Even my Book of Mormon was on the desk and did not burn. I did not see this as a sign. I did not tell Mama or Yu-wen about the fire. They would have said the same.

At that time there was not a Mormon church in Tai-Tung City. Usually we would meet in an office space under where the missionaries lived. It had a sign on the door, but no place for baptism. Baptism was how God could forgive you of mistakes. I made mistakes sometimes and wanted to be good, so I thought it would be ok to be baptized. But being baptized did not mean you were always good. And being forgiven for mistakes did not make one's actions good. That had to come from inside, I knew.

The missionaries said they could baptize someone in any water deep enough. I knew the water around here very well. There could be baptisms nearly everywhere, I told the missionaries. They laughed, but said they did not have a single baptized member in Tai-Tung City, and that they soon would go to another part of Taiwan. New missionaries would come to take their place, but they would not be the ones I already knew.

They said they wanted to see me baptized before they left. It did not matter much to me to get baptized, as I could not see how a little water would make me a good person. It was the teachings that helped me. I had been an investigator of the church for more than one year and had learned much. Baptism, the missionaries reminded me, was important to devote ourselves to God. To make a covenant, which was a promise between myself and God, which God could not break if I did not. This, I thought, would bring me closer to goodness, so I agreed.

I was still in high school and baptism would require a signature showing permission from one of my parents. Mama would not sign the paper, I told the missionaries. They insisted we try. They wanted to talk to her themselves. One day we took the train to the mountainside and began the long walk up the hill toward the Buddhist Temple and home.

The missionaries were surprised to see how close our house was to the Temple. I had told them I had grown up there, but they did not fully understand until now. I also told them my mother was very devout and would not allow me to be baptized. However, that day, Mama was not home.

Father said she was working outside tending the vegetables. He was home and happy to see the missionaries. He was always so polite to anyone who would visit our home. He was interested in these Americans and impressed that they spoke very good Mandarin.

The missionaries explained the importance of baptism to my father. He listened, but did not ask me what I wanted. "I cannot sign for Jung-yu," he told them. "His mother does not wish him to be part of any church except Buddhist."

"It's ok." I jumped into the conversation. "She doesn't have to concern herself with my religion too much. It can help me be a better person." We talked back and forth before Father changed his mind.

"I will sign for Jung-yu," he told the missionaries. "You must not tell your mother I am signing this today," he told to me.

"Yeah, ok. I will not tell her," I promised. I was very grateful to Father for helping me. I did not mention to the missionaries that he had been drinking that day. Perhaps they could not tell, but I knew how to know.

The day of my baptism, December 12th, 1971, I walked to the ocean to meet the missionaries. A few other people from church were on the shore. The two missionaries spoke, we prayed and sang, then they both walked into the water. I followed them.

They said their baptism prayer over me and dunked me under the waves. I stood up and was baptized. I had made a promise with God to be good and He would make me pure. Then the waves from the ocean came in. One rushed back and I slipped in the water. The wave pulled me toward the ocean and the missionary pulled me to shore. This happened once again before I could find my feet again and walk to the dry ground where the other investigators hugged me.

I was the first baptized member of the Mormon church in Tai-Tung City, which I took as a sign for my future. I felt I had been saved by these missionaries. They had given me something I had been searching for. They had taught me so much, and I felt a goodness inside of me I wanted to share. I knew then that I wanted to be a missionary to help others find goodness for themselves.

On My Own

Rarely my mom would cook. We mostly ate from cans like canned peaches, canned corn, and chips. And besides my mom's milk habit, we would often have surplus groceries from the Bishop's Storehouse. But when the food stamps came in, sometimes my mom would cook an elaborate meal. From the stacks of books along the wall she would pull out four or five cookbooks, then sit on the ground with them spread in front of her. She would turn the pages of this one and that one, looking at the pictures and occasionally reading the descriptions of the meals to us. Once she found the right recipe, the flurry would begin.

First the ingredients would arrive, bags laid everywhere there was space, and my mom would start cooking. The kitchen would transform with different foods and smells. Cut vegetables in piles, opened jars scattered across the counter, and warmth from the oven flooding out of the kitchen into the rest of the trailer. You could even smell it from outside. The whole trailer park knew that my mom was up to something.

It would take her all day back and forth in the kitchen while Victor and I watched. We would pull jars from the grocery bags, sneak a taste from one jar or another, and watch as the whole meal took shape. Finally, it would be done. There was roast duck, capers, beans cooked in butter, little golden potatoes sprinkled with green herbs. We would have a magnificent dinner. Like a fancy restaurant, but all for us, and we could eat it while sitting on the couch. It felt like we were royalty. We would eat so much. Then my mom would get tired, and she would sleep. We would all sleep. It was warm and safe and we felt abundant with our bellies full.

The next day the feast would sit on the counter, half-eaten, the glimmer of warmth and succulence faded a little. But we still ate. The food was ready and delicious, and my mom had put so much work into making it. The days after she didn't have as much interest in the food, but Victor and I would eat from the pans as we wandered by, never sitting down to a full meal.

Days would pass and the food stayed out on the counter, drying out. It would diminish through our grazing, but stayed served and ready for us. My mom would sleep for long periods during the day and would not spend any time in the kitchen. Victor and I would play Sega Genesis or watch television.

When the food was gone, we would return to eating from cans. But for a while we would have a gourmet meal reade for us whenever we wanted another taste.

One time a friend from school came over. She seemed surprised we would have food just out for us. She didn't do that at her house.

"Aren't you going to put that away?" she asked after refusing to have some.

"No, it is just here for when we are hungry."

"You aren't even going to put it in the fridge?"

I remember the look of horror on her face, and I knew that not only did her mother not do this, but that there was something distasteful about it. I felt ashamed, but I didn't know what to do. I couldn't change my mom, and this was our normal.

Bringing up the need to preserve the food or clean the chaos from the flurry of cooking would not have any effect. My mom would not change. Any commentary would be taken as criticism or explained away by revelation. I knew any effort would be left to me. After my friend left and my mom was asleep, I put the food we could still eat in the fridge and threw the rest away. Victor watched me in silence.

The food was taken care of now. Life could continue as normal. Or so I thought. As I saw more of my friends' lives, I realized ours was not normal. It never could be. My friends were not running from the cult. We were. And at any moment we could be found. This drove many of my mom's decisions for us. And G-ma's too. It had to. We were wanted and living in secret. I trusted that my mom's methods might be different. They had to be.

The cult could be anywhere. We had to be vigilant. Our lives could not be like the lives of those who had not been victims. We had survived. And to make sure our survival continued, we had to be constantly on guard.

I could not tell my phone number to any of my friends. Or my address. When they asked where I lived, I would only tell near where we were. I could not risk the information getting where someone could find us. "We are by the corner by the gas station," I would say. Or, "We live near a bunch of other houses not too far from here. A great neighborhood." Of course, their parents would find out whenever a friend came by to play, but my mom had told them, which meant she trusted them to be safe. More often I went to their houses. It was simpler that way. However, most of the time we stayed home, the three of us together. It was easier to live in our own normal than to try to justify it to others.

The only time we would clean the trailer was before having visitors. My mom didn't have many friends who stopped by, so that was never a concern. Instead of checking on us at church or via a phone call, one time the Home Teachers from church were actually coming to see us. We needed to clean. The Mormon church assigns each family Home Teachers, men who come to every house dressed in their Sunday clothes once a month. They would carry the Ensign, the church's monthly publication, and would share the central message, check in on a family's concerns, and ask to pray together. My mom would talk to them on the phone so they would not usually visit us at the trailer. This time they had insisted. It was so they could properly look after us as the Lord wanted them to. We could not deny the Lord.

Cleaning was hard work. We spent hours picking up trash. It was everywhere imaginable. Though it was months from

Thanksgiving, I found an old pumpkin that had been placed on a bookshelf and had withered and browned as it decomposed. Dark brown streaks ran down the shelf onto the floor and other books. It had been that way for months. There were so many boxes to move just to have a seat for guests. The couch had to be cleared off. The table too. We stashed stuff in cupboards, or under our beds. Victor's room became filled with things, but he didn't mind. Or so he said.

This went on for three days. Each day we would spend time cleaning, we would find things we thought had been lost or we had forgotten about. By the time of the visit the trailer looked entirely different. There were more spaces to sit than our three and the pathways through the house were cleared wide. It was almost as if we had moved again. We were ready.

One of the Home Teachers brought his son along with him, Thomas. I knew him from Sunday School at church though he was a year older than I was in public school. They came in and we all greeted them, happy to have a visitor. The Home Teachers and my mom sat down and began to talk. Victor and I talked to Thomas. I asked him about school, and about what classes he liked. I tried to talk about the things he might be interested in. He did not seem impressed.

I told him that we were happy to have him. I even told him we had cleaned and cleaned before they came. At this he paused. He looked around. "You've been cleaning in here?"

"For three days!" I was proud. Thomas looked at me in disbelief. I did not understand what he could be confused about. Then I did. This was so much cleaner than what we had become used to, and to Thomas it was still filthy. For him to think we had spent time cleaning and for it to still look as it did meant it had been dirtier than he had even imagined. I watched his face as he looked around. I began to see through his eyes. The trailer was still dirty. There were stains where things had spilled and were never picked up, piles lining every wall, and he hadn't even seen our bedrooms.

It hurt to see his disapproval. I had seen again that our way of life was not acceptable to others, was not the same as others, and in ways that had nothing to do with the cult. There was not any reason that we had to live in a dirty house. Later that night, after my mom and Victor had gone to bed, I cleaned my room. It took hours, but I folded my clothes, threw away so much stuff, and made my bed. In the morning I was tired but at least I had created a space where it was clean, organized, and mine.

I did not want to be ashamed of what we weren't or envious of lives we could never lead. I wanted to be proud to be me, to have survived. We had our trailer where we could all be together. It was full of stuff, but all of it was ours. We had birds and rabbits that lived with us. They didn't have cages and nested and ate and pooped wherever it was most convenient. My mom always was so kind to animals and wanted to care for them. It was not uncommon for her to rescue a hurt creature and nurse it back to health. We once had a crane with a hurt leg. It lived in the bathroom for a couple weeks until it was well enough to be set free. We had a chicken, Barbara, who would follow us wherever we walked. And we occasionally had a cat or two that God sent us. My mom would receive this revelation on the spot when we found them around the neighborhood.

We had our time. When we did not go to public school, our homeschool consisted of some TV, some Sega, and so many trips to the library. Some days we would go to the library in the morning and stay long past when regular school would have dismissed. My mom loved the library. She would spend all day there if she could, she often said. She would check out as many books as was allowed and bring them all home. We had stacks of books in the trailer. Stacks reaching to the ceiling. Still, my mom would bring more home. She spent more time collecting them than reading, but she liked the books around just the same.

We had our hopes. We knew that we were destined for great things—far greater than this single-wide trailer in this trailer park. That is why the Lord led us to safety. And we constantly dreamt of those days.

We wanted a farm with a little farmhouse and animals all around. It would be a place where we could all be, where G-ma would visit, and where the cult would never find us. We would have many chickens and rabbits. We would have mourning doves and even a goat. And we would have cats. How I wanted cats.

I would spend hours drawing out floor plans for the house I knew we would have someday. There were multiple different versions. Some had elevators, others had slides. But they all had rooms for the three of us and space for the animals. I would draw and dream of the day that we did not have to hide from the cult, when my mom would get a wonderful job, and we would have everything we needed.

We had the Lord. Each Sunday we would dress up in our finest clothes, except never anything red as that was the devil's color, and go to church. It was three hours long and was split into three different meetings. The first was the most boring. But also, my mom told me, the most important. That was where we would partake of the sacrament. It was little pieces of bread and tiny cups of water passed around by boys just older than me. It was a symbol of my baptism and the forever promise I made to Jesus. I would follow all of His rules, and He would make me pure. Every week.

Not only would Jesus make us pure, but he would keep us safe. We had to be extra careful to follow all of the commandments. It was by the power of the Lord we escaped the cult, and because of Him we could stay free from them. We had to be careful as well, but none of it would be possible without the Lord. We prayed each night and gave thanks for that.

And most importantly, we had our safety. Here in the smallest trailer in the park, the cult would not come looking for us. Here we could live in peace.

We had many things, and we were thankful for them. But we never had any money, or at least not much. Not because money was evil, though lots of evil people had money. The cult made money in evil ways, selling sex slaves and drugs and all sorts of things. But lots of good people had money too. G-ma and Grandpa Tom had money and land. G-ma was even looking for her dream house.

It would take money for our dream house. I didn't know how much, but I trusted my mom as she trusted the Lord. We had been promised that if we followed the commandments we would be blessed beyond our wildest dreams. This would come to pass any day, I thought, and drew yet another floor plan. I would meticulously describe them all to Victor. "This is where the chickens would live. And this is the slide from your bedroom, and this is the slide to my bedroom." He was always very impressed. I stacked up the pages in a neat pile on the bed next to my sleeping bag where I knew they would be kept safe when we needed them to start building.

We all loved to dream of our future home. It was the great hope we could move toward. If we weren't talking about the fright of the past and how we were able to be free, we dreamt of even more freedom and a bit of luxury. I went to bed many nights thinking that my mom would suddenly get a great job, buy a farm, and we were going to fix up a house together and be okay.

Then I ran out of toothpaste. The tube sat on the bathroom sink. Victor squeezed from the top, but I rolled the toothpaste from the bottom to get every last bit. Then it was empty. I told my mom we needed more. She turned from the television to look at me standing in the hallway. "Are you all out?" "It's all gone," I said. She was not pleased. "You have to tell me before you are about to run out so we can save up for new toothpaste."

I didn't know how much toothpaste cost. But I knew it couldn't be as much as a farm with goats and chickens. We were running out of food in the pantry, and what had been cooked and left out on the counter had been moldy for weeks. I realized then, as I brushed with only water, that the farm and house and land wouldn't magically come true. All of that required work, persistence, and money. If my mom couldn't even get us toothpaste, then our dream life would stay a dream. She wasn't going to take action on it. She was going collect books about it, watch TV, and sleep for most of the day.

Because we had escaped the cult, I thought we were chosen and would be taken care of. I thought that everything was going to change. That wasn't true. We had escaped the cult so that we could be cold in our leaky trailer, and hungry, and brush our teeth without paste. That was what life was, and that was how it was going to be. I pushed all my drawings of our dream house off of the bed. They merged with the trash on the floor. That is what had become of our dreams.

I wanted out of this life. I was so frustrated because as a fifth grader I couldn't be in college yet. College was the ticket out. Until then I was stuck here, hungry and cold. The other option I had in life was being raped and abused in a satanic cult. I had no other choices. Other kids could say, "I don't like this life. I'm going to live with my dad." But living with my dad meant death. Those were my only options: being really cold and hungry or being dead.

When I was ten, I thought how our lives would be different if we just had 100 dollars. Just that much could have changed our lives. I knew we weren't ok, and we had to be making money for everything to be ok. The trailer had become squalor. Food rotted on the counters and the birds and rabbits would poop everywhere. There were boxes of storage against the walls and stacks of books up to the ceiling.

I realized my mom would not change. This situation could have been different. This wasn't the fault of the cult. She didn't have to stay home in her room often all day. I would try to motivate her to get a job. I would be as encouraging as I could. I would ask her why she didn't work.

"I want to be home with you two. To take care of you and help you grow," she said.

"It's ok. We will be fine here. I will watch Victor," I assured her. I did not want our poverty to be my fault. She was firm that she wanted to be at home with us. She spoke with such conviction she began to cry.

I thought eventually it would get bad enough that she would get a job. Not only protecting us, but providing for us was also her responsibility. She was our mother, our protector. I always wanted to let her decide to take care of us. In the meantime, I needed clothes and toothpaste, and I needed to save for college.

College was always in my mind after that. I didn't dream about the farm anymore. I started plotting how I would get away. I would live somewhere else, cook for myself, and go to school.

I told myself that when I was on my own, I would have everything I needed, but for now I would save everything. I made a personal pact to save everything that anyone ever gives me. I said it in a prayer. I asked God for help and told Him I would save all I could. If there was money in a birthday card, I would save it. I would not ask for things, just money. I wanted to save all of my money so that I would have enough to get out! I had to have enough to support myself. If I started now, at ten years old, I would have enough for college and an apartment by the time I turned eighteen.

I did not know how much it would be for college and for an apartment. I just knew that my only option was to start saving immediately.

To save money I had to make money. My first business was feather pencils. I was in fifth grade and had a bag of craft feathers in all different colors. In my school many of the girls really liked having pens and pencils with different toppers. They would have fun, sparkly things decorating their pencils somehow. I saw a need and profit. I had a bag of feathers and could get another for a dollar. And each pencil only cost ten cents. I figured out how much I could make with each pencil. I started talking to some friends at school. I told them all about the pencils and how great they were. Then I made myself a really awesome feather pencil to show off. At school I displayed it proudly. "This is my pencil. Look at all the feathers." Everyone wanted to know where I got it. "I actually made it myself. I can make feather pens or pencils. I can make it customized to any sort of thing."

It was my first exposure to advertising, and it worked. People wanted me to make them one. That day I had quite a few orders. I told them to bring me a pencil and I would bring it back the next day as a feather pencil. I brought the pencils back and they paid me a dollar. I started making my own money. Just like that.

Then I noticed people were wearing hemp necklaces. They were the next big thing. Some kids at school were buying them, but I knew I could make them myself. I got a board and put a nail in the top, then tied hemp strands to it so I could braid necklaces. I would make different knot patterns and add beads, bringing them to school to show off. "Look how cool this hemp necklace is!" My classmates would gather around to inspect them. "Oh, that's so awesome," someone would say. "I want this bead!" "Oh, and I want that one!"

I would remember what they liked. That's when I started collecting beads. I even asked for beads for my birthday. I invested in different types and sizes, spending hours at the bead store to scour for unique ones. It was exciting to collect and display them. I organized them in a small box I'd found, and when someone wanted to design their hemp necklace, I'd open it to show all the options. "If you want this bead it's a dollar. These beads are only ten cents." I'd take their design and work on it that night.

My friend Sarah saw what I was doing and was impressed by how much I was making. She thought my business ideas were really cool. Then one day she came to school and announced she was starting her own hemp necklace business. I was furious that my friend would copy me and become my competition.

I completely abandoned the hemp necklaces. That wouldn't be my business anymore. I decided to do something skill-based that no one could copy. I took some money from my necklace business and invested in a little nail kit and special polishes with really thin brushes for detailed artwork.

My nail business, The Big Thumb, was born. I started painting my finger nails with elaborate scenes of a sunset on one finger or a little dragon spanning four nails on one hand.

People were amazed when they learned I did it myself. I told my mom I wanted business cards, and she said I could get them as soon as I made twenty dollars. I convinced my cousin at G-ma's house to let me paint her nails, upselling designs until she'd ordered twenty dollars of services. After completing her nails, I bought my very own business cards.

I began giving business cards to people I knew and had them share with friends. I created a display by cutting cardboard finger-nail shapes and gluing them to paper, making them larger than actual nails. I painted sample designs on a fingernail so people could look at all the options directly on the pricing sheet.

Soon people called the house asking for me to paint their nails. Some of my classmates' moms would invite me over to do their nails, sometimes for all the girls in the family. Sleepovers became my biggest moneymaker. I wasn't invited to stay at the sleepovers. I was invited to come paint nails. My mom would drive me to these parties where five or six girls would each want something fancier than the last. I'd show them the design sheets, spend hours paint-ing their nails, and then my mom would drive me home again. I could make quite a bit in one night.

I had a unique business and was earning more money than ever. My stack of bills grew larger, so I created a special bank from the cargo pocket of my brother's old shorts. I arranged the bills by denomination and kept them hidden in this pocket bank, only taking it out to add more money. I was on my way to financial freedom.

Then just like that, whether from a weird call in the night or because my mom learned the cult had found us, we moved back to G-ma's. We packed frantically in the night, stuffing everything into boxes and bags. I carefully packed my pocket bank with my best clothes before we left the little trailer behind. I never told anyone goodbye. Maybe they called looking for The Big Thumb. Maybe they wanted hemp necklaces. Maybe customers were waiting for me, wanting my services. I would never know, and I wasn't sure if it would ever be safe to come back again.

士兵

Soldier

Before I could serve a mission for the Lord, I first must serve two years in the military for Taiwan. It was mandatory for every young man. Some would later become officers as their career, like my brother-in-law married to my second sister. Most, like me, would wait for the date we could leave.

When I shipped out to training camp, Mama came to see the truck take us away. We loaded up in the back until we could not squeeze in another soon-to-be soldier. The truck started down the road. I could barely peek out, but I could see Mama running after the truck until we were out of sight. Many other mothers ran after the truck as well. It was a sadness to see their sons leave home. At the same time, they were proud to watch them go to serve their country.

We had been told we would only need the clothes we were wearing. The army would provide everything else. Turns out we did not hardly need our clothes. At training camp, we stripped to our underwear and sat down for a haircut. In under three minutes each, we were all shaven bald. We told our height and were given our uniform. By the end of the first day most soldiers did not have a single thing from home except their memories. I had those and also my Book of Mormon.

Training camp was mostly learning the rules for the military. And running. There was so much of both. The first rule we learned was how to make a bed. It had to be so tight. There could not even be one bean curd rumpling the smoothness. The second rule was that you do not complain. If you complained about the heat or the running, you would have the lining taken out of your steel helmet so there was no barrier between your bald head and the hot metal. If you complained more, you would lay on the cement outside in the sun where your head would burn. It would be very very hot. Many would cry out in pain, but it didn't matter to the officers. Military would make many things to punish you. We did not have a courthouse in the army. Whatever an officer said became the new law. He could give any punishment he wanted.

If you do something wrong, you can get punished. If you do something very wrong, you could go to jail for a long time. For as long as the officers wanted. After, you still have to serve your time in the army. Army is two years, but if you go to jail for three years it doesn't count. When they let you out you still have the full two years. If you kill somebody, you get executed. When they execute someone, they send notice to all other platoons. Every platoon had to send one soldier to watch the execution. That soldier would come back very sick, very upset, and tell their platoon what they saw. This was to scare all other soldiers into following the rules.

The military under Chiang Kai-shek was very strict. They had many rules and very quick punishments. You do wrong, you get punished. They think you do wrong, you get punished. You run away from army, you get executed. There was no judge, no court. Only the rules of the commander.

We were taught the rules, taught to fight, made to run, and told we would be stationed after training. We were given a rifle and pistol with our number on them and told they were our first life. We could lose our real life, which was second, but we could not lose our guns. After three months of training, the army organized us into squads in a platoon in a battalion under a commander. Then we deployed to camps. We were not at war with China then, at least not open war, but it was still very dangerous.

At the military camp there were many guards. There were two at the gates to guard who could come in and who could leave, a guard inside the camp armory who would watch the weapons, and a guard to watch the other guards. Sometimes they would send a spy to make sure the guards were doing their job. The spy would come and ask for their weapons. They would ask for their pistol that matched their number. They would say, "Just give me the gun for a little while. I give you lots of money. Five thousand." If you cooperate with the spy you can go to jail for a long time. Very strict.

Everybody must be a guard. I also had to take my turn. Every day there were three different guards for every post. At the gates you have to make sure no one comes in who isn't allowed. For example, you ask them what color today is. If they don't know the color of the day to get back in to camp, you don't let them in. If anyone tries to run inside the camp, the guards can shoot them, no problem. I sometimes stood at the gate to guard the camp with my gun which has my number. Sometimes I guarded the weapons inside the camp. This was better because it was more quiet and gave me more time to think and read.

If you are on guard and reading the newspaper no one would say anything. We were all from the platoon. But I didn't read the newspaper. I would read my Book of Mormon. In the army you could not read much, only military pamphlets and the newspaper. They don't allow any religious books at all. They don't allow any bible or anything. Other guards must have thought my Book of Mormon was just a magazine. But since it had one angel Moroni with a trumpet on the cover, it looked like religious book.

One day on guard at the armory an officer came to tell me that I cannot read any religious books anymore. I said, "Ok, I will not read." For a while I did not read, but once in a while I read my Book of Mormon again. It is a very good story and I learned a lot every time.

Every army camp has people who will go out and buy food to feed the soldiers. Ours was a soldier who started before me named Pai-han. He would negotiate with farmers to buy whatever the army needed. He would buy so much food at one time and the cooks would put it in their meals for us. Whatever was left over would be thrown away or fed to the pigs. Pai-han would tell me what he bought and give me all the receipts. I was the assistant accountant. I would write all the expenses down in my book. It was a good job to have in the army. Much better than training to fight. I had to take my turn on guard as well.

The real accountant would also check my book. He was a career officer whose job is to care for all the accounts and balances. His job was also to make sure the soldiers are not talking about Communism. I was just his assistant. I would write down all the receipts and all the money spent. If any other officer finds a mistake in the books, there could be a problem. They wouldn't check just on certain days. They could walk in at any time and ask for my book. I had to stay very up to date and write down all the details.

I got this job because my handwriting is very neat. I also had the job to make the poster for any bulletin across the camp. This was a very good job. Sometimes when I had to be in the office, I could miss a training. When other soldiers were running and running, I could be in the office writing down the receipts.

Pai-han was not an honest man, but he had help to get where he was. The commander of the platoon was older. He had come from China with Chiang Kai-shek's forces and was ready to retire. He could advance rank one more time to increase his pension. Everyone knew that was the only reason he stayed at the camp. It wasn't because he was a good man or a smart man. He did not even have grade school education. He gave Pai-han his job, and together they were dishonest.

One day, an officer from outside of our platoon came to visit. He walked straight in our office and demanded to see Pai-han and the full record of our accounts. The actual accountant was not there. Only me. The officer asked to speak to Pai-han. I did not say anything. It was just my job to write down the receipts, that's all.

The officer told Pai-han there had been a mistake with the books and money was missing. Pai-han said that perhaps someone had stolen money, but he didn't know anything. The officer was quiet for a minute. When he spoke again, his voice was calm and lower.

"I know what has been happening. I know everything. I have requested the records, but I don't need them to know what I know. If you are honest with me and tell me what happened, I can help you stay out of jail. If you are not, I cannot help you at all."

Pai-han told him everything. It was all news to me, who stayed shut. I had nothing to add. Pai-han told how they would ask a farmer how much to buy his crop. If the farmer would say 500, Pai-han would offer him 400 and have the receipt made for 600. The extra money he would keep. Same when they sold pigs. Whatever price they got, they would write down they were paid much less. The rest of the money would just disappear. Pai-han did not act alone. He told the officer names of others who knew this and the names of those who kept the money that was supposed to be for food for the soldiers.

I did not know this was happening. All I knew is I wrote down the receipts I was given and noticed that so many times there were different prices for similar goods. It made no sense why potatoes would cost twice as much as they did the week before. I made the record anyway. The officer asked for a copy of my reports. He told us not to worry and that we were safe.

Pai-han was worried. I was worried. I told Pai-han, "That guy said he knew everything, but I don't think so. You told him everything. He didn't know." I didn't know either.

The commander was very upset with me and Pai-han. But Pai-han was ok and he still had much money. When I was questioned, I said the truth—that I didn't know anything, and I didn't tell anybody what I didn't know. Everyone thought it was me who told that officer because he copied my reports. This was an order. All I did was make a copy for him as commanded. They were not happy with me. That did not matter. I was just there until my time was up. Then I could leave to serve a mission for the church.

I lived my life just as before Pai-han confessed. One day I was stationed on patrol guard. I had to guard the whole camp, walk the fence to make sure no one was sneaking in and out and see that the other guards were all in their places. I would walk my route and then sit at the main gate for a while before walking again. Early in the morning, about to be relieved of my duty, the commander came in to my guard post where I was reading the Book of Mormon. He pulled the book from my hands, saw what it was, and threw it on the ground. It broke into eight pieces.

He was very upset. I was very upset. He could tell me not to read, punish me, whatever, but he is not supposed to break my Book of Mormon. At that point I had nothing to read and could not retaliate. I continued my guard and walked the grounds again. The commander went back into his room and stood in front of the window. It was almost morning.

The commander was upset. Not only at me. Every day before training he would take us into the field. There he would keep us in line and just begin talking about nothing at all. We would stand for hours while he talked of his life, the war, what he saw, what he had to do, anything that is garbage. Nothing important. He said he knew there was a spy in our camp. He said this over and over.

He did not say the spy was me. The spy was not me, though maybe he thought it was. I had written my reports just as they had been given to me, and I made a copy for the officer that demanded them. It was all under orders.

He would keep us standing in line in the sun until someone fainted. He would talk and talk. He told us that if there was a spy during wartime, he would be executed. But this was not wartime.

At camp we had a small house with rooms as small as an outhouse. It was not a jail, but it felt like jail. The commander could lock people in there and have a guard watch over them. When they left the room to eat or go to the bathroom, a guard with his gun would follow them. I joked that one day it would be my time to go in there. Actually, I was right. It was not only a joke.

They told me I had to live in there for a while. They had a room for me. They said I was reading my Book of Mormon while on guard duty. That was true, and I was wrong. I didn't know it was such a big problem. They said I had been brainwashed and I needed to change my loyalty and be only loyal to my country. A guard sat in front of the little house. He told me that if anyone tries to run away or take his pistol, he has the right to shoot them.

"I will not steal your gun. I will not try to run away," I said.

The guard said that if I cooperate then I might only have to stay a few days or a few weeks, that's it. I said, "That's good. I will stay here." Soon the guard became my friend. He told me that all the officers were waiting for the next notice. They could be transferred to a different camp or a different platoon. Or they could go to jail. They could not know.

I wanted to say, "Why is it me staying here? I did not tell anything. Nothing happened to Pai-han, and he was the one who told the officer they had been stealing money. He has no punishment. He's ok. I did not steal nothing and I did not tell nothing. I was just there to record, that's all." But I said nothing.

Because we were not at war every Saturday and Sunday the soldiers had days off. We could go into town. Many would drink or smoke until late in the night. They thought it was so fun. I did not drink or smoke or chase girls, so it was not as fun for me. I did not always leave camp. When I did I mostly I went to the movie theater.

The little house was not jail, though it felt very much the same. It did not have a big lock on the door and many bars. It had a guard who sat there with his gun, that's all. I was let out to get food from the mess hall and to go to the outhouse. I was also let out for the weekend and had to report back to the house on Sunday night. For a few weeks I would come back and hope I could go back to my job in the accounting office. They sent me back to the little house without anything to do and nothing to read. I was not serving my country in there. I worried that I would go to jail. Then Mama will not be happy. She didn't want me to go to church. She would be very unhappy if I went to jail for reading my Book of

Mormon. I was afraid to go back to camp. One Sunday night I decided not to go back to camp, and I stayed in town.

I was very nervous. I did not look like everyone else. Usually, in Taiwan, people have hair. Many work in the sun, but not so many are so tan from running in the sun and training. If you were so tan from training in the sun and have no hair, it means you were army. In every city from Monday to Friday it would be easy to spot any soldiers. If the military police see someone very tan and with no hair, they would ask for your papers. If you have run away, you have a big problem. They would report you.

If you ran away with a gun, they would notify all MPs across the country so they can find you. If you don't have a gun, they would wait one week before beginning a reported search. I knew I could not walk around outside. During the day I would stay in the movie theater. It is dark, usually quiet, and the military police rarely come in.

After a few days of movies and hiding I felt that this was not right. It was a Thursday when I decided to go ask for help. I took a bus to Tai-Tung City to see my brother-in-law, an army officer. I told him the whole situation. I told him all about Pai-han, the stolen money, and the broken Book of Mormon. I did not tell my second sister. I did not want her to panic.

My brother-in-law said, "You have a big problem. If you had left during wartime, you would be executed. If you had a gun you would be jailed. You are lucky it is not a time of war. You still have a chance. The best way is to go back to camp as soon as possible. I don't know what the army is going to do to you next step. You are lucky I know some very important people in the army. We might be able to keep you out of jail, but you must return to camp."

He was right. I had to return to my fate. I hoped I would not go to jail. I was nervous. I didn't want to have a big, big problem. I wanted to finish my army so I could serve my mission for the Lord. I did not go back to the camp. I was too scared. I ran to the movie theater again instead.

There I saw one movie about the army. In this movie some of the soldiers ran away. When they finally were caught some of the soldiers were executed. I could not be caught. I decided to go back to camp.

About midnight, I got back and thought maybe I could sneak in to the camp, but could not without passing the gate. The guards at the gate all knew me. They saw me. "Oh my gosh," they said, "You are in big trouble. You have to come in and go straight to jail. You better get in as soon as possible." They said all sorts of things to make me more afraid.

"Yeah, I will go in," I said. Inside the camp, everybody was asleep. I moved without a sound to my bed in the darkness to sleep. People started to wake up, and they woke up the others. They saw I had returned and everybody started talking about me. The guard stopped by because of all the noise.

"Oh, Jung-yu has returned. You have to go see the commander. Everybody has been looking for you for a week. This is not good for you," the guard said to me. I followed him to the commander's quarters in the middle of the night.

The other men shouted to me, telling me that they will bring me snacks while I am in jail. That they will come visit once they return home. They shouted they hoped I don't get too old in jail to serve in the army when they finally let me out. All kinds of things they said.

I waited outside the commander's quarters wishing I could run away again. The commander already did not like me for reading my Book of Mormon, and maybe he thought I was a spy. Now I was a deserter. It was not good. What I did not know would save me.

There had been a transfer while I was hiding in the movie theater. Many of the officers, including the commander, were moved to a different camp. I had never seen this young commander before. He ushered me into his room.

I wanted to explain to him what had happened, but I knew better than to speak first. There are rules. Then he told me not to worry. He said he knew what had happened to me before I left and all that happened with Pai-han. He was here to fix it and to protect his soldiers. He said that if I had run away during a war or active deployment, I would be executed. As there is no war, he could arrange whatever punishment he saw fit.

I waited for my punishment, hoping I would not have to stay in that little room alone for very long. He did not punish me. His eyes were very kind when he looked at me. "Being a commander is difficult," he said. "I have to be respected and also understanding. But I chose this life.

"You should be careful. And kind, and patient. In two years you are going home," he told me. "Then you can do as you wish. In the army there is no freedom to talk how you like, do what you like, anything. It's army—you follow every rule every day until you return home.

"I want to see you on the last day of your army service," he said. He gave me a hug and told me to get to sleep.

No bed had ever felt so good. I was comforted by all the kindness the commander had shown to me. I could have been thrown in jail, or worse. I was so happy to crawl into my bunk and not worry for my future. I would be ok—and loyal to this commander.

The next day the commander spoke to us where we lined up after training. He said, "Jung-yu is home now. Nobody say anything about it. Just pretend everything has always been this way. If I hear of any of you spreading word that he left and came back, you will be punished. Jung-yu is your brother. In the army we protect our brothers."

This commander was a good man. He took a risk in not punishing me and showed us all his loyalty to his soldiers. We respected him very much. We did everything he commanded. I kept the accounting books for the camp for the rest of my time in the army. I worked very hard because I knew I served under a commander who was honest and who worked hard too.

Finally, it was my turn to go home. I had finished my service. I folded all my army clothes, very square, and made my bed—not a bean curd. I bought thirty feet of firecrackers. At the army camp gate, I lit all my firecrackers. Some of my friends were already there to see me leave. The rest came when the firecrackers went off. I stood in the smoke after the noise had stopped and looked at all the soldiers I had known. "Next time it will be your turn," I said. "If you are patient!"

The next thing I wanted was to be a missionary for the church. I sent in the application papers when my army service was over. But I didn't hear a response. I waited weeks, months. And nothing. The church had not written me back, and I had told them I was ready. All I needed was for them to tell me where to go. I was not even hard to find. I was living back at home on the mountainside next to the Buddhist Temple.

Every day I spent four hours walking to our mailbox at the post office down the hill by the river and back again. I prayed the church would write and tell me I could finally be a missionary. But there was no mail for me. Every week no mail. I was disappointed.

Mama said, "There is no reason you should wait to go on a mission. That church doesn't want you. You don't need to go on a mission for them. You better go find a job. You can go to Taipei with your brother. He is a truck driver. Go and find yourself a good job. Don't stay home. Your church, your mission doesn't want you."

I told her, "This week I'll get my letter."

"You've been saying that for the longest time. Go work with your brother."

After five months I still waited. Finally, I gave up on serving a mission. When my brother came home to visit, I told him I would go to the city with him to find a job.

Mama was so happy. I was dismayed by my church. To her this was good news.

My brother was very happy because I would be staying with him. He talked all the way from Tai-Tung City about the fun we would have together. The first day in Taipei, we went out to dinner then to a bar where a lot of girls hung out. I sat and drank my soft drink. The girls approached and flirted with me. "Your brother told us that you like telling jokes. Why are you so quiet?" they asked.

"Today is not my day," I responded.

My brother butted in. "Just because you can't become a missionary doesn't mean it is the end of the world. We can make lots of money together and have fun!"

I did not want to follow his lifestyle. I had committed to serving God. I wanted to fulfill my commitments. I enjoyed the Mormon lifestyle and searching for my inner goodness.

I worked for a few days with my brother before I saw two missionaries on the street. They gave me the address and phone number for the local mission office. Immediately I called the office and scheduled an appointment with the mission president, Brother Nielsen. My brother said he would not drive me to my appointment. Our mother had sent me to Taipei to help him, not to get involved with the local Mormon church.

"I have to tell them I am done waiting. They might be waiting for me to respond to them," I said. "They needed to know after two years of army service and months of waiting, I am working and no longer available for a mission."

Eventually my brother agreed to take me to the mission home for ten minutes.

In the office I was greeted by a couple young missionaries and an older couple. Each had on a name tag with their American name spelled out in Mandarin characters. I told them that I had been waiting for over five months for a mission call and now it was too late. I was going to find a job and would not be available.

The kind woman at the desk smiled at me while one of the younger men translated into English what I had said. I could speak English only very little. I spoke Mandarin to the missionaries as they all spoke my language to a different degree. She asked me to have a seat and wait for Brother Nielsen. She filed through papers in her open filing cabinet. Then she dialed the phone and began speaking in English.

We waited, and I began to get nervous my brother would be upset I took so long. I was there to say goodbye, not to wait for some stranger to have a conversation. The missionaries continued talking to me. They had so many questions. I told them my story of wanting to go on my mission during my time in the army, and how I had been waiting since then to serve the Lord and His children.

The woman still talked on the phone when Brother Nielsen greeted me. In his office, I spoke with him for over an hour with the help of the missionaries who translated for us.

The woman from the lobby came in during our talk and spoke quietly to Brother Nielsen. He smiled and thanked her.

Brother Nielsen told me that Salt Lake City had not received my papers. Perhaps they lost the letter. That did not matter, he said. He would allow me to leave on my mission immediately. I did not have to wait any longer. He told me that I should come back next week ready to become a missionary. I could finally fulfill my promise to God.

When I came back outside to meet my brother, I told him I had so many appreciations for the church and the missionaries. And that I could serve a mission. He was not happy.

"You should not go," he told me. "You should stay with me. We can do everything together. We will work, and cook, and go out to bars, have drinks, talk to girls. There are so many things to do together," he said. "I can teach you how to drive if you don't go. If you join the missions, I'll never see you again. You'll disappoint Mama and she'll blame me for your decision."

I declined. I wanted to go to my mission and learn from my Father in Heaven how to be a better man. Mama should be happy for me that I can learn this and not end up like my father here.

I did not have any things to get or take care of like they had said at the mission office. I only had family to tell. Then I was ready to go.

My third sister, Xinyi, asked how much the church was paying me for this. I explained my service was voluntary. She accused me of being insane. She could not understand why I would do such things without pay. I explained that I believed in God, and He would help me fulfill my dreams. I had made a promise to Him. I could not expect Him to keep His word if I did not keep mine. She agreed to help me finally, if I needed it.

I returned home to tell Mama. Mama was not proud like she was when I went to the army. She seemed sad. She did not come to the train station to see me go. She did not run after me as I left. She found no honor in my service. It was not for her that I went. I needed to go, to grow, to be a good man, and follow the Lord. Every day until I left, my brother tried to convince me not to go.

I went to my mission. I served my mission for two years without missing a single day. I was very happy for these two years; they gave me some kind of change. I learned to take care of other people. I learned to love God is to love all His children. All the scriptures, Bible, whatever, all are nice. The leaders of the church were very kind. I wanted to be around this type of people. People who want to help others, that respect family, that show love to all of God's creation. I wanted to have a family that believed these things. I served my mission for only two years, but I dreamt to have a healthy, happy, loving, Mormon family for all my life. And more.

During my mission I lived and worked with American missionaries. They were kind, very tall, and spoke loudly. I helped them with their Mandarin and they would help me with English. Many of them could not pronounce my name correctly. "Dzh-ung-Yoo," I would say slowly. "Junk-you," they would repeat. It was easier for them to call me Jack. This would be my English name, I decided. Almost everyone I knew in the mission field called me Jack.

Because of the church I became a more better person. The church taught me to love my parents, respect parents, respect elders. I feel it is a good thing to become a member, even though my mother wants me to walk away from the church. I can see the value of family and the importance of loyalty and honesty. I did not have all these growing up, I felt. I had to learn them from somewhere, and the Mormon church taught me these things. So I never felt bad about learning to love and serve others.

Leaving

We were used to not saying goodbye. Leaving was always sudden. After a suspicious phone call would alert my mom that the cult had found us, we'd pack and vanish in the middle of the night without farewells. If anyone knew we were leaving or where we were going, we might be in danger. Every couple of years, I would disappear from my friend group without a word. They probably still don't know where I went. One day I was their friend, and the next, I was gone. This pattern repeated over and over.

My mom stayed constantly vigilant. We prayed every night to know if we were in danger and to be blessed to stay far from anyone in the cult. Of course, we knew who they were, including many famous people, government officials, even some people at school. They were doctors and church members. We had to stay watchful.

At G-ma's new house, my mom assured us we would be safe. G-ma lived up on a hill overlooking the city. This gave us a good vantage point, but we still had to be careful. When leaving the house, my mom would scan the area for unfamiliar cars on the street or drawn windows where someone might be watching. She had Victor and me check under the car and in the wheel wells for tracking devices or cameras.

We knew the cult had advanced technology to spy on us. Sometimes I wondered if they had found us through my nail business, where I'd given my phone number to strangers hoping for new clients. If this was the case, my mom never mentioned it. Now at G-ma's, I knew I would have to start over. This time I would be more careful.

For starters, I changed my name to Jane Bee. This way, I was sure the cult couldn't find me. Not now, not ever. I had designed my plan for freedom and nothing could get in my way. At G-ma's, my goal became more important than ever. This was not only because my mom, brother, and I lived in two rooms in the base- ment. Worse than that was constantly hearing about all the abuse and trauma I couldn't remember.

My grandmother always had a "call." That's how she'd tell us. "Don't interrupt me, I have a call" or "I have to stay near the phone, I'm expecting a call." She spent hours talking to friends, sharing details about the cult and sexual abuse. She revealed things I didn't know, hadn't heard, details I never would have imagined, and they were things that happened to me. Her stories made me even more afraid of the cult.

I knew some of the things. I had been tied to a table with an upside-down star. Cult members circled the table, pointing a knife at my eye, threatening to cut me. They said they would cut out my eyes if I ever shared their secrets, they would find me and would do the same to everyone I knew. They told me that one day my mom would try to kill me, and that I could only be safe with them.

I knew this because my mom told me I had told her, and because of the pains. Once when my eye hurt, I told my mom. She dismissed the pain and said, "Yeah, that's because your eye was injured. One day I came home after you had been with your dad, and there were marks in your eye. I could tell the cult had drilled needles into your eye. That's what they do as a form of torture." There was never medicine for my pain. All I was offered was further evidence of my abuse.

My mom would tell me some experiences, but I learned far more from listening to G-ma's calls. From her telling others, I learned so many details about the ritualistic abuse, the gang-rape, how the cult would break my bones and then call upon Satan's great powers to heal me before my mom returned.

The cult had advanced technologies. They could torture someone, cut into their flesh, break their bones, make them scream until their personality split, and split again. Then they would heal them back together and not leave any marks. Only the hidden personalities remained, waiting to be triggered.

I had to be careful about any sort of symbols I saw. I had been brainwashed during torture, and certain colors or words could trigger me and switch my personalities, turning me into whoever the cult wanted me to be. Then my entire family could be in danger.

Staying safe from satanic symbols and the restrictions of our church limited what I could watch on TV, what movies I saw, and even what we talked about. We lived in fear. I could split into a different person who wanted to rejoin the cult, who wanted them to own and break me, a person who told The Fly where we were. We could all be in danger, my mom admonished. I had to stay safe and pure not just for myself, but for my family's safety.

However, G-ma kept telling everyone exactly what had happened to us. I heard the details over and over as she called yet another person to recount the trauma Victor and I had known and forgotten. Hearing these details, fortunately, did not switch me to one of my splits, but the stories formed my identity. I was a survivor, a victim of the cult. I was forever marked, damaged, and lessened because of it.

It wasn't much of a secret. G-ma talked about our abuse to everybody who would listen. The teachers knew, the people at church knew, and all my grandmother's friends knew every detail. I didn't want everyone to hear about it. I didn't want everyone to think about it whenever they saw me. In justification, she said, "Well, people need to know. People are caring about you. They fast for you. They have to know the details so they know what to pray for. You know we need lots of people praying for us."

This was true. We had survived the cult through prayer and by following God's guidance through my mom. Through prayer and faith, we knew when to leave California. Through the Holy Spirit my grandmother knew to leave her favorite house and move to Utah. And it was prayer that told my mom when the cult was getting close. Our nightly prayers kept us safe and my personality from splitting, or remembering. I accepted her answer. After all, the more people asking God to keep us safe, the more likely He would.

When my grandmother talked to her friends about what had happened, she called it "the abuse." That was better than when she used words like sodomize, gang-rape, ritualistic torture, and brainwashing. It was better to think of it as abuse. But when she or my mom talked to police or teachers, it became a security situation.

My mom would begin conversations with my teachers that way. "We have a security situation," she would tell them and follow it with all the other information. "This is their legal name, but this is the name they go by. Please call them only by this name. This will help with the security situation. If anyone calls or asks for them by their legal name, I need to be notified immediately. Or the police."

We changed our names nearly every time we moved. I soon started naming myself. If we were just making up new names, I could choose whatever I wanted. It could be anything. I became Eleanore Dalia Moishisha Whahespero Manera Barihera Smith for a while.

Moving to G-ma's had not stymied my plans for college. I wanted to make my own way into the world, and I would not be stopped. G-ma lived in a real neighborhood where people read the newspaper. At eleven years old I got a paper route. That was when I started feeling super rich. A paper route meant big, consistent money without having to advertise or give out my phone number. I just showed up and did my job every day.

My money piled up. I stored it all in my cargo short pocket bank and hid it on the top shelf of the hall closet where no one would look. I'd secretly add new money I had made. Soon the velcro wouldn't close.

This was the first time I had a regular income, and it felt amazing. I was making good money delivering papers, though soon I realized I could earn even more. While my route couldn't expand, I could increase subscriptions. The more people that subscribed, the more money I would make. On the weekends I would knock door-to-door on every non-subscriber's house. By the time I was done with that paper route, almost everyone in the neighborhood had a subscription.

I followed up with those who had declined at first and learned to overcome any objections they might have. When one woman said she was allergic to ink, I researched and found out that was probably the old ink they didn't use anymore. This was a newer soy-based ink that caused fewer allergies. I returned with this information and signed her up that day. I was signing everybody up. Even people who didn't care about the newspaper signed up.

I also could make more money by getting tips. I began finding out what everybody wanted, just where they wanted their paper delivered. I would give everyone amazing service. Instead of tossing papers randomly like others did, I placed each one perfectly on the doormat so they would be able to open up their door and be like, "Whoa! It's right there. That's so convenient."

I learned how to deliver more efficiently as well. I loaded up a big apron with huge pockets on the front and back and packed them as full as possible. Carrying all the papers on my shoulders, I would walk across lawns to deliver papers on my subscribers' door mats. I would go through their yards, but it was much more efficient for me. I got up at 5:30 in the morning so everyone would have their paper before breakfast.

There was one old man who was up before I got to his house. He would wait by his car and smoke a cigarette. Every morning when I came by, I would hand his newspaper directly to him. And every morning when I handed him the paper, he would hand me a dollar and tell me to, "Go buy yourself a sodie pop." Did I ever buy a sodie pop? No. I did not. I put the dollar in my Velcro pocket and I saved and I saved.

I ended up making more than any other paper carrier in town. And toward the end I made much more than in the beginning. Or how much Jane Bee made, as that was my name at the time.

新生

New Life

I had been working in Taipei for nearly a year when I was offered to come to the United States. An American man named Clark who ran a printing shop in Fresno asked me to move in with him. He promised there would be money.

I was working at an import/export company in Taiwan exporting sporting goods from the factory to businesses overseas. It fit very well with my accounting background from the army. After two years living with American missionaries, my English was good enough to speak with the clients. It wasn't great, but I could sell balls. We sold baseballs, soccer balls, basketballs, all kinds of balls.

Clark had contracts with many of the high schools in Fresno in the state of California to print their flyers for games, dances, announcements, whatever. He knew the schools and he knew how many balls they used up. He called to get them cheaper and sell them directly to the schools. He asked so many questions I invited him to come and visit the factory. He accepted.

Clark knew the printing business, but he did not know anything about the import/export business. He would not have time to run both businesses. He invited me to come to Fresno to be his business partner and manage the imports. A friend of mine here in Taiwan could manage the exports. I accepted.

Mama was sad to see me leave. She blamed the Mormon church for filling up my mind with fantasies. Fantasies of more. American fantasies. I wanted to make money to provide for the family I dreamt of everyday. America was the land of opportunity. Plus, I could help business in Taiwan. I barely had enough money for the plane ticket, but I felt it was very smart to go to America to make more.

Mama looked at me a long time like she would never see me again. I told her I would take care of her, but I had to settle down first. Perhaps she thought that I would get scared and turn back at the very last minute. I knew I would not. I was full of hope, goodness, and knew God loved me. I would go to America and make a success of myself and come back to Mama to show her it was smart and good. I would make it so good even Buddha could not deny.

It was ten in the morning on the day before Christmas of 1979 when I arrived in L.A. It was my first time on a plane and my first time outside of Taiwan. I felt strong though all alone in a new land. The only person I knew was myself. I was happy for the chance to create a future for myself in this land. I bought a couple hot dogs. They tasted different to what I was used to. Everything was so fresh and strange.

Later that day I took a small plane to Fresno to meet Clark. I had met him only once before moving across the world. He and his brother took me to Clark's house. They treated me to dinner, and I fell asleep exhausted and excited.

I stayed with Clark and his family. There I learned American ways. They were very kind, liked to have much fun, and smiled and laughed a lot. Like me. They ate American food in the ways Americans like it. They stop only for minutes at lunch and eat one small hamburger. I need five hamburgers to feed me. So, I was very hungry all the time, until I found a K-Mart and bought myself so so many snack bars.

Clark stayed so busy with printing that the new business was left up to me. But I did not have clients. I stayed with Clark and did not know how to drive. Clark would go to the printing shop every day, and I would help him. Clark was busy, so busy. He kept saying he would get the schools to make an order so we could begin importing the sporting goods. I knew it would be left to me.

After two months I told Clark that I had to renew my Visa to stay longer but we had no business. We had to apply for the company. I started our own import/export business called Chin-Tan USA.

The company was built. Clark said he had the money to begin importing the sporting goods. I went to the bank to apply for a letter of credit to send to the company, because you cannot just send money to the company. This requires the bank to issue a letter guaranteeing the money once the goods have been shipped. The bank had never heard of this before. I knew we had a problem.

I wired the money to my friend. This is very risky. But my friend at my old company sent the goods, and we sold them all. After that I told Clark I should go back to Taiwan.

He said, "Don't go back. I don't know how to do what you do. The business will fail without you." I told him the business would fail without customers, and that I must get a job which pays me money. I had nothing and did not want to ask my family for help. I did not even have money to fly back home. Clark and his family lived far from the city and I could not drive. I needed an apartment close by to find work but did not have money for an apartment. Clark said he would give me money for an apartment if I didn't leave. He said he needed me here to help run Chin-Tan USA.

I found a job in the Central Fish Company in Fresno. I walked in to apply. The owner said he would give me a job, but because I didn't have a green card yet he would have to pay me less. The pay was about $3 per hour. He would call when he needed me.

Every day I had to wait for his phone call. Sometimes I worked five hours a day, sometimes only two. If it was not busy, the boss would send me home. When business was good, he called me right away.

My job was to take fish from the freezer and clean them. I had to work inside the freezer. Every time I went into the freezer my pores would close. I had never experienced cold like this in Taiwan. There the weather is always nice.

Sometimes it would take longer to find a certain type of fish. My hands would freeze and my fingers would stick to the fish. My ears burned with pain from the cold. With cold hands I fumbled with the fish. While cleaning the fish some of their bones would pierce deep into my skin. My fingers would still hurt as I slept. I would often get up in the night and put cold water on my fingers to soothe the pain. I made between six and fifteen dollars a day.

I endured this pain and swallowed my pride because I could not ask my family for financial help. I wanted to prove I could be successful even though I had joined the Mormon church and moved to America.

I worked for three days in exchange for one of my boss' old rice cookers. Every day I ate rice and peanuts and drank water. I could not afford snack bars from Kmart. But I was happy because God kept me healthy, and I had a warm place to sleep. This was His special blessing. Because I was blessed, I was able to have many different jobs. Later that year I worked in the Lai Lai restaurant in Fresno as an assistant chef. I had plenty of food to eat then. I saved everything I did not have to spend.

I met Richard Lee, also from Taiwan, and we made a business importing toys from home and selling them wholesale at swap meets. The best ones were in Los Angeles. I found an apartment there and started a seafood company buying large quantities from the ships and selling them directly to restaurants. I knew what they wanted and could deliver it to them fast.

When I applied for a green card, I wrote that I could speak three languages and a dozen different dialects. They questioned me about this and thought no one could do it. I went to the

University of California in Los Angeles to talk with the professors there. After spending an afternoon with different professors, they called the immigration office to say that I could indeed speak all the languages and dialects I mentioned. The immigration department gave me a green card and another job. When other applicants said they were from an area whose dialect I spoke, they had to speak to me. I could tell if they were from the place they claimed. I talked to people from China, Taiwan, Japan, everywhere.

While I worked for the immigration office, I still ran my seafood company in the mornings and the toy company on the weekends. Every day I went to work with the rising of the sun and got off work with the rising of the moon.

I loved my new life in United States. I found a Mormon church where I could worship, read my Book of Mormon without anyone bothering me, and could meet others who wanted to follow God and serve Him.

After four years of working six days every week, I was finally able to buy a small house. My own house, bought with my own money. I felt I had made it. Mama would be proud, I hoped. Next, I wanted to find someone to share it all with. I wanted to have a family in America. This was the land of promise and freedom. Here I could work hard for my family and we could all be together and happy.

New Life

My new life was going well. I had a job, a new name, and was attending a new school. Instead of living in a trailer with holes in the floor to the outside, we now lived in a house on the hill. No one needed to know it was G-ma's house and that my mom, Victor, and I lived in the basement. This was my chance to start over. I was going to a new school, and I was going to be cool.

That year, before seventh grade, was the only time my mom bought me new clothes from a store. I was convinced that striped shirts were where it was at. That was going to make me cool.

Usually, I wore hand-me-downs from my one female cousin or clothes from thrift shops. This time would be different. We went to the mall, to one of those teenager shops like Deb's or Maurice's. I tried on everything with stripes and found five or six shirts that fit. I wanted them all. I had one in blue, one in green, one in a darker blue.

These would be my entire wardrobe. I had grown significantly, and none of my older clothes fit anymore. I clutched the precious shirts as we approached the cash register. My mom gave the cashier the credit card. We always bought everything on credit. It was so much debt. This time, the credit card was rejected.

My mom looked at me, a 12-year-old, and asked, "Ok. The card was declined. Do you still want the clothes?" I said yes. I don't know how she paid for them, whether she used another card or if she had some emergency cash, but she bought me those striped shirts.

I felt so bad. I felt so much guilt and shame for causing our family more hardship, but I desperately wanted new clothes. I felt embarrassed, and then sad for having to feel embarrassed. This was different from when my mom bought our food with stamps, or when Victor and I went down to the gas station to see which candies the stamps could actually buy. I felt guilty and believed I should pay for these things myself, knowing she shouldn't be getting into more debt because of silly things I wanted. Especially for clothes I didn't actually need.

I wore those shirts every single day of seventh grade. My guilt intensified when I realized stripes weren't as cool as I'd thought. By the end of the year, I didn't like any of my striped shirts. Still, I wore them because they were the shirts of sacrifice. "Okay," I'd tell myself unexcited about another day with stripes, "it's the blue one or the green one." Then the next day, it would be the other.

I felt sorry for my mom because of the cult situation she didn't ask for, and for the debt on top of everything. All the sacrifice. And I felt angry because I believed she could have done more than she did.

The summer I turned 14, I decided I would support myself and attend a private school. I was ready to move up in the world. I had hidden pockets of neatly stacked bills and knew that to attend college, I had to prove myself an excellent student. This would be easy, I thought. I just needed to calculate how many points each class required and make sure I earned them. Then college would be guaranteed.

I prayed daily, promising the Lord I would be more obedient and follow each and every commandment if He would keep me from the cult and help me attend college. That was all I wanted: to leave and to be cool. I knew the Lord would help if I did everything possible myself. I wanted to start at a new school without the striped shirts of suffering and be kind to everyone. That would help with being cool. Also, I needed to earn more money.

I found the perfect school, a charter school called Tuacon School of Performing Arts. It was private but required no tuition. I would need uniforms and supplies, which I'd have to purchase myself. However, I didn't want these expenses to interfere with my saving. I created a detailed list of required dance clothes, uniforms, and supplies with costs next to them so I would know exactly how much more I would need to earn.

The only business within walking distance of my house was a Sonic Drive-In down the street. I got a job there wearing roller skates to deliver food to cars. The work left me sticky. I disliked my co-workers. And I was miserable. However, it paid better than my paper route. The biggest downside was working Sundays.

We always attended church on Sundays. It was the Lord's day and we did not work, play with friends, go swimming (though that was because the devil lived in the water) or buy anything from any store. It was against the commandments. I had promised the Lord I would follow all the commandments—even the difficult ones. I'd always kept the Sabbath holy, but now after church, I'd put on my uniform, grab my roller skates, and walk down the street to work. It felt wrong. I had trusted the Lord with my safety, and He had trusted me to follow His commandments.

Working Sundays meant compromising my standards. This could not continue. In a great moment of faith, I called upon the Lord in prayer. One Sunday morning, when my shift would make me miss church entirely, I prayed fervently. I thanked God for my job and for teaching me to follow His word. I prayed in faith for a job that I could get to without a car. Though I saw no other possibilities, I promised God I would quit my job before knowing what else I could do for money. I needed money for school, and I committed to having faith that I would find another way. I thanked God and closed my prayer in Jesus' name.

I walked to Sonic in my church clothes and quit. I was so happy to quit that job. After that, the sunshine felt brighter. I was confident I had done the right thing. The next step would be the Lord's. I would wait.

When I returned home, the phone rang. A woman from church asked for me. After pleasantries, she said, "This may come as a surprise, but I've noticed how responsible you are in Young Women's. My husband is a loan officer, and we think you could do great work with him. He works from our home office and wants to know if you'd like to be trained as a loan processor." I could hardly believe what I was hearing. I agreed and started the next day. The summer before 9th grade, I became a loan processor.

Five days a week, I walked to their house and worked out of the basement processing loans. This was the financial boom with all the ninja loans and the sub-prime mortgages that later contributed to the housing collapse. I spent my summer processing all these loans my boss was selling to anyone who qualified. The pay was good, and I didn't work Sundays.

I thanked the Lord nightly for my job and for answering my prayers. And I thanked Him that now I understood how prayers were answered. I'd been taught the Lord would guide me, just as He guided my mom to free us from the cult.

He did not speak in the way I had expected. I did not hear a voice like I thought I would. This had worried me because I feared following the wrong voices, those the cult had programmed into my brain. The Lord's direction also didn't come through uncontrollable urges like I thought the cult's would. I had to be careful with my actions, constantly worried that at any moment I could be triggered into doing something against my will. But the Lord's speaking was different. It was a feeling. When I did what seemed right, I felt profound peace.

I now knew I could trust the Lord completely. I could find answers to my situations and problems by trusting my judgment, and He would confirm the truth. This was promised to me by the Book of Mormon. I could ask God in faith and receive the answers I sought. I could know truth. Now I could feel free.

I wondered if my mom's experience had been the same.

Love

I knew what it meant to have family. I wanted a family of my own.

On the mountain, other than the Buddhist Temple, we did not have many neighbors. There was the small group of houses down by the river where we picked up our mail. A few families lived on the hillside like we did, but not many. Farther up the mountain to the other side facing the ocean, lived many Taiwanese natives. My father was proud our family had been in Taiwan for thirteen generations. The natives had been there even longer. Many did not speak Mandarin. When they came to the house, Father would speak more with gestures and expressions. His kindness knew no language barrier. Sometimes native people would come to the house bringing food they had harvested or animals they had caught looking for a trade. Sometimes they would trade Father for some of his wine. Other times they demanded money, but we never had much.

Still, it was a good life.

Mama stayed at the Temple to seek Buddha's protection to break through her emotional pain. I knew my brother's death had been difficult on her, but I was small and could not fully sympathize. I did know that her beautiful smile disappeared for a long time. That depth of pain was out of her control. The only one who could comfort her was God. The only God she knew was Buddha.

Father supported Mama emotionally. He knew she needed her time and space to feel her loss. They would sit and talk through their thoughts and Mama's feelings. We knew not to interrupt them. Mama would cook special herbs for Father, and she specifically instructed us not to touch his special nourishment. Father would always share his food with us. We felt the warmth of his love through his care. Mama did not say much of her love, but she gave her time and effort to care for us. We always felt her love.

From our house on the mountain, we were woken up by the birds singing. We could explore, knowing we had a place to return to where we would be welcome and cared for. No matter how poor we were, we were happy because we were together. Money can't buy this kind of happiness.

Sometimes natives would come to our house to sell meat. Sometimes they brought baby animals to sell as pets for children.

One day a man brought three monkeys to our house. The father and the mother were at least fifty pounds each. The baby was about a month old. All of us at home reached into the baby's cage to touch him. He grabbed our hands just like a human baby. We asked our father if we could buy the baby and keep him with us.

Both the mother and father had clamps around their necks. Each had a broken leg that had not been cared for. The bones stuck out of their skin among dried and fresh blood. Even though they were hurt, the mother and father would shake the bars of their cages and howl every time we touched their baby. They were afraid we would harm him, though we just wanted to be friends.

After the dealer left, we continued to ask Father for the baby monkey. He finally agreed. My third sister and I went with him to the dealer's house the next day. It was a small hut on the other side of the mountain. It took hours walking to find it. The mother monkey was breast feeding the baby just like a human mother would. Flies buzzed around her wound. Her leg bone still stuck out. We knew she was in terrible pain. The father was not around. We imagined the man had killed him for food.

The baby monkey was happy to be with his mother. He probably did not know how much suffering his mother experienced. The mother's hair around her eyes was wet and my sister said she must've been crying. The mother was chained but the baby was free.

We watched them. The baby turned its head toward us and watched us while feeding. The mother turned to see us and became angry. She pushed the baby away from her and farther from us. Every time she pushed the baby away it would come back to her. The baby would climb onto its mother's back. He did not know she had a broken leg and a chain around her neck. My sister began to cry to see this.

Father could not afford to buy the baby monkey that day. He wanted to come back in a few days to negotiate a lower price. We begged him for it or to catch another for us. "They are very tricky," Father said. "And difficult to catch. This man must have been clever and patient."

The dealer told us the baby monkey would ride on its mother's back and play on small branches when she foraged. The man hid under a tree laden with fruit. When the monkeys came to feed the man jumped up and yelled. The frightened monkeys scattered leaving the baby behind. He grabbed the baby and ran away.

The parents would come back for their baby. The dealer chained the baby to a tree and put strong traps around him. When the monkey parents approached their baby to save him, they stepped into the traps. The monkeys would not leave their baby behind. The man waited for both to be caught. When he returned, both the mother and father were trapped but with their baby. The mother fed the baby though her leg was snapped shut in the trap and broken.

My sister was so troubled by the story, Father carried her home. He held my hand with his all the way to our side of the mountain.

A few days later my father and I hiked back to the dealer's house with money and cigarettes. We had decided to buy both the mother and the baby. Father assured me that he could treat the mother's leg.

The baby monkey held the bars of its cage and watched us. The mother was nowhere in sight. They had a storm and the

dealer brought the baby monkey inside. The mother was left outside. The dealer told us she choked on her chain. I imagined her
searching for her baby in the rain. She had to endure her broken
leg and the cold weather. She continued looking for her baby and
fought against the chain until she died. Her life ended with so
much pain inside.

We could smell meat being cooked inside the house. The
dealer was cooking up the mother monkey to eat. If we had the
money earlier, we could have saved the mother's life. I wanted to
cry for her and for her baby.

We brought the baby monkey home with us and named him
Anquan. We fed him milk and played with him. He was now part
of our family, and we wanted to keep him safe. Our faithful dog
had five puppies not long after Anquan had come home to stay.
She would feed her litter and the monkey would join the pups and
receive milk and cuddles. The dog knew this new monkey was not
her pup, but cared for him just the same. This way Anquan came
to know us and our family as home.

My father built a treehouse for baby Anquan and attached a
bamboo pole to the side so he could easily get up and down. We
kept him near and safe with a long rope that still allowed him to
climb freely. He would sit high in the trees with a mouthful of
food, eating everything he could find. We laughed at his stuffed
cheeks.

Anquan stayed with us for a year and a half. Then we set him
free so he could go back to the jungle and live in the high trees with
other monkeys. Occasionally he would come back to the house.

Other monkeys would not approach the house, but Anquan would walk right into the yard. Sometimes he climbed into the house to see us. We would play with him while he visited. Then he would return to the trees.

As we aged Anquan stopped coming to the house. When I looked at the high trees and could hear the chatter of monkeys in the distance, I remembered Anquan. I hoped we had helped him understand what it meant to have a family. Equally, I hoped he had found one of his own.

Miracle

The summer before my freshman year at Tuacon performing arts high school was magical. I had a relationship with God, I was making money, we were safe, and it was warm.

When I told my mom I was working as a loan processor, she was impressed. I mentioned wanting a second job to make more money, but there was nothing within walking distance. I had told her this before, but this time she offered to drive me to work if needed. I was overjoyed. This must have been because of the Lord.

I got a job in the afternoons at a mall kiosk as a spinal screener for a chiropractic office. I stood in the mall and convinced people to let me run a scan of their spine and then signed them up for an appointment with the doctor. Though I was paid by the hour, I still wanted to do the best job I could. Soon, I was recognized as the best employee and put in charge of training others.

Later that summer, I got a third job at the school I would be attending. They needed someone to keep things organized and on schedule in the admissions office before classes began. I had prayed for jobs and money, and now I had both.

My mom always expressed how impressed she was by my successes. She would tell me I would own a corporation and a high rise someday. Victor didn't say much about it. He did not want to help with the paper route or even start his own thing. I told him it would be so easy for him, but he would shrug it off and say that when I was in my high rise, he would come and be my janitor. I thought it was odd and not much of a dream, but he said that was all he wanted.

Working three jobs wasn't the only miracle of the summer. I had been praying we would be kept safe from The Fly. I had prayed this same prayer morning and night since I could remember, sometimes more. It was our primal concern. Now that I knew how God spoke to me, my prayers had become more sincere. He had spoken to me and given me these jobs, so I knew He was listening. I prayed and prayed to keep us safe from the Fly and the cult.

Then one day my mom came downstairs and told us that The Fly was dead. She didn't have any remorse in her voice for this person she was married to for a while, this father of her children. Her nonchalance didn't seem odd at the time because the news felt like a gift. This is what we had wanted, more or less. I felt relieved, but not happy. I had never wished for any misfortune or pain upon him. I wanted to be safe, that was what I prayed for. I had failed to consider what form that would take for my dad.

I told my mom it was great news and asked how she knew. We hadn't had any contact with him in years. We had effectively been in hiding from anyone who might know him. She told me the Lord told her. She knew it was true.

God must have spoken to her differently than what I had experienced. I realized there was still more to learn about how God communicated. I trusted my mom and her truth. She knew more about the Lord than I did. She knew more about how to keep us safe. She knew more about the cult. And she hadn't been split, so she could handle the things I couldn't.

I was grateful for her knowledge. What the Lord told her must be true. I didn't mourn The Fly. We didn't talk much about him then or after that. However, just because The Fly was gone and could no longer hurt us didn't mean that we were safe. The cult was still out there. The cult still wanted us back.

The cult controlled The Fly just like it tried to control us. He had been tortured and split so many times he was entirely theirs. We had been treated the same, but not for as long because my mom's prescience took us away from the danger when we were still small. Still, those things were inside me. More than I even knew.

We had always been told that the cult had advanced technologies. That summer I had an irritation in my ear. It stung for a while then would go away, then come back. It was a little hard spot inside my ear I could feel with the tip of my finger. I asked my mom about it. She examined my ear and pulled something out with tweezers and put it in the garbage.

I asked what it was. She told me plainly that it was a small tracking device of the cult. The cult had gotten to me somehow and put a tracking device in my ear. I asked if I could see it, but she told me it could trigger me and I couldn't look at it. She didn't want me to be split. She wouldn't know the right command words to bring back this personality that I was now, the one she knew and loved.

That wasn't all the cult had done. They had cameras all over the place—all over town, in school, in churches. They had helicopters that flew overhead and tracked where people went or who they talked to.

The cult had plants everywhere. There were people all the time observing and making sure everyone stayed in line. We were worried that now that The Fly was gone, the cult would want us, his own blood, to replace him in the cult. We had to be even more watchful.

I still went to work each of my jobs. My mom still drove me to the school or the mall. But we didn't invite anyone over to our house. We didn't tell anyone where we lived or give out our phone number. And we didn't tell strangers our names.

At the mall I would introduce myself as Elle. Not Eleanore, just Elle, or it could be just the letter L. It sounded the same. Many people would ask if it was short for something. But they could have been from the cult looking for me. I told them it was just what people called me and brought the subject back to their spinal screen. Sometimes I told them I was Jane. You could never be too safe.

家庭

Family

I missed Taiwan but began to love California. Los Angeles bubbled with energy. I felt that with drive and integrity, I could make a good living. In under five years of being in America I had bought a house and ran an honorable business. I worked hard at my seafood company and continued to get more clients. They knew me as dependable and honest and could get their restaurant the best fish. Pretty soon this took up so much time I worked only at that job. Still, it seemed there was more I could do. Doing enough was never enough for me. If I wanted to be successful, I had to do more. I skipped meals and sleep to make sure my fish was the freshest and ensured it could get to my clients before they needed it.

I invested all my time and most of my money in growing the business. I had very nice freezers in a warehouse to store many kinds of fish that were difficult to find. This way if my clients wanted something specific, I would not have to search for it on the docks or at the busy fish market. They could have it delivered to be cooked for their customers while other dealers still searched.

When the warehouse burned down because of a fire in the space next door, I lost everything inside. Insurance claimed they would pay for the equipment. But freezers were easy to replace. The fish inside the freezers was where all the money was. This, they said, could not be guaranteed because it had spoiled before it could be inspected. It was worthless at that point.

It was hard to see my efforts in ashes in a burned-out building. But this was only money. I was young, hard-working, and my clients trusted me. I could make the money back. I knew God would prepare the way.

After the seafood warehouse burned down, I had more time for myself. A church friend invited me to a church dance in Glendale. He said the change of pace would help me. I agreed. I loved to dance. I remember locking the house to leave. When the key was in the closing door, I felt that this house was becoming too large for just me. It was time to share it with someone. With family.

The dance was crowded. I knew many people there, and we danced to the live band. The band announced their last song and the dance floor filled with people. They did not want the night to end. Neither did I. I spotted a lovely lady standing by herself. I usually didn't ask strangers to dance, but this special stranger attracted me greatly. I wanted to ask her to dance, but could not find the words. The song was almost over. I gathered my courage and went over to her. In a gentle voice, she agreed to dance with me.

The song ended, but not my attraction for her. I had a special feeling I had never experienced toward any other woman. After the dance we talked for twenty minutes. Beth had grown up all over the world and had just returned from a Mormon mission in Japan. We had something in common. I told her I was a missionary in Taiwan. Then I asked for her phone number.

I had asked for girls' numbers before. Usually I lost them. I would put them somewhere and forget about them, or leave them in the pocket of my jeans while doing laundry. Even if I did not lose them, I did not call.

Beth was different. Her number I did not want to lose. I copied her number and kept it in three places: in my car, in my house, and in my wallet. I called her a week later. Her father answered the telephone. I was speechless and thought about hanging up the phone. "Hello?" he said again. "Is there anyone there?" Hanging up would be impolite, so I asked to talk to his daughter. We spoke for a while, slipping in a Japanese word here or there when the English was not coming as quick. I reveled that she understood a language I could speak with ease.

I asked to see her and she agreed but could not give me directions to her house. "It is difficult to find," she told me. "My mother likes it that way." Beth called to her father for directions. I thought he would get on the phone and interrogate me. After a pause she told me how to get there and said she worried I would get lost on the way.

I found her home easily. It was not as difficult as Beth's mother predicted. Beth often did not invite anyone to the house because she thought it was hard to find. It was a beautiful home in the

Hollywood Hills. I could follow directions very well and my path was clear to me. I knew where I wanted to be.

Beth and I went for a dinner. Everything went smoothly. When I took her back to her doorstep, I tried to give her a kiss on the cheek as in American custom. She let me kiss her hand. I had to see her again. She agreed.

The next time, Beth met me outside her front door. Her face was red like she had been running. She grabbed my hand and asked if we could get out of there. I was happy to go anywhere with her. Taking her home she would kiss me quick before getting out of the car, and she would run out when I came to pick her up. I never went in the house. She seemed happy to see me. There was also a great heaviness she carried. I wanted to carry it for her. I wanted to prove I could. I would show her every day.

After a couple months of our date outings, we spent a day at the Huntington Library in Arcadia looking at the peacocks and ponds. The ducks swam in pairs. They seemed so free and graceful. I joked that the male duck represented myself and the female was her. Then I asked if the ducks had marriage commitments.

Beth said all animals have marriage commitments and families, but only humans have marriages and families that last for eternity. Such unions were sealed in a Mormon Temple to be together forever. She talked a lot about family. She would be such a special wife to someone, I thought. I sat next to her and stroked her hair softly while she spoke.

One night on the drive up the hills to her home we pulled over to look at the view. I did not want the night to end and knew she would run inside her house as soon as the car stopped moving. We sat on the warm hood of the car and looked across the valley of lights.

"Such beauty could only be created by God," I said.

"It is mostly lights from the valley," Beth said.

"I'm talking about you," I said. She laughed and leaned against me.

One special day I invited her to a picnic and brought along my puppy, Wang Chan. We went to Rosemead Park where the weeds were so tall Wang Chan had to jump to keep up with us. We laughed, slowed down for him, and talked together. Lying underneath a tree, we talked of forever. I gave her a romantic kiss.

"Imagine if one day we had a chance to ride a white horse in a meadow speaking softly to one another as we stride through the grass with the blue sky as our fence and the flowers as our companions. The land would be our bed. Only you and I would be there creating an unerasable love story," I said.

"Jack, you are so eloquent. Where did you read such poetry?" She asked.

"I created it as I went along. But I think about it often and wish such a day would come."

Teardrops appeared on her face. Beth stayed quiet for a long time looking at the sky. I held her hand.

"I love you very much," I said after settling in the quiet.

"I love you too," Beth said, still crying.

"We both want the same things," I said. "I know it is a big responsibility to want something together. But I was thinking we might get married and create our own eternal family."

Beth was quiet still. After some time, she kissed me then snuggled against me. She told me she wanted some time to think and would respond very soon. I could tell it was a special day for both of us.

We took Wang Chan home and went to dinner to continue our fantasy of the future. To me it was not fantasy, I could see it as clearly as I could still see the green mountains of Taiwan. It was real, just not present. In the car, Beth took my hand and said in Japanese, "I can't believe I'm getting married."

"Let's create our own special relationship," I replied in Japanese. I could not wait to tell my family in Taiwan I would soon have a family of my own.

I was the most happy man.

Beth and I often went to the Los Angeles Mormon Temple to plan our future family. The beautiful grounds there hold many statues. We stood by one of a father, mother, and two children all happy, healthy, and following the Lord. Beth commented that our family could be like this masterpiece. We had many hopes for our life to come.

I already had a house to provide comfort. My seafood company was beginning to grow again. I remembered Mama working in the fields to bring in crops and food for our family. She would have liked to stay home to help us kids and go to Temple. Father worked at times, but spent and drank at others. The inconsistent support from Father made more work and worry for Mama. I would not fail in the places he had. I imagined beautiful Beth helping me grow our company and grow our family. She could stay at home and take care of things there, and I would go on all the deliveries. I would work hard every day.

Our love was new and pure. I looked forward to our wedding like it was the beginning of forever. Beth's mother, Angela, did not.

Angela did not know me. We had spoken but only for a short time. I felt she did not want to know me. While Beth and I dated, I did not see much of Angela. Beth would meet me outside and run in quickly. After the engagement, Angela took more notice of me, though from a distance. She would not talk to me as much as talk at me.

She was protective of her only daughter. Her son had become a ship captain and was at sea most of the year. Angela and her husband, Tom, did not spend much time together. Beth told me that her parents fought a lot and very loud. Beth would hide in her room or a closet and cry while they yelled. Now Angela was going to lose Beth as well. I sympathized for her.

I told Angela not to worry, and that when Beth and I get married, we would come see her all the time. I told her that family is very important to me. I looked forward to her being family as well.

Angela looked at me as though I had transformed into an insect before her eyes. "There's so much you don't understand," she said to me. Then she continued speaking, telling a story about how she used to entertain diplomats and princes while living in faraway countries. I listened, but could not understand what it was I did not understand. I wanted to show this woman I hardly knew that I could love her like family. I listened to her and did not interrupt.

At times when I would visit Beth before we married, I could not find her. I asked Angela where she was. She told me, "Beth is her own woman. She'll decide for herself." This did not help me find her. Sometimes I would find her crying in her bedroom. Every time I saw her tears, I loved her more and vowed to care for her. I wanted her to have no more reason to cry.

Once she was sitting in her closet, on the floor. "Are you hiding from me?" I asked.

"Not from you. Because of you." Beth did not explain further.

Later that day, we sat in the park holding hands and Beth told me she loved me and that God told her I was a good person. Her mother had said she was too young to get married, though Beth was older than Angela had been. Her mother threatened to cut Beth out of the family and the inheritance if she married me. Beth did not know what to do.

I wanted her to be happy. I saw her being most happy with me and our eternal family that God had promised. I told her nobody could stop our love. If a husband and wife are willing to be together, no one can tear them apart. She wept and nodded her agreement.

It seemed every time Beth and I were together there was some new story. Angela told me it was too much work to organize a wedding. She said we were being cruel asking her to do all the planning and preparation. It would take two years to do it properly, she said. I did not ask this or anything of her.

Angela had said the house could not be ready in time, that we should delay. Or that if we could not find the appropriate venue, we should call off the wedding. None of her excuses made sense to me. Sense did not stop Angela's comments from hurting Beth. Many times I found Beth crying from something her mother had said.

It was after an evening of consoling Beth that she suggested we should elope. Angela later accused me of planting this idea in Beth's mind, but that wasn't true. When Beth mentioned the term, I did not know it. I had not considered running away to get married. I agreed we could elope, if that is what Beth wanted.

When Angela heard of this plan, she changed her words. She claimed eloping would bring dishonor on their house. This I did not want to do. Instead, Angela suggested to host the wedding at their house. We agreed.

For a couple days Angela described the most beautiful ceremony. She had thought of so many details. Beth glowed; she was so excited. Angela wanted everything to be perfect. That is why, she said, they had planted trees that would be the best backdrop. We would only have to wait for the trees to mature before we married. I could not believe this. Trees take so long to grow. Our children could be grown before those trees were.

All the plans fell apart. Angela's excitement was set up to delay our union. Beth was furious and disappointed. I felt bad for Beth and for Angela. I imagined how difficult it would be to have one's only daughter leave home. I knew I couldn't understand Angela's pain. I also knew I wanted to be together forever with Beth.

In the Los Angeles Mormon Temple, Beth and I knelt before the altar and held hands in a sacred ceremony. There, on September 24, 1985, Beth and I made a sacred promise with God to always love and honor one another, to hold one another's hand through an eternity of righteous devotion to the Lord and our family. In turn, the Lord would bless our home and family forever.

The most valuable experience in my life to that point was going through the temple of the Lord with Beth to start an eternal family. We told nothing but the truth in this Holy Temple. That was the way it should be, I knew. Our marriage would be based on this truth for all eternity.

We spent the first day of our honeymoon in Hollywood then departed for Hawaii. "The islands reminded me of home in Taiwan," I said. "Though my home is now in California," I corrected when I saw how Beth looked at me. I told her I wanted to take her to Taiwan to meet the rest of my family. She would love the green mountains and weather.

"I do not want to leave California," she said.

"I do not either," I told her. "But it doesn't matter where we are as long as we follow God. The lifestyle that allows us to enter God's kingdom is the best way of life. It is priceless. No other culture can offer anything comparable." Beth hugged me and began to cry. I hoped her tears were from happiness. She apologized for crying and I held her tighter.

One day at the hotel in Hawaii, Beth began to cry on the patio. I hugged her and told her, "We're married. You don't have to cry anymore."

"Look at those palm trees. Look at how they grow," she said. She was moved to tears.

She could not be crying just because the leaves were growing. There must be some deeper reason. She didn't say. I made a decision to take care of her for the rest of my life.

Living in my house in Los Angeles, Beth and I developed a routine for every day. I would wake early and go to the docks to buy fish. Then come home for a late breakfast Beth had cooked. Then back to work. To expand the business, I began selling to the public at the fish market. The profit was much better. I had hoped Beth would work with me together to build the business, but the smell of the fish market made her feel ill. I would do the work myself. I did not want her to feel anything but health and joy. We soon found out she was pregnant.

I could not be happier. Life was so good. Beth told me she wanted to be a full-time mother and raise the children at home. This meant more work for me with more financial responsibility, but I was going to be a father. I was ready. I worked hard and was already planning how to make a better future for our children. I knew there would be more. I envisioned kids of all ages surrounding us in our home. It was my dream. Beth and I were excited to see what our children would look like, my Chinese heritage blended with her red hair and broad features. Her people had come from

Scotland and Germany, but had been in America since before it separated from England.

Beth was sick in the mornings carrying our child. She would feel better in the afternoon, but the mornings were hard. She stopped making breakfast for me, so I stopped eating. I would come home at noon and eat double what she had made. About that time, I began to get sick as well. My stomach would constantly hurt. Sometimes my lips would turn blue from the pain. Beth would rub my stomach at night. She would bring me tea. The pain would go away in the morning most always, then return again later in the day. We thought it could be cancer.

Soon the pain began to interfere with my work. I was too tired at the market and could not carry or sell as much. I wanted to prepare the house and our finances for our child. The doctor tried many different things, but nothing helped. This continued for a couple months while Beth's stomach began to grow. She was carrying our family, and I was worried I could be sick enough to die. God could not let me die before I could give my children, His children, the best possible life here in America. The pain hurt so bad. Sometimes I would have to pull off to the side of the road as I could not drive in so much pain. I did not know how I would live the life I had promised to Beth and God.

The doctor I saw could not help me. He recommended I see a Chinese doctor. The new doctor was kind, and it was a relief to be able to explain my symptoms without a language barrier. The doctor listened and asked after my diet. Beth cooked and I always found what she made very delicious. It was full of flavors I was not used to and sometimes very sweet. I confirmed for him Beth used dairy quite often in her cooking.

"Yes, yes, I thought as much," he said in Mandarin. He explained I was allergic to milk sugars. The lactose made my belly swell and sore. He did not prescribe medicine, only to change my diet. I stopped eating anything with milk or cheese or yogurt. I did not want to offend Beth and her willingness to prepare food for us. I told her as much. I promised it did not change the way I loved her or how much appreciation I had for her. But I could not eat those things. After only a few days of following the doctor's recommendation, I began to feel much better and get my strength back. I was happy to have some solution.

Our child grew daily, and Beth spent more time with her mother. I was working as much as I could. Beth did not want to stay alone all day. Angela did not like to visit at our house. So, in the morning after I would go to the dock to buy fresh fish, I would take Beth up to the Hollywood Hills. Then I would pick her up when I had finished work for the day. I was very busy but so happy to be building life for my family.

Angela and Tom had a beautiful home in Los Angeles. They also owned a very large ranch in Nevada. Every year their family gathered at the ranch for a reunion. Beth told me about it and was very excited to go. They would stay for days and ride horses enjoying the wide-open spaces so unlike Los Angeles. I wanted to meet all these new people I could now call my own. That night Angela called our home.

"Actually, I want to speak to you," she said when I offered to find Beth. "It's your health. I want you to know the right thing to do is stay and take care of yourself. Beth can travel with us to the ranch. We don't want to strain you."

"I am feeling much better. It wasn't anything but the dairy," I told her.

"I understand, but you also have your business to think of. You wouldn't want to miss out on the opportunities here."

"Thank you for your thoughts. But family is important. The fish market can wait." Angela was quiet for a long time. I could hear her breathing.

"Well, you know," she started. "You know, there will be so many people there. You might feel out of place. I wouldn't want you to be uncomfortable."

"I'm very good with strangers."

"It's not that. It's just. Well, you know. At the ranch we haven't had a, well, a colored person before. I would feel such shame for you if anyone mistook you for the help. I couldn't bear that for you."

Then I understood. I did not think I was colored. I am Chinese from Taiwan. I had experienced racism before especially when I fumbled with English. I thought family could see past that.

"I see," I told Angela. "I would not want to cause embarrassment." Then I hung up the phone. When I told Beth I would not be going with her to the ranch because her mother would feel better if I didn't, she did not seem surprised.

When Beth returned from Nevada she had changed. The happiness I saw in her when she left was missing. I worried it was from discomfort of the pregnancy. I worried for the health of our child. Sometimes when I came home from work, I would find Beth hiding in the closet crying. She would not tell me why. I never heard the whispers.

Beth and I began to fight. They were small things. She thought I was ruining her garden by opening the tops of the corn to check if they were ripe. Once she was upset that I picked strawberries that were not yet ready. I enjoyed them just the same. She thought I avoided her cooking just to insult her. I told her I was happy to eat everything that did not contain dairy. I thought these issues were small. But the small voice on the telephone changed them, made them larger.

The days Beth spent with her mother were the same that were the hardest between the two of us. I worked hard all day. I wanted to provide a solid life for our family and our child soon arriving. Beth said she worried constantly that I did not love her enough. I told her I would devote everything to her. I said she was so young, so pretty, that she shouldn't worry about such things. I told her I would love her until all her hair was as white as snow. Then still I would.

She said she didn't feel safe. That she did not have anything of her own. If I left, she would be stranded. I promised again and again I would not leave. Never before in my family history had someone divorced or left their marriage. We understood commitment. We understood love is devotion and work. I would show that to her.

She needed more proof. She needed to be included in all things. She said she wanted to be named on the house deed in case something happened to me.

I loved her. I wanted her to be happy. I did what I was asked.

Our child was nearly due when we went to the bank to refinance the house with Beth's mother. Angela spent time caring for Beth while she was so close to childbirth. I was so grateful. In the office, I signed the deed over to Beth, putting the house I bought before we met into her name along with mine. Beth began having contractions at the bank. We thought we might have a baby at the bank. We signed the papers quickly and helped Beth to the car. There the contractions stopped.

Angela did not say anything during the signing. Afterward she asked for the papers to file them. She wrote on them that the house had been a gift from me to Beth. This was to avoid paying taxes, she assured us. It seemed like she knew what she was doing. I was busy caring for Beth who was breathing hard and sweating from the pain. She held her stomach, and I held her.

Ten days later I became a father.

Guilt

My mom didn't give me many rules even though I asked for them. I wanted to know what I should do and what would be best. I wanted a system I could make more efficient. This is why I enjoyed school. There was a finite number of points in each class, all awarded for specific tasks. I could figure out exactly how many points I needed for an A and how I could make sure I had that many by semester's end.

This skill served me well at my different jobs. I wanted a system I could follow to perfection and then to perfect the system. I had just turned fourteen when Tuacon began classes. Even while attending school I worked in the administrative office. Days into my first semester, I was called in by my boss.

"Eleanore, how old are you?" he asked, looking quizzically at me. I told him. "Oh. Well, don't tell anyone else that. I thought you were older." I later found out he wasn't supposed to hire me until I was sixteen. I didn't tell. I needed the money.

G-ma didn't have rules as much as orders. She expected things of us, but we never knew what they were until she commanded. Sometimes we were to be invisible when her friends visited; at others, we were to join the conversation as long as we listened and only spoke to praise her. I was invited to these conversations more as I got older and had accomplishments to brag about. I didn't speak of them, she did. My presence made her boasts more significant.

Any expectations were inconsistent. We never knew if the dishes left in the sink would be cleaned up, or if Victor or I would be called in to wash them in front of G-ma while she complained that we were treating her like a maid. Being the maid was her most common complaint. Something would be left on the table and she would call us all in to see it. "I can't be expected to clean up after you," she would say. "I'm not the maid."

She would stand over us and tell us what to clean and how to clean it while telling us she wasn't the maid. Often it would be dirty dishes or crumbs from the large table with the ring in it. Or little pickies. Little pickies were small bits of balled up fabric that would stick to the carpet. I think they came from the carpet and wouldn't be picked up by the vacuum. They had to be picked up by hand.

"Come get these little pickies," she'd tell me. Then she would stand over me while I was on my hands and knees and point them out. "Over here there are more. And there's one." I would crawl across the carpet pulling these tiny puffs from the carpet with one hand and collecting them with the other. When G-ma grew tired of pointing them out, I would be dismissed—at least for the moment.

At church there were plenty of rules. Enough to make up for having none at home. As devout Mormons, we didn't smoke, drink, or swear. We didn't drink coffee or Coca-Cola. We didn't lie, although false names to keep us safe were necessary. We didn't date until we were sixteen, didn't kiss much even then, and did not look at pornography. There were many rules.

There were rules about how long your shorts and dresses had to be, what movies you could watch, how late you could be out, and who you could be alone with. The most serious restrictions were about sex. Premarital sex was one of the worst sins, second only to murder. We did not talk about sex, think about sex, or have sex until we were married.

Any sexual involvement before being sealed to a worthy partner in the holy temple for time and all eternity could mean being cast from the presence of the Lord forever. No impurity could ever get to Heaven. No righteous man would want to marry me. And I needed a righteous man with the priesthood to get into Heaven. I had to stay pure for the Lord and for my future husband. My eternal salvation was at stake.

I sat in Young Women's, which was the third hour of Sunday services, and listened to my teacher talk again about the importance of sexual purity. She used the example of a piece of gum. No one would want a piece of gum that had already been chewed, she told us. We had to stay pure and follow what the Lord wanted for us. The Lord commanded each of us women to be righteous mothers for our children and worthy wives to our husbands. This was the primary rule. We were born so that we could bear children. It was our calling and, we were told, the most holy of responsibilities. I hadn't envisioned myself as a mother, but I wanted to serve the Lord. This was my duty. And I would do anything I was commanded.

I wanted to serve the Lord perfectly, but I was already impure. It wasn't even by my choice. I had had sex before. So much. With so many people who I didn't even know or remember. My gum had been chewed. And worse, it had been chewed by the satanic cult for their dark purposes. Now the Lord and any husband would know I was tainted. No one would want me then.

I cried myself to sleep. I hadn't wanted all the sin that happened. I hadn't been asked. I couldn't even remember it. It could be much worse than even what I heard. I would lay in bed at night and think about all that I had suffered. All the rape, all the abuse. I would cry and cry and feel so horrible.

There was no telling all that had been done to me. I would lay in bed and my stomach would hurt. It was because of all the rape and the constant trauma. Then my leg would start hurting because the cult had broken it. The cult would do such horrible torture to split my personalities, but the power of Satan could heal me up to hide any evidence of their deeds. But their dark magic was never perfect. It was corrupted, just like they were. They never put me all the way back together, just enough that my mom wouldn't know when she picked me up from The Fly's house. Their violence stayed in me along with all the trauma. They had stolen my purity and tainted my future, my eternity. They could never give that back to me. I could never be perfect. I could never be whole.

Sometimes it was easy to forget about the cult. Since my mom's revelation, we weren't afraid of The Fly finding us, and we had known the secret symbols for so long they were easy to identify. We would communicate between us in hushed voices when we recognized about what was happening. It was our family secret that we knew, that other people didn't know, and, most importantly, that the cult didn't know we knew.

I'd forget about the cult when I was having fun, when everything felt right. I could forget at school, or when I was practicing for a play. I would forget that I could be triggered at any second and turn into someone else unaware of what I might say or do. It was easy to forget when I was working, though I remembered when I added my paycheck to my college savings.

Perhaps I forgot too easily. One of the rare scoldings my mom gave were to say to me, "Eleanore, you're not watchful enough. We take all of these precautions because of our security situation. You should be more careful. You should be more afraid."

When I was a teenager, sometimes I would give my friends my phone number or tell them what our plans were. I didn't feel that scared. But my mom would remind me, "You're not afraid enough, Ella. You could get us all killed."

My family was devoutly afraid. Enough so that they were afraid for me. One night in high school I was out with friends and got home later than anticipated. We were having fun and time flew by. When I returned, the feeling throughout the house was somber panic. My mom couldn't reach me by calling my friends' houses. She also couldn't tell them why she was calling. My family was convinced the cult had taken me. They suspected someone had recognized me after all this time because of my carelessness. They feared I was being tortured again, or locked in a small box and on my way to China to be a sex slave. When I finally arrived home, my mom was upset, but she didn't yell. She didn't punish me. She was furious in a really silent manner. I could feel her anger and noticed how she avoided looking at me as though my negligence was an offense directed at her.

I looked in my brother's room. He was fully dressed—boots on, hat on—sitting on his bed grinding his teeth. He was so upset, but not in an angry way. He was upset in a protective, dutiful way. He was ready to go. Ready to save me from the cult. He didn't know what he would find, or if it would be safe to come back home, or if any of us would ever return, but he was prepared. Because if I was late, of course the cult had taken me.

But they hadn't. I simply forgot to watch the time and came home late. That was all. It happens to every teenager, I supposed. But at my house, everyone was angry. And afraid. But no one spoke about it. We all went to bed. I was still not afraid—not enough.

I sometimes forgot about the cult mentally and even spiritually at times, but never physically. I couldn't remember what they had done to me, but my body did. It kept a painful record. I still felt with the same flesh they had tortured and abused so many years ago.

Devices had been implanted throughout my body. My mom pulled one out of my ear, accessible only because my ear was so small when I was younger that they couldn't put it very deep. There were other things inside me as well. When the cult cut open my body and did tortuous things, they put objects inside to claim my body as Satan's. If my hip hurt, then there was probably some object implanted to cause pain. The pain would remind me of the torture and could trigger a split. I didn't take medication for the pain because it was a spiritual ache. If I gave way to the pain and suffering, and tried to hide it with medicine, it would be giving into the cult's designs to separate me from the experience of my body. I needed to bear it.

My body did not feel like my own. It had been used by the cult. It had been tortured and cut open and broken, then healed up by the power of Satan. It had been raped for ritual. Even now, while I felt more free, the cult hunted for my body. It wanted total control again.

I had to maintain control by separating from any weakness. I taught myself to distance myself from physical sensations or urges. What my body wanted or told me could be from the cult. I could not trust it, and had to rely on the Lord and the mental palaces of a promised heaven.

One time at the dentist, the technician came in and said that I had shorter than usual roots on my teeth. My mom asked where that could have come from. The technician told us, "There could be many sources. If you have been in a car accident and your teeth shift that could be one way, or it could be from poor nutrition. But sometimes it's just, you know, the way that you were born."

Afterwards my mom told me, "You haven't been in any car accident. Looks like there has been a lot of trauma with your jaw and your teeth." I added abuse to my teeth to the long list of all the tortuous things I had survived.

The summer before my final year of Dixie High School I went in for a sinuplasty. My septum deviated and restricted my breathing—probably the cult keeping me weak. It needed straightening and to have polyps removed. We were on Medicaid at the time, so surgeries like this were free.

They took X-rays of my face and showed us what the procedure would do and why it needed to be done. My mom started asking questions of the doctor. She didn't ask about the surgery procedure or the healing process. There was no discussion of how this would affect me. She only wanted to know the cause. "Where would this come from?" she asked. "How could this be?"

The doctor assured her it could be a common thing, a natural part of growth. He said he'd seen many cases like this, and it was not out of the ordinary. My mom looked at me as though to say, "We know what this is about."

The doctor cut me open, removed the polyps, straightened my septum, and made it so I could breathe more clearly. I went in for a checkup a few weeks after the surgery. The doctor examined me and was pleased.

"Bruising is minimal. Airways are clear. Everything looks good. She is healing wonderfully."

My mom looked right at the young doctor and said, "Thank you so much for fixing that. It had been a problem for a while. I mean, Eleanore went through satanic ritualistic abuse where they broke her nose over and over and tortured her by cutting open her sinuses. It's so nice to finally have this repaired."

The doctor stepped back and paused, not knowing what to say. He responded, "Alright. Thank you," which sounded more like a question than gratitude.

In the car I asked my mom why she had to tell him that.

She smiled at me and said, "Did you see his reaction? I said that because I knew that he was in the cult. I wanted to check and see his reaction, and you could see he is obviously a cult member."

"Ok," I replied. My mom always knew.

一起

Together

I was the happiest soul to ever live. Our baby girl was perfect. She was healthy and beautiful. All memory of struggle was gone from me. I sat next to Beth's hospital bed and held her hand. I wiped her brow. I wanted to do everything for her. For the both of them. I had wanted to name the baby girl Tsen Fei, an old family name. It was still odd to me that family names came after given names in English. Beth wanted to name her Eleanore after an ancestor queen from Europe. She would have my last name, so I agreed with Beth about the first. Baby Eleanore. Ella we would call her. She had a tiny shock of black hair, Beth's light skin, and beautiful almond eyes that looked like mine.

The nursery in the house was ready. When I brought Beth and Ella home for the first time, I realized I never wanted to leave. This was family. This was heaven. I did not even have to die to find it. I thanked God for everything. Every breath was a gift. Every heart-beat in Ella's tiny body was a miracle.

The miracle lasted forever. The happiness did not.

We loved our little Ella. Beth was a very caring mother, always there to rock and soothe the baby. She would get up in the night for feedings and stare into Ella's face for hours. I loved our family together. I wanted it to never end.

I told Beth it would be so great for Ella to go to Taiwan some-time. She could get a taste of her cultural heritage. Beth stared at me.

"My mother told me you would say that," Beth said. "It's not a good idea." After that Beth would watch me anytime I held Ella. I wanted Beth to be able to sleep while I took care of the baby after work. She did so much. Beth did not want to. One day in her exhaustion, she told me her mother had warned her about me. Her mother said that I would take Ella to Taiwan and never bring her back. That I would steal her away and raise her there.

I told her this was not true. I had never thought of such a thing. We were family, and I wanted us all together everywhere. But her mother had told story after story about kidnappings in this country. I told her I could not bear the thought of being away from Ella. I would never do that to her. Beth said she needed some time away from me. It was too much. She took Ella to her moth-er's house in the Hollywood Hills.

When I came home to find only Wang Chan waiting for me, wag-ging his little tail, I cried. I called to the house and spoke to Angela.

"You should leave her alone," she told me. "You got the green card you wanted."

I told her very specifically that I wanted my family. It was important to have my wife and my daughter in my home. This wasn't about immigration. I had that handled.

"If you truly loved her, you wouldn't have bought her a used wedding ring. You can't marry someone with a second-hand ring and expect it to last," Angela said.

I did not know what to say. The ring was new, I bought it myself. But there was more within her statement. A ring was just the symbol of our vows we took before God in His holy temple. There I had pledged the rest of my life—the rest of eternity—to Beth. She did the same to me.

"All I want is to love my family and together we can love God," I said. I did not want to argue small things.

"Then you should talk to Beth. She's grown up now. She can make up her own mind."

"Yes, ok. Can you get her on the phone?"

Angela hung up.

I cried that night. And I prayed. In the morning I went to work. I would work hard and build a good life for my family. I did not have as much as Beth's parents. Our house was not as large or as nice. We had no ranch in the desert. But I could work hard so those comforts would not be so far away. I tried to focus on my work. Married couples had problems, I knew. But they could not be solved if they did not work together. Every night I came home to find it empty I called up to Angela's house. Most always Angela answered and said Beth did not want to speak to me. Until one time Beth answered the phone.

"I am so happy to hear your voice," I said.

"It took you so long. Did you not miss me?"

"I miss you and Ella. All I want is for you to come home."

Beth was crying on the phone, quiet and muffled. I waited. "I will. I want to. Will you come get me?"

Beth's face was red from crying when I picked her up. She did not want to talk then. Eleanore was sleeping and Beth rocked her back and forth. We drove home mostly in silence. Later she asked why it had taken me so long to call. I told her I called every night and talked to her mother. Beth's mother did not tell her I called. All those nights alone worrying that Beth did not love me, and she was up in the Hollywood Hills worrying that I did not love her. I felt sorry for Beth. I wanted to protect her. I wanted to grow our family and provide much happiness every day.

"I will love you every day," I told her. "I wanted you here every day. That is the most important thing to me. I know there will be problems. But let us pray about them. There are no problems that we cannot solve if we love our marriage and our family. If we are not going to stay on this earth forever, why would we fight over something that is not important in Heaven?"

She began to cry. She touched her face and was surprised by her own tears. I did not continue. I wanted to tell her that some people make their lives more difficult by letting their problems become something bigger, more frightening, and more complicated. Some choose separation instead of facing their problems.

I did not say these things. I said, "I want to be with you here. I love you now just as I did that day in the temple when you became my eternal wife and I became your eternal husband. This is a bond that is not broken."

We held each other. That night I stroked Beth's long hair while she fell asleep. I was happy once again.

I would come home from work and bask in joy with my family. I loved to hold baby Eleanore and bounce her on my knee. Her dark hair was thickening and she had the most beautiful eyes. I could not wait for my family in Taiwan to see her. We took her to Sears for baby pictures. I sent these to Father and Mama with extras for each of my sisters and my brother. I wanted them to be proud of the life I had in America.

Sometimes I spoke Mandarin in response to Ella's baby babble. It made Beth uncomfortable to not know what I was saying. She said I could speak in Japanese if I must. But Ella was not Japanese, and it did not sound right to me. Mandarin was her culture, at least half, and I wanted her to be able to speak to her grandparents one day. I stopped speaking Mandarin to her when I saw how much it disturbed Beth. I did not understand, but it was a small thing to keep my wife happy.

Family revolves around the mother. She is the seat of the home. When Mama moved to the mountain to live at the Buddhist Temple with two of my sisters, the rest of us followed. Father built a house near where she wanted to be. One day in church Beth had said that if a mother was educated the entire family would be. She knew her influence would most impact our family. I knew this too, which is why I had determined long ago to marry a Mormon girl who loved the Lord. If she was righteous, the entire family would be lifted up.

Beth was the giver of life to our family, and it made sense that she was center to the home. I tried to support her in this. I tried to support her in all things good. I worked hard so she could stay at home in comfort with our daughter. The happy days passed quickly.

We soon found out Beth was pregnant again. I was again over-joyed. I lifted Ella and swung her around. "You are going to be a sister," I said in English. I felt that I had won some sort of award. I did not know what I had done that would gift all this to me. I had my family in my home. Our family was growing. It was better than I had imagined.

I remembered sitting at the house by the riverbank as a young boy. Mama had moved to the Temple. Father was nowhere to be found. It was just three of us kids in a house with no food. It felt like this desolation would last forever. I remember crying and having no consolation. I thought life would be like this forever. Or perhaps we would all die alone, without ever finding our family again. I wanted to blame someone, but I could not. It was not Mama's fault any more than it was Father's. It was not nature's fault either. This was life.

When I sat next to Beth and rubbed her stomach which grew our second child, I remembered being that young boy feeling scared and alone. I remembered how much I wanted the peace of a family that would work and play and laugh and cry together. Now this was my life. I had a beautiful and sweet wife, a home, a healthy baby daughter that I promised to love and never leave. I never wanted her to wonder what had happened to her family like I had. I held Ella later that night, changed her and put her to bed. Beth needed to sleep. Then, with the house quiet, I sat with Wang Chan and thanked God for my every breath. I thanked him for every day I had lived which brought me here. I was the happiest man.

Different Stories

I always believed my mom. She had kept us safe, protecting us with her life and risking everything to keep us away from the cult. She had studied their ways so we could be on the lookout. We uprooted our lives and moved so many times to remain hidden. I believed when she told me what had happened that I couldn't remember or hadn't seen. She knew the world better than I did and shared her knowledge freely. There was no limit to what she would do for us. Plus, she seemed to know everything.

The years we were homeschooled, the library became our second home. My mom would bring home stacks and stacks of books, checking out as many as she could and they would be on the couch, on her bed, beside the television. She always loved learning and discovering something new.

It wasn't until high school that I noticed something odd about those books. While my mom brought them home by the dozens, she did not read many of them. She'd flip through some pages, but most just stayed in their stacks until they were long overdue. Then the piles would be replaced by a new stack on various topics. Still, my mom always had an answer for any question I asked.

I believed my mom when she said she hated my G-ma. And when she said she loved her. I knew love existed between them, but we spent entire evenings talking about how horrible G-ma was and all the little things we despised.

My G-ma resented us for needing her, yet we often lived together. She seemed to find comfort in feeling used and mistreated. It was her emotional home. My mom, meanwhile, found hers in feeling controlled, stifled, and targeted. Their stories often seemed incredible, but they told them with such conviction. Plus, they had lived in so many exotic places and had seen so much.

I believed them both. I accepted their words as truth, and my trusting had served me. We were far from the cult; The Fly was dead; we were safe; I'd attended my chosen school with money I had made myself; and I could commune with the Lord. Trusting in the ways of my mom and grandmother had taken me this far.

I listened to their arguments, understanding and believing both of them. But their biggest fight erupted over a watermelon.

It was late summer in St. George and watermelons were popular. They were everywhere. Supermarkets had them in outdoor bins, and I saw them being sold from roadside trucks during rides between my jobs. Someone had bought a watermelon, likely G-ma, or perhaps my mom using G-ma's money, as that was how the grocery shopping was done. The fresh, ripe fruit had been cut in half and sat on the counter, cut side up. The red flesh glistened, black seeds dotting the edges.

Someone had carved a bite out of the watermelon's center. It was not a proper slice, but a scooped-out portion from the sweetest, seedless part. This much I witnessed firsthand. I hadn't taken the scoop, but I saw the missing piece. The rest of the story was told to me later.

My mom described how G-ma exploded upon seeing the scooped watermelon. G-ma yelled at her, "How dare you eat the center! With all that I do, I should have the heart of the watermelon. Instead, you leave me the pig's portion and expect me to be your maid." This all aligned with my experience.

My mom, fed up with these familiar complaints, nudged G-ma aside and began carving up the watermelon to prove how much good watermelon remained. Not all the good part was gone, just a scoop out of the middle. G-ma, lighter and frailer than expected, stepped back easily. She continued lamenting about how she was left with the crumbs while we feasted on her dime. When my mom couldn't make her listen, she placed the large knife beside the watermelon on the counter and left the kitchen, knowing she could do nothing more.

Later, G-ma pulled Victor and me aside, speaking in hushed, serious tones. She told us that she was terrified of our mother, who she said had "gone a little crazy" and turned violent. She did not understand why. G-ma said that she was disappointed because she was looking forward to having some watermelon, but when she went into the kitchen there wasn't any watermelon left.

After making such a simple observation, my mom grabbed the watermelon knife and charged her. My mom forced G-ma to the ground and shook the knife in her face. G-ma insisted she'd never been so afraid in her life. Even after all the violent things that had happened with she traveled while my grandpa Tom was a diplomat in dangerous foreign countries, seeing her own daughter charge her with a knife sticky from the watermelon that she provided was the most terrified she had ever been. It was scarier than when The Fly attempted to break in and kill us all and G-ma had to hold him there with her gun until the police arrived. It was more frightening than any threat of the cult. This was worse, she said, because it came from her own daughter. She was afraid she was going to be killed right then, in her own home.

Now G-ma felt uncomfortable living with us because she did not know what would spark more violence from my mom. G-ma had to be very meek and tiptoe around to avoid triggering my mom's rage.

I knew both versions couldn't be true, but I did not know which to believe. My understanding of what I knew of my own experiences came largely from G-ma, while my worldly knowledge came from my mom. There must be truth somewhere, but I wasn't sure where. I knew that neither G-ma or my mom would lie. Lying was against God's commandments.

My mom and G-ma didn't speak for quite a while afterward. If my mom's account was accurate, the lingering anger seemed excessive. If G-ma's version was true, we would have moved out very soon after that. Instead, we stayed right there—together in tense silence.

低語

Whispers

I never heard the whispers. I only saw how they destroyed my family.

Ever since I had been baptized into the church, I understood the full power of words. I knew they were strong. The fact that an agreement and some water can wash away all sins and make one clean again in the face of the Lord is power beyond what I can understand. But it strikes of truth.

Lies have just as much power.

I did not think words would be used to create such harm. I told my wife I loved her when I meant it. I told my daughter I loved her every day. I always meant it. I did not tell one thing to one person and then something different to someone else. That is not what I thought words were for. I did not understand how someone so close to us would use her words to hurt her own family, her own grandchildren.

Some days when I came home from work, I would find Ella in her playpen and Beth in a closet crying. Sometimes she would share what had made her sad. Other times I was met with silence and deep stares. Beth began spending more and more time at her mother's house. Her father was busy with his work and away often. I did not want Angela to be alone. I offered that she can live with us. It would be helpful to Beth, and Angela would be taken care of. It is traditional in Chinese homes to have everyone together.

Beth agreed at first. After discussing it with her mother, Beth said that I only wanted Angela to live there so that everyone would be where I could watch and control them. This was not my thought, I told her. I wanted Beth to be taken care of while she looked after Ella. Our second would be born in a few months. Being together would give them both company, and Angela could help with the new baby. I assured her that Angela would have every comfort and her own bathroom. Beth was not convinced.

Beth stayed with her mother for a week because she was not feeling well. When she came back home, she was overjoyed. Her grandfather who lived at the ranch in Nevada was giving her a horse. She could hardly believe it. She always talked about having chickens and goats and horses. Now her dream was coming true. She talked about how she would ride it, brush it, and teach Ella to ride. It gave me great joy to see her so happy.

Days later Beth asked when we could bring the horse home.

"I don't think we have a place to keep it? Does it not live at your grandfather's?"

"It is my horse," she said. "It should be with me."

"I want you to have it. But this is Los Angeles, we cannot keep a horse in our small backyard."

"My mother said you would deny me. She said if you really loved me, you would let me keep the horse."

"I do love you. I just don't know where we would keep a horse."

"Then I guess my mother was right all along." Beth left the room. Ella began to cry in her crib. I went in to see her. Beth pushed past me and picked her up.

"Don't," she said. "With how you are right now you cannot be a good influence."

I did not understand. I understood even less when Beth said she wanted to go to her mother's. We only had one car which I needed for work. I drove her up to the house in the hills. I did not see the luggage she had packed until she asked me to unload them from the trunk.

Then I understood.

The whispers had become too loud for Beth to ignore. They were constant and worked to break down the happiness of our family. Angela did not care for me, but she had never taken time to know me. Our conversations were always about her. I wanted to be polite so I listened. Perhaps I had done something wrong, but I was never let in as family far enough to have caused offense. I was cut off from the beginning. I hoped that our union before

God in his Holy Temple would have shown Angela that I too am God's child and worthy of love. If from Him, then even from her. I feared she could not see past my culture and my race. Now she had used her words to poison our relationship. I did not know what to do, but I refused to accept failure in my home because one woman did not like the color of my skin. Still, I held no ill will. My family's care was important, and Angela was my family.

Tom did not share his wife's opinion. One day I called Tom to come help move a freezer I bought for the seafood company. It was a good freezer for a good price. Tom was helpful and good-natured as always. We went for the freezer in Tom's truck. He had a few bruises on his arms that I had not noticed before. I was concerned about his family and my family. Beth had told me of his temper. I worried for Angela. I did not ask about the marks on Tom's arms. I did not want to embarrass him. I also did not want to confront him about something that could be so sensitive.

With the freezer set where it would be most useful, I thanked Tom. Then I drove up to Angela and Tom's house in the hills. I wanted to make sure everything and everybody was ok. No one answered the door when I knocked. I knocked on the windows. I called out for Angela. There was no response. I went home still concerned about her. I did not know until later she was at home the entire time.

Beth lived full time at her mother's. Wang Chan and I stayed at our house. Before I had met Beth, the house seemed large for me, ready for a family. After Beth took baby Eleanore with her, the house felt deserted. It had found its purpose, had come into its own, and now did not know how to readjust to being so unused, so empty.

Beth's garden still grew. Most of the plants would bloom again in spring. I sat outside with Wang Chan and imagined Beth back in her garden, tending the plants and touching their leaves. I saw Ella toddling behind her, curious about everything. Wang Chan licked my hand where drops had fallen. I did not know how long I had been crying.

One day Beth called with a panic in her voice. I was happy to hear from her regardless. It was her brother, she said. He had been working as a repo-man and went into Koreatown to get a car. There he had been beat up by some guys. Now Tom was headed there to make things right. She was worried for him. It could be a dangerous part of LA. I volunteered to go search for Tom.

In the white van I had bought for the fish market, I drove into Koreatown. Up and down the streets I drove. I did not see Tom or his truck. For hours I searched. I retraced my drive to make sure we had not looped one another.

When I called Beth, she said her father had not gone to Koreatown after all. I searched those streets for nothing. I was not mad. We were all trying our best to help.

I mentioned the holidays were coming up. All I wanted was for her to celebrate them in our home, just as we had the year before when Ella was so tiny. Now that she was walking, we could decorate the house for her to enjoy.

"We have to start making memories for her. She must know that her family loves her," I said.

"I want that too. We will have to see," she said.

"And I want to spend those days with you. We should make our memories together," I said. I recognized the sniffle of her crying.

"Yes, I want that too. We shall see." She hung up the phone.

That night I sat with Wang Chan outside again. This time with hope.

I didn't like to come home to an empty house. After working hard all day, all I wanted was to see my family and hold my baby. I would call Angela's house to find Beth. They were too busy for me to come by, either going to a gourmet restaurant or shopping. I would come home late, tired, and make my own dinner, feed Wang Chan, then sit outside. It was my one chance to recuperate for work the next day. Sometimes I would see Beth and Eleanore at church. I would go to Angela's church meeting house to see them. I didn't pay attention to the speaker and lesson. I would bounce Ella on my legs and play with her. I would offer to take her into the hallway where she would not disrupt the services. I was always denied. Beth would stand up, her belly heavy and uncomfortable, and take Ella out. Then it was just church services. I tried to think about Jesus, but all I wanted was more time with Ella.

We spent Christmas together. Our second. I went to Angela and Tom's house. I gave a present to Ella. She grabbed at the wrapping not knowing she should pull it apart. She ripped off a piece and stared at the colors. I tore a little to show her how it was done. She laughed and put her hands on my face. I could have stayed like that with her all day. Ella's hair was long enough for little pony-tails on either side of her head. And it was dark. We had wondered if she would get Beth's red hair and green eyes, or my dark hair and brown eyes. Her skin was so light, but it made me happy to see she took after her father. Though I was exhausted from every day of struggle with the fish market and no help and no one at home at night, when I saw little Eleanore I knew everything I did was for her. It was a happy day. Even Angela was kind to me. We exchanged gifts and ate.

At night Beth and I stared at the lights of the tree and talked. I never celebrated Christmas before coming to America. It was in the American movies and on posters but was not part of our culture. Now, sitting with my beautiful wife pregnant with our second child while the first slept peacefully, I understood what Christmas was about. I played with Beth's hair. Everything was so perfect I thought it would start to snow, just like it did in the movies.

"Come home with me," I said. "Let's be together. I can see how happy you are when you are with me."

"You work so much. I wouldn't want to be so lonely. Plus, my mother helps with Ella."

"That is true. But maybe she could come stay with us. I've offered before. Our home is open."

Beth pat my hand softly between hers. "I'm going to stay up here," she said. "Mother needs me. And as big as I am, I need her as well."

I did not press the issue. I was happy just to be where I was.

The new year came and went. I worked, but the fish market was not keeping up. The overhead was too high. I had already put all of my savings into the business and paying our bills. Even though Beth stayed at her mother's, she needed money for food and diapers. In my exhaustion, I found someone who would take the business. Not to buy, just to have. Then I could start over with something else. A wonderful lady took the inventory and supplies. I made notes on how I got the best deals for fish and who to talk to down at the docks. I told her everything I had learned. She seemed very grateful. Now I had time to spend with my family. I wanted to be around so Ella could know me. She would be speaking soon. I was excited to get to know the person she was becoming and to help her grow.

It was mid-January when I called Beth to tell her I had ended that business. I would not have to work so many long hours and could be home more and be less tired. I could help raise Ella while Beth took care of the new baby. I could see the future plainly. Beth answered the telephone at her mother's house.

"Oh, it's you. Good. I have something to tell you."

"Me too," I said. She did not pause.

"I won't be coming back there anymore. I'm going to stay up here with my mother. I'm sorry, Jack. I filed for divorce months ago. My lawyer has drawn up papers and they are ready for you to sign."

She had decided to leave me. Months ago. All the sweetness she had shown lost its flavor. All the hope and kindness of the holidays was not true. She did not plan to stay with me. She had made up her mind about me and did not even say. I could not believe this was happening.

I thought back to our time together. I thought about everything closely to find what had gone wrong. I wondered when the divorce papers were filled out. Did Beth go alone? Or did she have her mother there, guiding the ink of her pen? I questioned if it was after I could not get a horse for her or after I ate the strawberries.

I did not know what I could have done to make a woman turn away from her covenants she made before God. Beth was not only divorcing me, she was betraying her promise she made to the Lord on our wedding day.

I felt broken. I was broke, had medical bills, no business, and no family. That night I sat with little Wang Chan on my lap and I wept. I did not know what I had done, and I did not know what to do now. I could not call my family in Taiwan. It would be dishonor. I was the first of thirteen generations to leave Taiwan. I was the first to marry a white woman. And I was the first to get a divorce. I could not fathom how my life turned so upside down. Just when I thought I had everything I had dreamed.

I cried myself to the bottom. I might have sat there with that faithful dog for hours or even days. I would not have noticed. I wept until I could not. Then, with nothing and no one to support me, I remembered my daughter. I saw Ella's face. I saw her ponytails and her smile. I saw the eyes she inherited from me. I saw how she blinked at me when she first was born. She was my flesh and blood. I could get divorced, but I could never not have a daughter. And there, at the bottom, surrounded by the emptiness of a Los Angeles night without love, I picked myself up for Eleanore Tsen. She deserved everything I could give her.

If her mother decided to break apart the family joined by God, then Ella would have to have extra love and extra care. She must know how important she is. The new baby as well.

The next day I called up to Angela and Tom's house.

I called again the day after that.

All I asked for was to speak to Beth and to see Eleanore. Angela denied me. I asked Angela to talk with me, so she could understand how important it was to keep family together.

"It would be a pity," she said. I did not know if this referred to the break-up or the marriage. I wanted to believe Angela had Beth's and Ella's best future in her intention. Perhaps somewhere in her fear she did. Perhaps she was too far in her hatred to see the damage she was doing. I did not know. I only know she stayed cold and emotionless unless she burned with rage and threats.

I went to the Hollywood Hills. I knocked on the door. I waited, then I knocked again. I was sitting on the ground near the pond at the bottom of the stairs when Angela came out.

"Oh, you are still here. Hold on," she said. I asked to see Beth and Ella, but she had already gone inside. Minutes later she came out again, her arms filled with small objects. I recognized them as the gifts I had given her. "Take these. I did not want them." She poured them into my hands. A jade carving of a family symbol fell to the ground and broke.

"Also, one more thing," Angela said. "You should get a lawyer."

I did not take the gifts back into my home. It was a disgrace to have them returned. If Angela did not want them, she could have thrown them out. She wanted me to know she did not want them. This was her way of severing ties with me. It was more than gifts;

gifts always are more than the object. It was dismissal. She wanted to show me she did not want anything to do with me anymore.

I did not call Beth that night.

I went to church every week, even when I had to leave immediately and get back to work. It was important that I show God honor. I wanted to be faithful. This institution taught me families can be eternal. It showed me how to find salvation. In the church were good people with strong family values. I met with the leaders to appeal their help. I told them everything, how Beth had left, how I wanted to see my daughter and could not, and how I could not bear to walk away from the covenants I had made to God. I asked the leaders to try to talk to her. They could remind her of the importance of keeping family together.

When they called up to the house, they spoke with Angela. She was a leader in her ward. She had been the Relief Society President and a member all her life. They talked for a long time. Angela told them how I was cruel to her daughter. She told them I mistreated Beth. Angela said I had done so much wrong that she did not see any way we could ever get back together.

This was not true, I told them. They nodded their heads at me. I don't know if they believed me, but they said they could not help me anymore. God would provide the way. I must trust in Him and have faith, they said. I would have faith. I also wanted to have my family. The leaders told me again they could do nothing more.

Angela came one step closer to getting what she wanted: me gone.

I called Beth. I wanted to see her and Eleanore. Finally, she agreed. We planned a day at the beach. I would pick them up. We could lay in the sand while Eleanore scooted around and explored. She could walk now, but barely. She would wrap her whole hand around one finger of mine and slowly toddle. She would fall often and how she would laugh. It was music to my ears, those tiny sounds of joy. We put her in the car and drove toward the beach. I had prepared everything. I had towels, sunscreen, diapers, toys, and a lunch for Beth and myself. It would be a perfect day, I thought.

We started talking. Beth was more quiet than usual. I had many questions. I wanted to know why she had left, why she would not talk to me when I called. I was distressed. I wanted this day to be perfect, but I also wanted to know how to resolve the conflicts.

Beth did not want to talk about it. I still asked. Soon we got into an argument. Beth wanted to go back home. She called it home, but it was her mother's house. I dropped her off and drove away. I came back a few minutes later.

"You don't have to spend time with me," I said when Beth answered the door. "But let me see my daughter."

Ella had followed Beth and Angela outside. I picked her up. Angela pulled her from me and gave her to Beth. "She needs her mother," she said. They refused to let me see her though we had planned this day to be together.

Upset, I paced back and forth in front of their house. I slipped into the pond not far from the front door. I was hurt and tired. I grabbed one of the smooth rocks near my wet feet. Childishly, I threw the rock at the front door in my anger. I was wrong to do it. It made a loud bang and scratched the door. I already thought how I could repair the door.

Angela came outside with a pistol. She pointed it at me and told me not to move. I did not. I did not want to be shot for throwing a rock. I did not know what Angela would do. I had misjudged her before.

"I have called the police," she said. "Don't do anything before they get here or I will shoot."

Beth came and stood by her mother. I looked at her worried I would be shot right there. She looked worried too.

The police did not arrest me, but they took all my information to file a report. I was charged with trespassing and vandalism of property. I told them I had been invited that day. I told them I would fix the door. They did not care.

The church counselors told Angela she should not have called the police. She shrugged them off. "It was standard procedure," she said. Now, she had a report from the police that I had committed a crime. Soon I would have to apply for my green card renewal.

I saw a shift in Angela. Before she was polite and calm. She talked a lot, mostly about herself, but she would pretend her kindness. Now, she was harsh and cold. She would accuse me of things I had never thought of.

When I came by her house to check on her, she said I was searching to kill her. She said our wedding ring was used. That I only married Beth to stay in the United States. That I was dangerous.

After this, I did not see Beth or Ella for a long time. Beth would not talk to me. They would not let me come to the house to see Ella. I would be arrested and deported if I tried, Angela said. I knew I should not cross her. I did not know what she was capable of.

Another

I didn't meet another victim of the cult until after high school. I had seen hundreds of cult members who were indistinguishable from victims. My mom pointed out television stars, singers, radio hosts, and people in the community. There were police officers, teachers, church leaders, and even people who had visited G-ma at our house. There were so many. But none of them had ever admitted to being in the cult. That knowledge was reserved for later, shared between us in bright-eyed whispers when we were alone. We kept our distance and never confronted anyone about what we knew. They would deny it anyway. That's what the cult told them to do.

That all changed with Gina Hughes. I met her in my first singles' ward. I was excited about being a college student. I had saved enough money and worked hard for grades good enough to be admitted to Dixie State College. Even though I lived at home, I wanted to be part of the college culture, so I joined the ward I'd attend if I lived on campus. In the Mormon church, there are regular family wards with kids of all ages, married couples, and older people. The college wards are different. They have singles' wards meant for young Mormons between 18 and 26 years old, most likely to encourage young marriages. Once married, couples transfer to a family ward.

My singles' ward was just college kids. We were the leaders, the speakers, and the congregation. We had all been taught our roles and now ran the meetings, with little oversight from a bishop. There I met Gina. She was the Relief Society president and all around amazing. I wanted to be like her. And I wanted to be her friend.

After an evening fireside, everyone left except for Gina and me. We began talking, sharing. It was exactly the kind of college experience I had hoped for. We fell easily into deep discussion. Gina was smart and engaging. But nothing could have prepared me for what I found out that night.

I told Gina about my backstory, how we were in hiding from the cult. How I had been abused and raped by the cult. How my father had tortured my brother and me when we were young because he had split personalities. And all because of the cult. Instead of fear or even placid acceptance, Gina looked straight into my eyes. "Me too," she said. I was stunned. I couldn't find words to ask more. "In fact, I'm still involved with the cult. My parents are both in it. They have been for years. I'm still tortured and raped sometimes."

We stayed up all night talking. Finally, I had found someone who could understand me, someone who could validate all I had experienced and share in my silenced trauma. We told stories and shared worries. Gina knew even more than my mom about the workings of the cult, who was in it, and who was in charge. She had been involved for years, she told me.

I had found a friend. She had been split, like me. She could be triggered, like me. She had been victimized, like me. But she had not gotten free. I knew I wouldn't be a good friend if I didn't help her. I had a responsibility to free her from the cult. She didn't live on campus, still stuck at home with her cult parents. This sounded so horrible to me. My heart hurt knowing what she was surviving. I had only heard what I had gone through. It was one of my splits that remembered. Gina had to remember it all, and she was split as well.

I got to know Gina and her splits. They had different ways of talking and different memories. Some of them knew jokes, some couldn't speak. There were frequent splits, so we named them. I got to know Gina, but also Bobby, Edmund, Carol, and little Reina. Of all these, Bobby was my favorite.

To help Gina, I offered that she could move in with us. We understood what it took to escape the cult and we could help her. It would be a difficult process, but we were there.

Gina accepted, and we went to my apartment complex to tell my mom. My mom agreed easily to have Gina live with us, though we did not reveal Gina was still in the cult. I didn't want our security situation to jeopardize Gina's escape. Besides, if no one knew what Gina was running from it would be safer. That much I had learned from my mom.

It was great to have Gina live with us. She was a great friend. Victor got along with her, and my mom thought she was very nice. Gina was always polite and seemed to know what to say to everyone. I didn't know a single person who disliked her. We grew closer by the day and I was proud she was out of danger staying with us. I didn't realize I would be the one in danger.

Gina had been with us for a couple months, knew us all well, and was becoming part of the family. She slept in my room and we went to school and church together.

Then one day I felt groggy. Not sick, just forgetful and woozy. I had slept for so long but was still so tired. I couldn't quite remember how I had gotten into bed. When I woke up, Gina was there, just as she usually was, sitting on the chair we had brought in from the kitchen.

"I'm sorry," she said. "I had to do it. But it wasn't me. I promise. I didn't want to hurt you."

"What's going on?" I sat up, alarmed.

"I drugged you and raped you," she said. "But I had to. I wasn't myself." She meant she had split. Some of her splits were controlled by the cult. We knew they were in there, but most of the time they were friendly. I didn't feel like I had been tortured or violated. Just confused. I didn't know if I should be scared or angry. Perhaps both.

My mom could sense something was wrong. She came in the room and demanded to know what had happened. I didn't know what to say. Gina did. She told her everything.

"You see, Beth. I'm part of the cult. I have been for years. And I have never left. I told Eleanore I was leaving, but I couldn't. This whole time that I have been staying here I have been part of the cult. I poisoned Eleanore so that I could sneak out. I go back to my parents' house at night so they can rape me."

My mom wasn't surprised. She didn't freak out or yell. She didn't show any surprise. Her eyes lit up as she listened. "You poisoned Eleanore?"

"One of my splits did."

"What did you poison her with?"

"A needle."

"Where did you stick the needle?"

"In her neck."

My mom flipped my hair in front of my shoulders and scanned my neck.

"Oh, I see where you stuck the needle in."

"Really?" said Gina, now seeming surprised.

"And you have been sneaking out?"

"Yes. Out of that window." She pointed to the window near my bed. It was a sharp drop to the bushes below, but not too far.

My mom opened the window with a creak and stuck her head out. "Yes, I see where the bushes have been poisoned too, to make it easier."

"Um. Yeah," Gina said, unsure. "I did that. I'm sorry."

"You really have thought of everything," my mom said, more curious than alarmed. I worried the cult now knew where we were, who we were, and that we were actively in danger of being taken, of being split. I thought my mom would be upset that I had not been afraid enough to keep the cult at bay. I thought I could help Gina and it would all be ok. We would be safe and Gina would be free.

I didn't think that the cult could possibly have a plant living in our house. I worried I had undone all the work my mom had struggled through for these nearly twenty years. None of this surfaced. My mom seemed fine. She and Gina opened up about the cult. They talked for hours about signs, symbols, ritual, and the constant abuse. I heard Gina say things I had not known, but my mom agreed with her, as though it was common knowledge. They were becoming friends.

There was no anger, no dismissal. At the end of their conversation my mom thought it best that Gina not stay in my room anymore. Gina walked out our front door and waved to me. I watched her walk past the other apartment buildings, around the corner, and out of our lives for good.

被告

Accused

My baby boy was born in a hospital without his father. It was in the spring. I did not know where or when he came into this world. I could not see him. I sat with Wang Chan alone at the house and wondered what he looked like. I wondered if he was healthy. He needed his father. He needed to know who I was and where he came from. It was my responsibility to help him grow. I only knew his name.

I cried for my babies. I cried to be with my babies. Even though eighty percent of my body's water content had turned into tears, I could not stop the painful feelings of losing my wife and my children.

The first time I held Victor he was already months old. I stood in front of Angela and Tom's house. Beth brought Victor out to me. Ella ran to me and held on to my leg. Victor looked like me and like Ella. I could see myself in his face and knew we were family.

Nothing Beth or Angela did could change that. I held him. He did not cry.

Beth and I talked a lot. She was very kind. She hugged me and said that we should get together soon. I looked forward to that moment. I wanted all the time with my kids that was possible. I did not go in the house.

After one year of separation, there was a time when my wife seemed intent on reconciliation. She called sometimes. We talked. She worried for the safety of the children. I said I would do anything to provide for them and keep them safe. Beth thought I should write a will. I did. Beth suggested we buy a pair of gravesites. I said I was not preparing to die just yet. She did not think this funny. She asked me to get a life insurance policy in case. I did all these things.

Beth asked to see me away from her mother's house. My prayers had been answered, I thought. My family was coming back. I took off work. I was selling seafood wholesale to restaurants again. I had a truck and could drive the route myself. This way I would not have many expenses. I could save again and provide for my children.

One time together, with Victor on my knee, Beth asked me to sell the Los Angeles house for some place better for the children. She asked that I place half the cash from the sale in her personal account. She said she worried that I would waste the money or put it into a business. She wanted security. I told her I was willing to do this. I wanted her to feel safe.

We had a picnic in the park. Ella picked up everything nearby and brought it over to show it to Victor and me. I hadn't seen them in so long. Ella now pieced together real sentences, instead of broken strings of words.

After, we all came back to the house, back to our home. I showed Ella where she used to sleep. "This is your room," I told her. She did not go in. Looking up at me she asked, "Why does Mommy not live here in this house?" She wanted us to be together.

When I told this to Beth, she smiled but did not comment. Beth said she wanted me to be happy. She knew these times had been difficult. "Would it be helpful to go home for a while?" She asked. "You talk of Taiwan so fondly. Would some time with your family help you heal?"

"Thank you. But this is what I need to heal." I motioned to where Ella played and Victor slept in his bassinet. "I want to stay close by my family here. This is so good."

Beth's smile went flat. Suddenly she needed to go back home. It was not late, I told her. She said it was important.

We had not been fighting. The kids were happy and fed. I did not understand why she wanted to leave. I drove her home. She seemed bothered but not unhappy. When she got out of the car she began to cry. "I really wish you would visit your parents, Jack. I want so much for you to be happy."

I did not want to see her cry. "I am happy when I am here," I told her. "Besides, I don't have the money to go back. And I must work." She looked away, picked Victor up in his bassinet, and walked to the house. Ella hugged me then ran after her mother.

Three days later my phone rang near midnight. I was asleep. I had to get up at four and drive to the docks. I woke to the phone continuing to ring. I thought it was Beth. She might need me. Perhaps something happened to one of the children.

A man was on the other end. He introduced himself as Beth's attorney. I knew him from when Angela pressed charges against me. I did not think I would speak to him again. I had hoped not.

The lawyer informed me there was a restraining order against me. I would not be allowed to be alone with my children, sell my house, or have any contact with my wife or her family. Additionally, I had to appear in court in two days. He suggested I bring a lawyer.

I did not have any money. I worked all day to pay off the last lawyer to keep me from jail. And the house bill. And the money that Beth needed for the children. I told Beth I had no money, and she responded by engaging lawyers. Perhaps they thought if I did not have money, I could not have adequate representation in court. I still stumbled with English.

I must not lose my children. There was nothing I could do to come up with more money. I tried to sell my blood to the Red Cross. However, the Red Cross only accepts donations.

The next two nights I spent with eyes wide open and my heartbeat lurching. My wife did not want me to return home for my happiness. She wanted me to be absent for the custody and divorce hearing. My wife and her mother planned to cripple me financially and emotionally. As I pondered their lack of human feeling I recoiled in horror and amazement.

I wore my only suit to court. It was black and felt like I was going to the funeral of Beth's and my union. I could not believe it had come to this. I was not able to speak to her to gain any understanding. If she wanted out of the marriage, I could do that for her. If she wanted to rebuild our union without her mother's interference, I would do that for her. But if she wanted to take my kids away, I could not do that.

The hallway outside the courthouse was cold and uninviting. Government buildings in Los Angeles were different than in Taiwan. Everything was distant, built tall and blank to make you feel small. I sat on a bench when I was too tired to walk, and walked when I was too tired to sit. I rubbed my eyes. In the blur I saw Tom, Angela, and Beth come in. Beth held Victor. Ella walked by her side. Ella ran toward me when she saw me waiting there. Angela picked her up and put her body between us so Ella could not see me. Ella cried and cried. She crowed so loud I thought we would be asked to leave. If she had been able to come to me, it would not have caused this disruption. Plus, I wanted to see her. I wanted to tell her that her father would always be there for her. That I would always love her no matter what.

Tom approached me and put his hand on my shoulder. Ella still cried for me. "I know this is hard," Tom said. "I've always liked you, Jack, which is why I am telling you this. Don't fight this. This isn't something you can win. You have not seen what Angela is capable of. But your children will find you someday. You just have to let them."

I had thought Tom was my friend. He was a father and a member of the church. He knew how eternally bonded family is. I could not believe he would advise me to let my kids go. I realized then this was not just divorce. They were trying to take away my children.

The judge looked over his glasses at us after we were seated. He read the case description then asked to hear from Beth. Angela interrupted, "I'll be speaking for her."

This is how the entire mess started, I thought. Angela argued that I was unsafe, threatening, and a bad influence on the children. She waved the charges she had filed previously against me at the judge.

"I have a copy of those, ma'am." The judge then looked at me. "How would you care to respond?"

I told my lawyer I would like to speak even though my English is not perfect. I told the judge I was sorry for damaging the door. It was wrong of me. I only did so because I was frustrated by not seeing my daughter. I told him I made money. I had a house with rooms for the children. I loved them. I wanted to be in their life even if they did not live with me. It was important they have their mother while I worked, I told him. And I would do whatever he ordered so I could have them with me when I could.

"This case is not settled," the judge said. "I see no reason to separate custody during this separation. Mr. Tsen has full right to see his children until ordered otherwise. The restraining order still stands, but does not apply to Mr. Tsen's children."

"His children are afraid of him," Angela yelled. "Didn't you hear how Ella cried when she saw him today?"

"I understand divorce proceedings are underway. This can be a difficult time for everyone. This order will stand until a new one is ordered at the decree," the judge replied.

I felt as though I had finally been seen. Like my new home accepted me. Beth and Angela did not look at me before they left.

"This is far from over, Jack. But today was a victory," My lawyer said when I shook his hand.

One day my wife wanted to talk to me about an urgent matter. We met at Forest Lawn in Hollywood where we had spent many great nights while courting. There Beth informed me that her mother had agreed to sign the house back to me and that I would not owe her half. I could sell the house and keep all the money. But the children had to stay with her. I could only see my children when it was convenient for Beth and Angela, and I could not take them out at all. I understood why Angela had agreed to returning the house. She thought money could buy anything. I rejected her offer and left.

Every time I called to see my children, Angela reminded me I should not and had to wait for Beth to call me. Beth did not call. It was months before I saw my children again. Beth called one day to say I could see them on very specific conditions. I agreed before I even knew what they were. I had to be home alone. She would bring the kids over to the house while she remained close by at a neighbor's during the stay. Then she could come by quickly if she was needed. That was fine by me.

It had been so long since my children were in my home. This would be the first time for Victor since he was just a tiny baby unable to move around by himself. He was now one and could walk short distances. Little Ella was almost three. She was so curious. She would ask about everything and always had something to say. Victor was very quiet. He never cried.

Beth dropped the children off. I carried Victor inside and held him. Ella played. The toys I bought from the open-air market were in a basket. Ella took each one out before deciding which to play with. I loved to watch her piece together her world. We had a peaceful and easy afternoon. I showed Ella her bedroom. I showed her my room, and the room we had for Victor. Each had beds, and I put toys in their rooms so they would feel comfortable. Ella asked, "Where is Mommy's room?" I did not have an answer for her.

"I'm just glad you are here," I told her. Ella went in her room and came back out again. She preferred to play at my feet. I sat on the couch holding Victor while she played. The hours passed quickly as Beth arrived too soon. I wanted the children to stay near me longer—always if possible. Victor was asleep, and I carried him to the car. Beth buckled Eleanore in her car seat and drove away. I slept well that night.

In the morning I still felt great from having spent time with the children. Love was meant to be shared. I could not hold on to my love and only tell Wang Chan about it. Love must be given. It was not only a word—it was action. Love was years of devotion, care beyond sacrifice. I felt like it had been received. Ella had held my hand. Victor slept in my arms.

I've always had one wish for my children: to grow up in a healthy environment. This wish could only come true if they have their father in their lives. I had glimpsed what I could do for them and how it had felt to be there together—as family.

The next day passed in pure light. There was much work to do, but seeing how it could benefit the children I had held yesterday made all my efforts a joy. My fingers did not burn from the frozen fish. I carried my own warmth. At least until I received a call from my lawyer.

"Jack, did you see your kids yesterday?" His tone was more weighted than the question.

"Oh, it was so great. I want them to spend every weekend here." I still beamed.

"Jack, I have to ask you this. And I need you to think carefully before answering. Was your fly down?"

I could not remember so I said nothing while I thought. The question was odd, and not something I gave any attention. "I don't know. What is that supposed to mean?"

"It means we are going back to court. Your wife, it seems... now don't get mad, Jack. Your wife has made some troubling allegations against you."

I had to sit down while my lawyer continued. I could not believe Beth as I knew her would lie like this. And with such awful sickening things. She knew I loved those children. She knew that they were the most precious to me of anything in this world. I was willing to work my entire waking moments and give everything to them. To lie that I had sexually abused my little girl. It was impossible. She knew I would not do anything to harm a single hair on Eleanore's head. And she lied about this sick sick abuse!

I was confident the court would see the truth. I was hopeful they would see it takes a sick person to invent such things. I prayed the court would allow me to keep my children safe and teach them trust, honesty, and respect. It was clear Beth could not.

The day at reconsideration court of Los Angeles I drove my Dodge van to court. It was a family van, but I no longer had a family. I waited on the second floor of the courthouse and felt very depressed. When Beth and I had knelt across from one another at the altar of the Lord's holy temple, I never dreamed I would see this day. I sat for half an hour before Beth walked in. We did not say anything to each other.

The court showed a video instructing us not to hurt the children emotionally while obtaining the divorce. The video did not create any hope for a successful marriage. I thought of my wife's family and their history of marriage. Beth's grandfather divorced her grandmother two times and remarried her three. Her mother's marriage had lasted but they separated often and yelled at each other more often. It was not a healthy lifestyle.

After the video, we went back into the reconsideration room. Beth sat behind me so I could not see her. Perhaps she did not want me to look at her face or eyes while she lied to the judge. Reflecting upon how she was raised and the example of marriage she had, I began to pity her again. With my pity also came my love and protection. I wanted to help and take care of her. Until she began talking to the counselor.

The counselor introduced herself as Anna and interviewed Beth first. There, in the presence of lawyers and the counselor, my wife began to cry and accused me of sexually molesting my three-year-old daughter. I turned to look at her while she was crying and lying and crying and lying some more. Sick! Very sick! Very evil! Very sly! Very dirty! I could not believe she would repeat such a thing she knew to be false.

Beth said she could only permit me to see my babies in the presence of a professional monitor which was forty-five dollars an hour. The counselor knew that I was spending all the money I could make on lawyers and supporting the needs of my children. I could not sell the house because it was half Beth's and selling it had been prohibited by the court. The counselor asked if there was any way the church could help with the monitoring.

"If my wife wants someone to watch me, I have lots of friends who would be willing to help," I told the counselor.

"I know who he is talking about. He wants Dr. Chou. He's a child abuser. I went to his home a couple times and saw him hit his son with a pencil. He's mean to his son," Beth said.

"Would someone else from your church be available?" the counselor asked.

"Church people aren't professionals," Beth told her. "Jack sees a counselor there. But he's not qualified."

"Does he speak with you two about your marriage?" The counselor asked me.

"He did before. But Angela has prohibited him from calling her home. Every time he invited them for a discussion, Angela would say her daughter is sick. She would say anything to not cooperate."

"He is not a professional counselor. He's a football coach," Beth said. She continued to negate any offers I had of childcare.

The counselor said she had to listen to these complaints of abuse and safeguard the children until the accusations were proven otherwise. I could still see my children, she said, but in the presence of a court-trained monitor. "For now," she told me. I had hope when the truth was revealed, I would have my children with me as much as possible.

I had loved Beth. I had promised to love her forever. Had she been a woman of God, I would have. She made this impossible. Now I pitied her more than I loved her. I felt very bad for her. Hopefully she could love herself one day.

I confided in my church leaders again. I told them Beth and Angela were trying to take away my children. I did not know who else I could ask for help. One of the church leaders told me, "You have just run into a very wicked family."

I had thought this family to be good. They were leaders in the church. They were returned missionaries, a temple worker, a Relief Society president. If I cannot trust this kind of religious family, I did not know who I could trust.

I was wrong in putting too much trust in Beth. The only reimbursement I could give for my children's hurt was to spend more time with them and make more money for their future.

My children will always receive one hundred percent of my love. No matter what. I brought them to this earth, and I will always do the best to love and take care of them. I will always be devoted to them. I hoped for their bright future.

Dan

My mom didn't date anyone from the time she was divorced from The Fly until I was nineteen and about to leave home for the first time. I was in my second year at Dixie State College, preparing to transfer to BYU, the Mormon school where I felt I was supposed to be.

I loved college. I was good at it. I would read the syllabi, calculate exactly how many points I needed for an A, and get them. I organized study groups and social groups at my singles' ward. I spent less and less time at home, always finding reasons to be at school. Meanwhile, Victor went to high school and then retreated to his room with his video games. I guess my mom must have been lonely. She spent more and more time at the public library. She had often said, after leaving a long day among those books, that she would want to live there. She did the next best thing and started volunteering there a few days a week. That's where she met Dan.

Dan was a brusque, bald guy with short, worn-down teeth from years of spitting tobacco. He always wore a white cap with a large flat brim and a cloth neck panel fringed by wisps of his pigment-less hair around the edges. He wore T-shirts and faded jeans and carried his hands in a fist. His fingers had become arthritic and boasted large bulbs of beat-up knuckles, which he attributed to countless fights.

He'd lived rough. He had lived everywhere, he said, but most recently Colorado. There, he'd had a change of heart. He was giving up his rough living, his drinking nights, and his rambling days to find a respectable woman in Utah to marry. He wasn't subtle about it. He walked into the library in St. George, saw my mom at the help desk, and told her exactly that.

"Alright," Dan said, grinning through his nubs, "I'm here to find a good Mormon woman. Is that you?" Two months later they were married.

The marriage was sudden. My mom called while I was at work. Her voice, so much like mine, asked, "Hey, we're getting married. Do you want to come?"

"When?"

"Today."

"Yeah. I'll come. I'm off work at five." I was neither surprised nor prepared. It just was.

I went to the mall after my shift to get a new shirt for the wedding. My college boyfriend came along, and the five of us drove down to Las Vegas. My brother came too. We went to the Little Chapel of Love. It was the cheesiest of ceremonies. It wasn't even Elvis marrying them, which was either a step down for a Vegas wedding or a step up, though no one seemed to care. It was marriage. It was legal. They said their "I do's," and we went home.

Soon, Dan started pestering my mom about his teeth. He couldn't chew properly. This affected his speech and, he felt, his "stature as a man." My mom dutifully racked up $40,000 in credit card debt getting him all new teeth.

A couple months into the marriage, Dan decided to reach out to his estranged son, Lance. My mom encouraged their reunion, saying it was important for Lance to know his father. This would have mattered for Victor and me too, had our father not been a cult leader and abuser—now deceased.

Dan hadn't seen Lance since he was eight or nine. Lance, now twenty-two, lived in Colorado smoking pot and avoiding school. Once they reconnected, it wasn't long before they wanted to live together. Lance left his life in Colorado to move in with us. It had not been six months since Dan arrived in Utah, and he now had a wife, new teeth, and an adult son. Crammed in our little condo lived my mom, Victor, Lance, Dan, and me.

Most days, Lance and Dan sat outside in folding chairs while Lance drank beer and smoked weed. I would return from classes or one of my jobs and they would be out there laughing. My mom would be inside watching TV or in bed. Victor stayed in his room.

Dan was genuinely nice, always ready with a smile and a compliment. Although much of what he said seemed expected, he had a way of making each expression feel authentic. He befriended

Mormon missionaries and showed interest in all things that had to do with Mormonism. He was going to get baptized, he had said. He'd sit with me some evenings asking about Joseph Smith, usually turning the conversation toward something he'd read in his big book about the prophet.

He had not always been like that. Lance shared stories of when Dan was younger. Dan was sitting right there to confirm them. Once, Lance told us, when Dan still lived with Lance's mother and the both of them were using drugs, Dan came in the room where Lance was sitting with his friends.

"Hey, what are these candies?" Dan had asked. "They are terrible." He held a handful of little blue things and tossed some in his mouth. Crunch. Lance said, "Dad, those aren't candy. Those are fish rocks." Dan had been scooping the gravel from the bottom of the fish tank. "Oh. Weird." Dan said. Then he shrugged and tossed what he still had in his hand into his mouth to eat even more fish rocks.

One day, Dan tried whitening his new teeth by swooshing bleach. It burned and burned and Dan ran around the house swearing from the pain. Lance just laughed it off. Soon after that, Dan decided to trim off his chest hair by setting it on fire, thinking it would burn off in one poof and be gone, but instead he burnt his chest.

None of these events seemed to bother Dan at all. Mere days would go by before Dan and Lance would recount these tales as though they happened to someone else entirely. They would both laugh and laugh. Dan would look around like a joke had been played on him and say, "Yeah." With a shrug of acceptance and zero shame, he would continue laughing. It was impossible not to find him at least entertaining.

My mom began spending more time at G-ma's. Victor retreated further into his room. Between my jobs, school, and church, I rarely was at home except to sleep. Dan and Lance stayed at the condo all day, laughing and telling stories. When my mom was home, she often was in her room on the phone with G-ma.

With my two-year degree all but guaranteed, I prepared to transfer to Brigham Young University in Provo, three hours north from all the family I had known, and away from everyone I knew would protect me from the cult. I would be living out of the house for the first time. It would be the full college experience I had craved since starting my first business. I didn't know if Victor would go to college after he finished high school. Unlike my eagerness to leave, he seemed to withdraw further into himself, becoming more and more solitary. It felt like everyone did.

Soon my mom began confiding in me about Dan. She was convinced he was deceiving her about being a practicing Mormon. She questioned his testimony and his intentions, suspecting he had returned to drug use. He smoked weed with Lance, that much I knew. I sympathized with my mom. It had to be hard in ways I couldn't fully grasp. "He's lying about all sorts of stuff," she told me. Then, without warning, she added, "You know, Dan is poisoning me."

My brain halted on those words.

"How do you know?"

"I just know it. I see all the signs," she insisted.

Though I didn't know Dan well—neither did my mom—something about him poisoning her did not quite make sense. Yes, he might have been a freeloader who didn't follow the Word of Wisdom, the Mormon doctrine prohibiting drugs, alcohol, tobacco, and coffee. But he did not seem malicious. There was no evidence beyond my mom's suspicions, which she presented as divine revelation.

This echoed how she spoke about The Fly. She never witnessed his misdeeds, or attempts to poison her, yet she claimed with 100% conviction that, "There were so many signs."

I pondered: What would be the chances that both men my mom married would try to poison her? That is a lot of poisoning. Of all the things in the world, poisoning seems like a less common thing to happen to someone. Out of all the people to choose as a mate, my mom had married not one, but two people who would want to poison her.

I did not disagree with her, though I chose not to believe her totally. It was hard to doubt my mom. She had guided us through countless challenges and taught us so much, and now to see her words as not the whole truth was not something I could fathom. I began to be suspicious of Dan in case he was poisoning my mom. I also began to be suspicious of my mom.

I remember one day after church, Victor, my mom, and I visited G-ma's house for Sunday dinner. Dan had attended church without Lance but returned home afterward to join him. I suspected Dan didn't feel welcome at G-ma's. I would not have if I were him. G-ma made no secret of her disapproval, telling us directly he wasn't good enough for us. All her other reasons he should go, we heard her tell my mom or her friends on the phone.

That night, unprompted, G-ma began describing how my grandpa Tom had poisoned her. I don't know if Victor was paying attention, but I absorbed every detail. Her account matched my mom's allegations about Dan perfectly, and the same as The Fly. Either I was naive to trust that any man I was with would not poison me, or there was something suspicious about what they were saying. I kept my mouth shut but listened intently.

Pretty soon my mom and Dan divorced. Their marriage lasted roughly a year. They had gradually spent less time together until one day on the phone, my mom simply announced their divorce had been finalized for weeks and Dan had moved out.

She showed no sadness. Dan had come and gone. I did not know where he went with his new teeth, and I didn't ask.

遺失的

Lost

My wife has taken my babies from me. This hurts me very much. I have to ask permission to see my babies, and they have completely refused to let me see them. This is a cause to my extreme emotional pain.

I have not had an opportunity to sit down with my wife and talk because of her mother's interference. The church cannot do anything because Angela does all the talking. I can't sleep and feel ill. I have to carry this broken heart and soul around while trying to make enough money to pay all the bills.

My parents are not in this country, and I have no relatives around. I have no one to discuss my problems with. A little concern and love is very important to my life. Family means a lot to me. To me family means love, concern, and care. After more than a year of separation and lengthy court battles, I need more love and devotion rather than more anguish.

Visiting my children was my most profound joy. I would save every Saturday away from work, even though I needed the money. I would call and arrange with the monitor some time when I could be present there with both Eleanore and Victor. Then I would call Beth to confirm. So often she would cancel. Either she was sick or the children were fussy. There always was an excuse. Some of the time she would not answer. I would wait and wait at home with Wang Chan. I would call Angela's house again and again. Too often I sat at home waiting for the children and they never arrived. My heart hurt, and I worried I would never see them again.

After I had missed Victor's second Christmas, I called nearly every day to set up a time when I could see my children. It was the end of February before Beth was well enough or had any time. Or perhaps she had run out of excuses. My friend Henry had an infant, just younger than Victor. I wanted to take them to visit. I told my intentions to the elderly woman next door who served as the court-approved monitor along with her husband. I gave them Henry's phone number and assured them I had two car seats available.

Beth pulled up to the monitor's house late. She went inside and called me from their house. Beth asked why I had not put the "For Sale" sign on the house yet. I did not want to sell this house, but Beth reminded me that she needed the money. I agreed to fulfill her wishes. Before she hung up, she threatened to have her attorney come after me if I did not put the sign out.

It was half an hour later than expected before I saw my daughter running toward my house. My wife had finally agreed to let me see my babies. I was so happy to see my children. Henry would be too. It had been ten months since he had seen them.

I gave Henry's phone number to Beth so she would know exactly where we were. I prepared what the babies needed and drove to Henry's home. Within a few minutes all the babies were playing together. Henry's wife told me she had spoken to Beth on the phone and she sounded happy. She had called to make sure the children were there.

We watched the children play and enjoyed lunch. After lunch, Eleanore wet her pants. I went out to my car parked along the street to fetch her a clean pair of pants. When I walked back to Henry's apartment, I saw three policemen standing at the door. Beth was holding my babies as she walked out.

The policemen told me I had to obey the contract and stay with the monitor. I told them I had notified the monitor and my wife in advance. Henry's wife told the policemen that Beth had sounded happy on the telephone when they spoke. She was surprised when Beth arrived in such an angry mood. They were unfamiliar with being deceived by her.

Ella was scared because her mother was taking her away in a forceful manner while surrounded by policemen. Victor woke up as he was being taken from Henry's. I was quiet for a while. I did not know what to say. I went to my car, retrieved Henry's car seat, and returned it to him. "Thanks" and "Goodbye" were the only words I could find. Then I left.

Before walking into my house where Wang Chan waited for me alone, I went to the monitor's home. I told them both what happened. The monitor said, "I don't know why Beth did that. She had asked to use the phone after you left. Then she called Henry's home to ask the address. She sounded very happy. After that she called her mother, her attorney, and the El Monte police department. They came to your home and Beth went outside to talk to them."

I asked them to write down what had happened that I may show it in court. They discussed this and the husband refused to let this go any further. He told me Beth was a problem person, and they did not want to be involved except that they wanted the proper care for my kids. I told them not to worry about my personal affairs and assured them I would find another monitor. I knew the monitor and her husband would miss my babies. I'd let them visit as much as circumstances permitted. I didn't want Beth to give them any trouble. I didn't want any trouble myself.

Trouble was here to stay. For almost two years I had been hurt when I should have been celebrating my family. This caused much physical, emotional and financial strain. All I had wanted to find was a loving, church-going family to support and care for. I cared for them. I cared for Beth. I cared for Angela and Tom. Most of all I cared for Eleanore and Victor.

That is the way of love. Love is not a word you say once and then forget about. It is not a word you repeat when it feels good. Real love does not hang off one's mouth, it takes time to be proven. It takes years of understanding and sacrifice. It takes work and care. From

the days of Adam and Eve until now, love has always had one com-
mon theme: care.

I had no one to care for me. Wang Chan was a comfort, but he
could not help me get free from the things which wrenched at my
soul. I dreamed of having Ella and Victor with me at home, taking
them to the park, watching them play, helping them walk and learn.
I wished to care for them as I wished for care for myself. I would give
everything I had and all of my time to my family in return for love,
time, and care. Instead, all I received was more pain and loneliness.

Soon we were back in court. This time I could not be in the same
room as my children. Beth's attorney had argued that the children
would not be able to testify if they saw me. My being there would
interfere with their words. He said that they were afraid of me.
This was not true. My children loved me and loved to spend time
with me. Somehow Beth knew that Eleanore would not tell the
lies they had coached her to say if she saw me sitting there.

It was a difficult day in court. Angela saw me walk in and
turned away. I did not see Beth or my babies. I wanted to see them.
I wanted to see more of them. I thought this was what the court
date was about. When I reached for the door to the courtroom
and two policemen stepped forward and grabbed my arms, I
learned differently.

People I knew were coming to court that day to recommend
my personality. Henry would be there, and Dr. Chou. My old
business partner Richard Lee and my neighbors. They came to tell
the judge that I deserved more time with my children, that I was
stable and caring. Beth and Angela had something else in mind.

My lawyer came from the courtroom to tell me they were putting my daughter on record. Beth had her lawyer, a psychologist, and someone from Child Protective Services there to question her. I did not know what Eleanore could possibly say about her parents' divorce. What I did not know ruined me.

I was not allowed inside to hear the lies. If they were truthful, the psychologist would have testified to my wife's fragile emotional state and her difficulty with her mother. They would have told the judge how they tried to damage me emotionally and financially. They would have said they trained our daughter to tell lies in court before she was aware of what she said.

Instead they pleaded with the judge to not let me inside. They claimed they could not conduct a proper trial while being afraid of me in there. I was not scary. This was only so I could not object to their lies. Then they asked the judge for full custody and twenty thousand dollars from me so they could pay court fees. They wanted me to pay for the damage they caused to my life and my family. They wanted me to pay more than I already had, more than I could.

Then they talked of my daughter. They told the judge Eleanore had been molested. That I had hurt her. They trained her to say that her daddy had "poked her butt" in a sick effort to keep me from my children. They asked her questions about how she had been hurt then listened as a young, sweet girl, innocent in the eyes of God, tried to make the adults happy. She was only three. She didn't know what she said or why she said it. Her words were coaxed from her by her mother who was coached by her mother. It was a sad, sad day.

My friends waited with me in the hallway. They were there to support the truth, but their story fell on deaf ears. Before they could testify, Beth's lawyer spread lies about them as well. He claimed they worshipped the devil, and were part of a cult which hurt children. They said we were all in on it and could not be trusted. Then he did something even more wicked.

Their lawyer told my lawyer they would call recess before any of my friends could witness for me. They were present and ready. We were told it would not happen that morning, and the court would be dismissed for a second day of trial. Everyone was to return the next day. My friends were sad for me, but they promised to return when needed. Upon leaving, Henry said to me, "This is strange. We're here already. So why can't we testify?" I thanked them and they left.

After the recess my attorney and my wife's attorney went into the courtroom and came out with some bad news. Beth's attorney wanted my witnesses to come back. My attorney was furious because he felt that this was a dirty trick. My witnesses had already left for home.

Beth's lawyer argued that they had left because they could not support me in a court of law. That they would not lie under oath. This was further proof, he argued, that I was guilty. My lawyer denied this and requested of the judge a longer recess to recall witnesses.

I was angry, but I could not show it. I wanted to yell. I wanted to tell the judge how this family I married into were not the righ-

teous church members I had thought. They had worked together
to destroy my family and my happiness. The judge needed to
know they had hired immoral attorneys and psychiatrists to testify falsely in court. But I could not tell this. My ex-mother-in-law
continued to use my money to make her sick lies appear like truth
and make me look like the guilty party. If Angela's deeds could be
stopped then two generations of people could live happily. But
nobody could stop her. I could not prove she was lying. I could
only testify my truth.

We called my friends to come back. But they didn't answer.
They might not have had time to get home. I drove to Henry's
house. I got there about the same time he did. He said he would
return to court. From his house we called Dr. Chou. He would
also return. I left a message on my neighbors' answering machine
and drove back to court. I did not want to give any truth to Beth's
lawyers statement about my witnesses leaving, but had to return
with only half of who were there previously. I tried to keep myself
calm and to stay under the speed limit. Both were a struggle.

Back in court Angela still testified. They had taken five hours
to tell their lies. Before Angela testified, she raised her right hand
and promised to tell the truth. She told the judge she had been
a nurse for thirty years. She testified she could know what had
happened in her absence. Angela told the judge that her granddaughter, my Eleanore, was sexually molested. She also told the
judge that she discovered my son, Victor, was sexually molested.
She said she discovered this right after my son had visited me and
my friend, Henry. My son was one year and two weeks old at the
time. This was untrue, and Angela looked straight before her and

lied in court. Angela later took my son to the emergency treatment center to gather documents to prove her accusations.

Angela also told the judge that I had called on July 15 threatening to kill her if she did not let me take my children to Taiwan. My ex-wife said this as well. They wanted their scheme to take my visitation rights away. They also wanted to smear my name. I promised to fight for the truth, even if it left me financially crippled. Perhaps Beth and Angela thought that I would not tell others because I could be embarrassed to be accused of such horrible things. Those who knew me knew this was absurd. I would not be frightened by them. Spending time with my children and helping them prepare for the world would always be more important than anyone's thought of me.

Beth and Angela did all these things without spending their own money. The lawyer, the psychiatrist who told untruths, and all the expenses were paid using the property fund they cheated away from me. This way they stole from me to perpetuate their lies. I had to continue to spend to argue for the truth.

Finally, my witnesses were able to testify. I anticipated their truth being heard in court and all mystery absolved. I should not have put my faith in the court. It could not deliver what I asked from it that day. The first witness on the stand was Leslie, the monitor. Beth's attorney argued that she was unsuitable because she lived in a neighborhood not suitable for children and if she did not realize this, she could not be trusted to guard over children or understand what proper care for children would be.

The second witness was Henry. He began by answering the judge's question about his occupation and family background. Beth's attorney suddenly accused him of being a devil worshipper and part of a cult which harmed children. When the judge asked for proof, the attorney handed a letter written by Henry to my wife about reconsidering the divorce. He wrote this because I had asked. Beth's attorney said it mentioned blood and that was proof he worshipped Satan. Henry referenced a Bible verse about garments being white after being scarlet with blood as an image of the power of repentance. He was asking Beth to repent. The judge read the letter and saw nothing wrong with it. He was upset at her lawyer for twisting the meaning of the letter.

Dr. Chou testified on my behalf. He was the president of the Hollywood Chinese branch of the Mormon Church. He was a physician and had a wife and two children. He said many positive things about me and about my ability to care for my family. He was accused of being a child abuser because my wife told the court that she saw him hit his son with a pencil. Beth's lawyer argued this should strike his testimony from the record. They tried to make sure their telling of the story, with all their carefully plotted lies, was the only side to be considered.

The judge did not change the court order. I could see my children with a court approved monitor on the days it was possible for me and for Beth to arrange it. I could not be alone with them. I could not take them to a second location. I had to abide by the judgment of the monitor.

It didn't matter how much my wife's attorney lied. The truth always stays the same. The untrue performance in the courtroom couldn't help their lie come true. I still would be able to see my children. Neither Beth nor I were granted the decision we wanted. The only people who won that day in court were the attorneys making money.

It is one offense that my wife and her family emotionally, financially, physically, and politically crippled me as well as racially treated me like a second-class citizen. However, I could not put up with the heinous lies Beth and Angela created that I sexually abused my children. Not only did they falsely accuse me, they also told my children their father had done this evil thing to them. No lie can stand up before God in front of the truth. And nothing could ever stop me from loving my children.

I have tried many times to forget my past. But as long as I am living, it will continue to haunt my mind. Every time I think about what happened, I feel I have irritated a wound deep in my soul that has yet to heal. Sometimes I ponder over these events in a lonely room or in a quiet park. This kind of serenity cannot mend my broken heart. What could mend it is seeing my children grow up with me, have a good education, have their own families, and have a good job they like. I wish they could grow up soon. I wish my care for my children would not be taken away by the court because of false testimonies.

On April 24, 1989 at 12:45 pm I went to see a psychiatrist in a courthouse. Before I went, I had to fix my car. Fortunately, my friend Henry helped me take care of all the paperwork that the doctor needed. I was upset at my attorney for not helping me with these papers. He seemed to be irresponsible and slow with this matter. Perhaps it did not matter to him. It mattered to me. This was my entire life. It was the lives of my children. I had no choice but to make up for my attorney's faults.

I got the car fixed and made it to the courthouse by 1 pm. I ran inside, out of breath, and tried to relax. They wanted to take my picture for their files but the secretary was out of film. The doctor asked about my family, my relationship with my siblings. He asked about their employment and ages. Then he asked why I didn't get along with my wife. I was dismissed at 1:30 and told to come back at 2:30. I walked around the courthouse to pass the time.

When I was walking back through the courthouse, I saw my beautiful Eleanore playing on a bench. I called out her name and she called out, "Daddy!" She ran toward me, and I reached my arms down to pick her up. Angela grabbed Ella by her arm and lifted her up. Ella cried, "Daddy, Daddy!" Angela carried her and walked away.

I was angry at my mother-in-law's attitude. I walked into the doctor's office and told the secretary what had just happened. She said, "How could a grandmother do such a thing?" Later the doctor wrote in an official report that Angela took Eleanore away from me to protect her. My father-in-law saw the entire spectacle and said nothing. I was disgusted at his attitude to allow such fraud and deceit happen in general, let alone in a courthouse. If I were him, I would have stood up for righteousness. He was ordained with the priesthood of the most high God and was tasked with shepherding his family toward holiness. This cannot be done by supporting their lies and the destruction of my family unit.

Beth's family had many problems. They did not start with trying to separate me from my children. When Beth saw me in the courthouse, she told me that if I came any closer, she would call the police.

"Your entire life has been filled with calls to the police, courtrooms, attorneys, and psychiatrists. They're your regular friends," I told her. She repeated the threat and I did not approach. This was something I could not fix. This attitude could not be healthy.

Beth went in to see the doctor with Eleanore and Victor. I waited in the hallway. After forty minutes Beth came out. Our children remained inside with the doctor. Then I was called in.

Victor was crying when I entered the room. I picked him up but he continued to cry. He was so small and wanted his mother. That was ok. The doctor saw me holding him and asked if he is always upset with me. Eleanore jumped with joy when she saw me. She hugged me and skipped around the doctor's office. After a few minutes, in a sweet sing-song voice, Eleanore began to say, "Daddy's mean. Daddy's mean. Daddy poked my bottom." I asked her who had taught her to say that. She said her grandmother told her. Then she seemed to become confused. "Mommy told me to say it. Grandma told me. Daddy told me. Baby told me." She had been coached into lies by her mother and grandmother. Only sick, desperate people would manipulate a child and lie to her in such a way. I knew I needed to be more involved in Ella's life and protect her from such cruelty.

I briefly told the doctor about Beth's and my marriage. I told him about the wonderful days with the children and how they need more time with me. For the last interview, Beth joined me and the children in the doctor's office. When Beth came in, she told two different lies almost immediately. One was some story that my brother had cut off someone's arm in a fight, and the other that I trained in martial arts in the military so that I could kill people. She said this made me dangerous and that I could not be alone with the children. Neither of these were true. Though, if I was a martial artist, that should make me better suited to protect my children. But I could not claim that title. I was a fish salesman, an importer, and a hardworking man of business who just wanted to spend more time with his children. I was not the monster they said I was.

The doctor asked Beth if she coached Ella to say the things she had. Beth denied this. I said that Eleanore was only three and could not have known these words had Beth not taught them to her. Anyone could tell that my daughter had been lied to and prompted to say hurtful things. She did not know what her words meant, and could not know that they could keep us separated. But there was nothing I could do.

The doctor dismissed us and we left the courthouse. I could not believe what I had just witnessed. A religious family who attended church who served missions. They prayed daily. Yet, none of this mattered. This did not make them good people. It did not cure them of their selfishness and their lies.

Angela and Beth used religiosity to mask their deeds, but thier masks cannot last forever. False masks stink and are unpleasant. It is difficult to breathe wearing such a mask, and they were not born with them on. It is just a matter of time before the masks comes off.

Then I will see my children again.

Found

Finally, my dream was coming true. I was leaving home to go to college. After two years at Dixie State, I transferred to Brigham Young University. It was where good Mormons went to study. As the official university of the Mormon church, each class began with prayer, and many classrooms doubled as chapels on Sundays. I felt the Lord wanted me here, exactly where I had wanted to be for years.

I took all the pockets of neatly stacked bills I had saved for this moment and found an apartment within walking distance of campus. I would live with three other girls. Boys and girls couldn't live together, be in one another's apartments after midnight, and never, even for a moment, go in one another's bedrooms. I wouldn't have wanted to live with guys anyway. I was at BYU to be a good Mormon girl alongside my roommates, study, make good grades, and follow the Lord's will. For the very first time, I had roommates other than family, and I loved it. I loved living away from home and sharing space with others in the same stage of life who had similar ambitions, goals, and beliefs. I loved my little neighborhood and my student ward. Best of all, this was the first time I had legitimate records in the church.

Due to our security situation, we had never allowed our records to be discoverable. It was incredibly inconvenient. This might not sound like a big deal, but every member's entire history in the church was kept on their central database in Salt Lake City. It kept track of callings, addresses, interviews with authority figures, and even worthiness. Keeping our records undiscoverable meant they only had paper copies and couldn't duplicate them in the digital records. When we moved from ward to ward, we had to request our official records by letter, which would then be mailed to the new ward. We did this for years. This made it difficult for the church to assign us home teachers or give us callings.

I never felt like we were part of the ward. People didn't really get to know you if you stayed secret, especially as we were often living under false names. I wanted to participate fully, receive all the blessings, and I wanted to be able to serve. We stayed under the radar of much church involvement because all our information was in one file locked in the bishop's office. We couldn't get church callings because we weren't in the system.

Everyone in the Mormon church had a calling. It was a way to serve the Lord by serving others. I always wanted one. When I moved to BYU, I decided I would get one. I would be a normal student and a normal person in the ward. I didn't want any special considerations.

I was free from The Fly. After my mom's revelation about his death, we weren't afraid of him anymore. And after Gina, I wasn't as afraid of the cult either. If they had wanted me, Gina could have told them where I was. But they did not show up. They didn't come for Victor or for me.

Every time we moved to a new ward, we'd sit down with the bishop to explain: Yes, our record is protected because of a security situation. Yes, we want to be part of this ward. Yes, we will have the records mailed over. Many bishops had never dealt with a protected record before, much less a security situation. My mother would explain in detail how our secrecy was vital, that our lives were at stake. She sometimes shared details of our abuse from the cult, other times she hinted at possible dangers in case the bishop had satanic allegiances. I was tired of hiding and all this rigamarole. We'd been doing this because of the cult since before I could remember. We always remained cautious. We always hid and were afraid. I was constant. And now, I wanted to be done with our security situation.

I didn't want to have that conversation with this bishop. He led a student ward where members changed every semester. I didn't want to explain my entire situation to him. And I didn't want to have any special consideration. More importantly, I didn't want the whispers of others sharing my story of abuse. I was ready for reinvention. After working so hard to get here, I wanted college and relationships on my own terms. My bishop should think I was just another student. That would be best. With so much turnover, bishops couldn't know everyone. I wasn't close to him; he might not even remember me.

I called the church office in Salt Lake City and spoke with the one guy who was in charge of protected records. After confirming my information, I had my records added to the database and sent to my college ward. I could now be like everyone else.

College life felt wonderful. I loved walking between campus and my apartment. I found my favorite study spot in the library. I got involved in the ward. And, I had a calling. When my records transferred, the bishop called me to his office for a brief interview. He asked about my studies and how I liked BYU. Then he asked me to be the ward's piano player. I wanted to accept. I knew the Lord had a plan for me. I told the bishop I would play the piano if he wanted, but admitted I didn't actually know how.

He laughed. "That's alright," he said. "Why don't we have you be the choir director?"

"If that's what God wants, then awesome. I'll do that. But I would've learned to play the piano if that's what God commanded." I became the choir director. I was overjoyed, having my first church calling of my entire life. I had watched girls I grew up with become leaders and teachers while I couldn't, until now. Every week I stood in front of our small congregation in a survey classroom and waved my hand in beat to the hymns we sang. It felt wonderful. I was part of the congregation. I was part of the school. Life was normal. I had roommates who had never been afraid of the cult.

I still thought about my past, but I did not tell my roommates. My worries had shifted from fear of the cult finding me to concerns about how my trauma would affect me now. I knew it made me different, someone to be felt sorry for, but I didn't want to be seen as pitiful or damaged. Still, the physical trauma haunted me.

My tailbone would ache sometimes. This had to be remnant of all the rape I endured at age two or three. I thought I must have some really awful damage that I had not discovered yet. I was really worried about having sex for the first time. It could be so painful. Also, I had been warned my wedding night could trigger flashbacks. When I would have sex for the first time, or the first time I could remember, an experience that should be holy and special, my mom repeatedly told me my personality would split and reactivate the dormant cult programming.

I did not share any of this with my roommates, keeping silent through my worry. I didn't want to seem different, so I couldn't ask. And I didn't want to seem impure. The shame would be too much to bear. One evening, as we all talked in the apartment, one of my roommates shared a story about her older sister who had broken her tailbone in a sports accident. When she had her first baby the doctors had to re-break her tailbone because it had healed incorrectly and was blocking the birth canal.

Her story sparked my own fears. If my tailbone had been repeatedly broken during ritualistic cult abuse, it would have also been healed by the cult which took pleasure in doing things wrong. Though there were no visible marks, the occasional pain was evidence of the cult's imperfect healing, leaving me broken inside where they still could hurt me. I was so scared of having kids, even though I knew God's purpose for me was to "multiply and replenish the Earth." I was so worried about having to have a child because it sounded so incredibly painful. Not just the labor, but the possibility of a broken tailbone complicating the delivery.

I expressed sympathy for my roommate's sister as we discussed how awful reliving that experience must have been. But also how we were all so excited to have babies. I couldn't reveal my fears or their source. I wanted to appear normal, like them. They didn't know what I'd been through, and I doubted they could understand. I didn't want to be treated differently. I convinced myself that if I ignored my past enough, it wouldn't impact my future.

One Sunday the bishop asked me to come to his office after the three meetings of Sunday Service. I had been directing the music with earnestness to prove I was ready and willing for more. I was certain God wanted me to actually become the piano player for the hymns. That was God's plan for me, and only the bishop knew.

I sat down in the small bishop's office that doubled as an adjunct professor's office, dreaming of my new calling and hoping the Holy Ghost would give me the abilities I would need. He looked at me and said plainly, "So, I got a message from your dad. He's trying to get in touch with you."

Everything stopped right there. Gone were my previous thoughts, gone was any remembrance of church that day. My vision contracted until nothing else around me existed. I could not focus on anything except the bishop's face as he spoke. All the blood drained from my face. For the first time ever, I was frozen stiff with fear. I couldn't move.

The bishop could tell something was wrong. We both sat in silence for a minute. Then I asked, my voice scratchy and small, "What did you tell him?"

"Well, he was looking for you. I told him you were having a great time in the ward and that you just started helping with our music. I told him I would pass on the message that…"

Heat rose through my neck and ears, boiling in my brain. I interrupted him there to say, "My dad is an evil person. He is a rapist. Do not tell him anything. Do not say anything about my location. Do not say you know me, or ever knew me. You have compromised my safety. I will not be in this ward anymore."

I stood up and walked out of his office. Reflecting on it later, I would imagine he was shocked, but I didn't care to see his reaction.

I walked out of the university building and off the hill campus was built on. I sat on a bench at the edge of BYU, where I had long dreamed of sitting. There I called my mom who had moved north to a nearby town to be near me—"just in case," she had said at the time. As the phone rang, I knew what she had meant. When she answered, I just said, "He found me."

"Don't do anything," she told me. "Don't go home. We don't know how close the cult is. I'm going to come there and pick you up right now."

I didn't go back to my apartment. I didn't move from my bench until my mom pulled up. I got in her car and told her everything the bishop had told me.

"You need to move back home. This isn't safe for you to be here."

"Yep, I get that." I agreed. I knew she was right. If my dad had already found me, the cult wouldn't be far behind. I was afraid I could be found, and then who knew what they would do to me? Surely, they would be furious I had hidden from them for so long. Surely, there would be additional torture and punishment. I thought of all the awful possibilities and knew I could not live back at school.

Moving back in with my mom was devastating. I had worked so hard for so long to get out of my house, and now I had to move back in with my mom and brother. There was no other option. My life was in danger. So were the lives of my roommates.

I hadn't told any of them about my history. I wanted them to think I was just like them. Now I had to. From my mom's house I called them. "You guys," I said, though I was only talking to one of them. "I'm so sorry. I know you didn't know about this, but there is a stalking situation. I've had it for a while. And, um, my stalker has found me. So please lock your doors. I don't know if somebody will try to come by. I'm so sorry. You all might be in danger. Um, I don't know what else to tell you, but I am moving out." I couldn't apologize enough for what I had done to them. I hoped and prayed to the Lord that the cult wouldn't come to that apartment and hurt one of them. It was devastating that I had unwittingly put them in so much danger and was now powerless to help them.

I couldn't find another renter for my room. I didn't try. It didn't feel right to put someone else in my place. It could be just as dangerous for them. In the end, I didn't sell my rental contract.

I lost all the money for the remainder of the semester. At least I was safe.

My mom and I went the next day while it was still light and would be less dangerous to move everything out of my apartment. We went in and, in a flurry, gathered all my stuff. We packed everything up in the car. We spent most of the day checking every spot to not miss anything I had left in the kitchen or hung up on the walls. There could be no trace of me left for the cult to find. When it was complete, I was out. I moved back home. My freedom had been so short. I didn't want to leave my ward, my apartment, my calling in the church. But it had to be done. I had to go back into hiding. We put my church records back in the protected records, and I called my bishop to tell him not to give any more information to whoever had been calling for me.

Then we started the rounds with the police departments. There were a lot of towns merged together along that stretch of the mountains and each had their own police force. We had to visit every one of them to ensure our safety. We went to Lyndon, Orem, Provo, Pleasant Grove, Lehi, Alpine, everywhere. At each station, we sat with a deputy and explained our situation: we had a dangerous stalker who had found us again and threatened our lives. We mentioned possible accomplices and gave them all the details we could, though we didn't specifically identify him as my father.

We contacted the police department closest to home, requesting special patrols of our neighborhood and to watch out for any suspicious activity. We told them there was a threat on our lives and needed their vigilance to keep us safe from our stalker. We did not tell them that he was a leader of the cult because some officers could be members themselves. If they knew what we were running from, they could help him find us.

I decided to tell the BYU police about the cult. I didn't want to drop out of school. I had worked too hard to be there. My mom and I met with campus police, and I requested special protection whatever that would look like. I wanted to speak with someone in charge to make sure I was not in danger by attending the school I knew God wanted me to attend.

The BYU campus police chief sat me down, looking concerned. I waited for him to speak. He stayed silent for what felt like endless seconds. I had so much to tell him that he needed to know. This was my life we were talking about. My safety and my family's safety.

"I know you're in... you feel you are in danger," he finally said. "We know this person, like you have told us, is somebody who has threatened your life. We also know that the biggest predictor of future behavior is past behavior. We want to keep you safe, so we're going to talk through this. It might be painful, but we need to know everything." He motioned to another officer in the room. "This officer will help you. He'll be on your case and we want you to talk to him."

I left the chief's office and followed the officer with the thick mustache to another room where I sat, again, across a desk from him. I began explaining everything.

"Okay, so this security situation is my... you know, my father. We've been running from him my whole life. We haven't had contact with him for so long. We thought that maybe the running was over. But he's found us and is trying to kidnap us."

I remember sitting there in that small space with my mom and this gruff officer, feeling strange about sharing these details. Usually, we only warned about a vague security situation. The authorities only needed to know just enough to help. But my family could share all the details when we were alone, when no one else could hear. It felt normal. We all remembered running for our lives, moving at night, being suspicious of everything and everyone. This was not something I said very loud very often, though it was in my brain every day.

I told the officer my truth: "My dad is part of a satanic cult. He's a rapist. He's killed and murdered people. He's threatened to kill my brother and me. He's attempted to kill us multiple times. We were sexually abused and gang raped by his cult friends. We've had to run our whole lives from him. And now he's found us again. If he knew we were here talking to you, he would have us killed. He might even have you killed just for knowing this."

When I finished, I paused. I didn't hear the officer's response, if there was any. I reflected on my own statement. I could almost hear myself think, like a whisper to myself, "I hope this is true," while wishing it didn't have to be. I felt the weight of making such serious accusations about another human being. I hoped what I was saying was true because it was a lot to implicate about a person.

I left the BYU police station still feeling heavy for admitting what I had. I had entered an official police report containing all these accusations about my own father. Heavy things to say about anyone. I cried that night thinking about how I didn't want my own father to find me and because I didn't want him to be the evil man he was. I cried, wishing my dad could just be like any of the other dads. I couldn't understand why mine had to be a murderer-rapist-cult member.

The police officer assigned to my case seemed to drag his feet. I kept following up, wanting to know if he'd tracked down my dad, checked his location, or confirmed if he'd been in the area. I wanted him to do the private investigator work I had seen on television and find out exactly where my dad was and confirm he'd been arrested or made to leave. I needed something, anything to feel safe at school again.

The officer had no news. He wasn't responding, and I still felt in danger. I was furious. This was the system that was supposed to keep me safe. This was all I had besides God.

I requested another meeting with the campus officer because I felt he wasn't doing his job. This time it was just the two of us in a room with closed doors. I told him I wanted to record our conversation.

"Okay. That's fine."

"What's going on?" I asked. "I haven't heard anything back. There's a person that has found me that is trying to kill me and I don't feel like we've been able to get any information."

"Look," he said, "I got the information." His mustache wiggled and he handed me a printed-out email, my dad's driver's license, and a picture of a little girl.

"What is this? This is not what we were asking for."

"Hold on. I want you to listen to me. And I want you to just be open to this." He paused for a long time. I waited. I was angry but stayed quiet. He continued.

"I heard what you told me and I read the reports. I got this information about your dad. And when I was looking at this case... You know, I'm sorry that it's taken so long, but when I was looking at this case it just... something didn't feel right. And I got in contact with your dad and..."

"You did what? You got in contact? You did the exact thing that I told you not to do. You've endangered my life again by getting in touch with this person."

"Just listen for a minute. Listen to me," he insisted through his mustache. I quieted. "I have gotten in contact with your dad. And Eleanore, you might just want to be open to something besides what your mother and grandmother have told you.

"Your dad seems like a nice guy. This picture is of his daughter. Your little sister. And he's not close. He is not anywhere near here to put you in any danger. He's in Taiwan. He lives there with his wife and their young daughter. He's been very cooperative. He sent me this picture, and a copy of his license, and his address, and any information I asked for."

I was livid. I couldn't see straight or hear what the police officer continued to say. I watched his mouth move, unable to believe he'd been fooled too.

"I told you he was a very charismatic person. He has tricked people over and over into thinking he is an alright guy, and they would give him what he wanted, and now it has happened again. You have given him information about us. I'm completely disappointed. Now I am more in danger than when I came in here. You were supposed to help! How could you do this?" I was so mad. I got up to leave. I took the copy of my dad's license, the picture of the girl, and folded email. "You have killed us all," I said before walking out.

I didn't want to be triggered by anything in the letter or the recording I had made. Perhaps I was already triggered, which was why I felt so furious. Perhaps the officer was part of the cult, trying to convince me my dad was fine so they could access us again. Maybe he was just terrible at his job. But that mustached officer had given us all a death sentence. A literal death sentence.

It was somewhat comforting knowing my dad wasn't in the country. He couldn't show up at my door. But my life had been altered again. I stopped participating in BYU wards. I had my newly input records taken off the database. I went back to church with my mom and my brother. Every day, I took the bus from Pleasant Grove where my mom lived, and now I did too, to Provo to school. Every day, I thought it could be the day that the cult would find me. I desperately wanted to have the college experience, but all I felt was fear. I lost sleep, I lost focus, and so much of what I had dreamed of.

Now I knew firsthand that authority figures couldn't be trusted. Neither bishops nor police could keep me safe. Anyone could be fooled by the cult or be a secret member. No one was to be trusted except family. Only they understood the danger and all we'd been through just to stay alive. I remembered my mom's words that I could only trust her. The danger of the cult was out there and since I couldn't recognize it as well as she could, I had to trust her knowledge as my own.

When I got home from the police department that day, I handed my mom both the email, still folded, and the picture of the little girl. My mom read the email silently to herself.

"Yeah, there was too much in there," she told me. "You could have been triggered by this. And this picture he sent of this girl was definitely a scare tactic. You know he hurts little children. They sent this to make you afraid she'd be hurt, hoping you'd want to stop it. You probably don't have a little sister. This is all part of his manipulation.

"And let's hope you don't have a little sister," my mom continued. "If you did, it would be horrible because she would be so raped and abused. She's part of the cult if she's even real."

This was all careful planning to frighten me. My dad, The Fly, had plotted well and knew that officer would believe him. He sent the picture to the officer to appear benevolent, but it was really a message to me because he knew I understood what he did to little girls.

It was a scare tactic. And it worked. It was a good thing I handed my mom that email, or who knows what could have happened. That night I prayed and thanked the Lord I hadn't read the email and that I had not been found by the cult. The Lord would keep me safe. The Lord and my mom.

傷害

Hurt

How much divorce hurts me?
Too much.

My wife and her mother planned this divorce and crippled me economically, emotionally, and physically. They no longer can reimburse me for the harm they did to my life.

I have lost $300,000 during four years of mental and emotional torture.

Before I was a very outgoing person. Now I am quiet.

Before I had a very good memory. Now I am forgetful. This has affected my job and income.

Before I was a sound sleeper. Now I often wake up at midnight thinking of my children and cannot go back to sleep again.

Before I was very ambitious in business. Now I need time to cover the hurt.

Before I had a beautiful family. Now my family is breaking apart and the ending is misery for everyone.

Before my heartbeat was regular. Now my nerves are affected, and my heart will beat irregularly.

Before I used to love children. Now when I see children, I am reminded of my own and the hurt comes back.

Before I used to respect Mormon families as a special group of people. Now I don't think they are.

Before I used to think a Mormon Temple marriage was a serious commitment. Now I don't because my ex-wife just walked away from our marriage.

Before I used to love to play with babies. Now I am afraid I might be falsely accused of harm.

Before I used to believe in the power of truth. Now I see well-paid lies are more likely to become law.

In all cases, I have been disappointed and shocked. This is not the fault of God. But it could be a reflection of the organization I had so much faith in. Perhaps it is not formed of God as I had been told and believed.

This is not what God had promised me. When I devoted my life to following his goodness so that this life would be filled with it, I did not expect any of this. I did not expect to be turned away from the covenants I still want to keep.

All of this hurts.

All of this strives to steal my joy, my future, my hope, and my life. But I must continue on to provide for my children. Even if I cannot be with them. I must prepare for the day when I can care for them and be near to them. I pray for the day when they can feel my love.

Who is hurt the most because of the divorce?
My two lovely children.

The Evidence

Life went back to normal. Or at least as normal as my life could be. I pretended it was more normal than it was. I finished semester after semester with good grades, organizing study groups and making sure the professors recognized me and my efforts. Though my church records remained protected, I had moved back to an apartment near BYU. We had to arrange for the lease to be under a different name than my own. At least I could live with girls my age and attend school. I couldn't trust anyone with my truth. I kept my history, my fears, and the fact that I was still in hiding to myself. I didn't tell my classmates or the boys I dated.

At BYU it is commonplace, and instructed by God, to find a partner to marry for time and all eternity and to have children with that person. Every young man who had returned from their two-year mission dedicated to serving the Lord was actively seeking a wife. We women were taught that our path to salvation required finding a worthy priesthood holder who would love God above all else, even above us. Without an honorable man holding God's priesthood, we couldn't reach the highest levels of Heaven. While I loved college life and wanted to focus on my studies, I also felt compelled to follow these sacred commandments. My eternal salvation depended on it.

I met the man I married my senior year of college. Alan was a devout, returned missionary who had served the Lord valiantly on his mission to Mandarin speaking people in Houston, Texas. His passion for the church was evident, and he had received personal revelation from the Lord that we were to be married. Though I hadn't received the same spiritual confirmation, I trusted in Alan's priesthood authority and his personal revelation to guide us back to Heaven. We set our date for immediately after my graduation.

BYU maintained strict rules to avoid sexual temptation. No boys were allowed in the apartment past midnight, and never could they ever go beyond the living room and kitchen area to the bedrooms. That is where sin might occur. During our engagement, Alan once excused himself to use the bathroom and secretly peeked into my room. I didn't know he did this until he came back to the living room, took my hand, and asked me in a serious tone if I planned to continue sleeping in a sleeping bag on top of my bed after we were married.

My roommates never questioned my unusual sleeping arrangements, though none of them did the same. I hadn't really thought about it before, but I realized I probably shouldn't keep sleeping on top of my bed covers, even though I'd been doing it for so long. The bed always stayed made so it would be possible for me to vanish. Even then, I had to stay prepared to leave at any moment.

It was my duty to get married. I must serve the Lord in the way He wanted. That meant to marry and have children, or as they said in church, to multiply and replenish the Earth. But I was still so scared. I didn't know what would happen to me. The commandments were given to all, and I was no exception. However, my upbringing had been different. My first night with my husband might be something I wasn't prepared for. All my life I had been told that sex would be the ultimate trigger. Because of the rape and trauma in my early childhood, I believed that my first sexual experience would definitely split me and make me obedient to the cult again. I had heard most words; they had not triggered me. I had seen many potential triggers; none had pushed me back into my cult mindset. But I had never had sex. I knew that it could be so traumatic that, even if I wasn't split completely, it might change my personality forever. I could become a different person after that first night.

Alan and I knew each other for six months before we were married. I hoped if I changed, he wouldn't notice too much. Still, I didn't tell him everything that had happened to me. He knew some things. He had been accepting of what limited details I shared, but I didn't want to seem impure and unworthy of our marriage. I didn't want him to see me as a bruised fruit or a chewed piece of gum. I did not tell him all I had survived, and I did not tell any of this to his family. G-ma did.

The night before my wedding, my grandmother hosted a party for our families at her home in St. George, where I had spent so many years hiding in the basement rooms. We did not have many people there. Alan's mother, step-father, and three brothers came. These people were about to become my family, yet I barely knew them.

Hours before I was to be sealed to them for time and all eternity, my grandmother sat next to Alan's eldest brother and began her stories. They always started as compliments before quickly becoming dramatic and much more than anyone would expect. The listener rarely was able to interject or pause her.

"It's so great to see how far our sweet Eleanore has come," she started. "She hasn't always been this way, and we were very worried for her with all that has happened." Then came the details. She told him how I had been raped and abused. How I had been programmed by the cult, and how my father had tried to kidnap me and my brother when we were small. When he failed, we were forced into hiding so he and his cult legions couldn't find and kill us.

I was horrified. Horrified and hurt. Not by what had happened. I had made peace with who I was. I was offended that my grandmother would share these details with near strangers. I didn't want them to see me as the poor girl with a tragic history. I didn't want them to see me as damaged or pitiful. I wanted to stand for who I was. I wanted them to see that I was a good student, that I was righteous, that I was a woman of my word, that I was capable, loving, and funny. I was beginning a new life; I wanted it to be founded on my own terms. Now G-ma had undone all of that in one night. I ended that night crying to myself, wishing my history had been different. Wishing my family had been different.

Alan and I still got married as planned. Our honeymoon came and went, and I did not feel any different. Nothing triggered me, no splits surfaced. I was still very much myself. Even Alan said so. This gave me strength. Sex, which I had feared my entire life, became ordinary and unthreatening. Since this deepest fear couldn't harm me, I felt less afraid than ever about the cult finding or taking me. I had worried they would target any future children of mine, trying to program them as compensation for losing me. I was certain the cult still wanted me, still searched for me, and was still was angry I had left. Now, with my new legal name, protected record, and complete separation from the cult and my father, I was not afraid they could find me.

There was still a risk, however. If they found us, especially after Alan and I had children, we would need to flee immediately. We would change our names and move. We would do anything to stay safe, just as my mom had done.

This wasn't a burden I could carry alone. I had to be open about what could happen. I felt obligated to tell my in-laws, my new family, about this reality. They knew some details about the abuse, but didn't fully grasp what running from the cult meant—how we could never stop our vigilance because the minions of the devil wouldn't stop theirs.

One evening, I sat with my mother-in-law, father-in-law, and Alan to share my story of growing up in the cult. It felt as vulnerable as it did important. They needed to know. I wasn't sure how they would react, but I hoped for understanding and love.

My mother-in-law watched me intently as I spoke. When I finished, she asked, "How do you know that's true?"

"Well, I just know. Like I just know. Obviously, that's what happened. I've known my whole life." I didn't know what else to say. I felt so completely insulted. I had opened up with this really intense story that I rarely told anyone in my life. The fact that my new mother-in-law doubted me really bothered me.

All those horrible things had happened, but her question planted a seed in me to examine how I knew. Of course, I knew; I had known for years. We all knew. From the time I could speak, I knew of my traumatic childhood as a cult victim. My mom had told me some things. I had heard G-ma tell her friends again and again. We had fled, moved countless times, hidden from the cult, changed our lives. It must have happened the way I had always known.

We had boxes of evidence. My mom kept everything. Boxes lined an entire wall, filled with threatening letters, recordings of my dad threatening to kill us, and documents detailing the cult abuse. There were the examination papers from when we were children. An expert on children had examined us and had documented how we had been raped and molested. Our abuse was so severe that she had to clear her schedule for the rest of that day, unable to handle anything more. There were all the court documents saying why my mom had custody of us because the law wouldn't allow us children to be hurt anymore. That's what the judge had said. Or what I had been told the judge had said. Surely it was written down somewhere in one of those boxes.

I had not seen the boxes. I had not wanted to see them. Any one of them could trigger me into an unknown split. But I knew they were there. I knew exactly where they were. About ten boxes were stacked along the wall in G-ma's garage, filled with evidence. I wanted definitive proof so that Alan and my mother-in-law would believe what I told them. I did not know how else to convince them of the truth of my childhood. I had lived it and knew how present the cult was. I knew how we had to be on run all the time, unable to form attachments to anyone or anything except family because we might have to leave at any moment without saying goodbye or keeping in touch. I wanted Alan and his mother to understand this reality.

I decided to examine the evidence, knowing it could be dangerous. I knew it could trigger me and split my personality. That was a risk I was willing to take. I needed to see the proof.

My entire life I had been terrified of my wedding night. Everyone assumed the first time I had intercourse would trigger flashbacks. That was expected to happen. That was a risk I took for love and to follow the commandments of the Lord. Miraculously, through the gifts of the Spirit and the Lord's blessings, I did not have any flashbacks on my wedding night. I didn't split. It was just a regular, normal thing. My whole life was leading up to flashbacks on my wedding night. Nothing traumatic happened. I was fine, and it made me feel stronger.

I felt I was strong enough to see the evidence. Maybe the Lord would protect me there as well. Maybe by some miracle, I wasn't as damaged as I thought. Maybe it wouldn't be so frightening. I was an adult now. Even though it might be difficult, I deserved to know what happened to me.

I went to my G-ma's house, where my mom and Victor were living, and approached them in the living room.

"Hey, you know what?" I began. "I know this might be a strange request, but you know, I haven't had any flashbacks or splits so far. And I'm an adult now, and I want to know my history. I just want to know where I came from. So, I would really like to see the evidence. You still have it, right?"

My mom confirmed what I thought, and what I thought she would answer. "Yes, we have boxes and boxes of evidence. We've kept everything. But we cannot endanger you that way. You could be triggered. You could split and literally never be the same again. We have no idea how intense the brainwashing from the cult has been. There's no way. We just can't let you do that. I'm sorry, Eleanore."

This felt wrong. I was an adult. I was married. I was strong. What I could and couldn't handle should have been my decision. It made me upset she wouldn't let me decide these things for myself, but I didn't argue. I accepted that my mom was trying to protect me.

Months and months went by. Then it started bothering me again. I did not have anything solid to tell Alan or his mother. It was my right to know, and my new family deserved to know too. After praying about it, I felt peace assuring me I could handle the truth. Opening my eyes, I decided I should know. It would be for the best.

Soon after my decision, Alan and I went back at G-ma's house. We had driven down from Provo for the weekend. When we arrived everyone else was gone. We called for G-ma, my mom, and Victor. No response. We went to the garage where the boxes were stacked and decided to look at the evidence ourselves.

The boxes I remembered toting from one house or storage unit to the next were stacked waist-high against the wall. I pointed them our to Alan, but could hardly move. I was frozen still, knowing I was breaking a rule by looking at these boxes, and girding up my strength to be able to withstand whatever I would see inside.

Alan took one down and began looking through the contents. Most of it was not any sort of evidence of anything. Most of the boxes had papers about houses, old bills, and journals. It was not related to my childhood or the cult at all. We opened them all up and narrowed our search down to one box.

When we started exploring its contents, it was the first glimpse that I'd ever had into my mom's marriage. I had never heard about it as a marriage. I had only known her time with my dad from the cult perspective. There were court records and countless letters from my father. He wrote her so much and so often. "Beth, we can make this work." "Why won't you talk to me?" "I was supposed to see the kids, but you never came." "I miss the children so much. Will you give them these gifts?" "I heard you said this about me, that you know is not true." "I just want you to come back." "Whatever I can do. Whatever we need to do. We can work through it." Letter after letter pleading to save their marriage.

The letters filled 75% of the box. The rest of it was legal court stuff from what looked like a couple years of proceedings.

Documents of what my dad was being accused of, visitation terms, custody arrangements, and divorce papers. It was all so mundane. It was not the horrible images or items that would send me into an irreversible split. And it was the first time I had any information about my dad as a regular person and not some dangerous cultist. In the letters he wrote practically begging to see his children and to save his marriage. They were not threats or satanic spells.

There was only one file about the cult in this box. Finally, I had found it. Inside was a single hand-sketched drawing from a nurse's examination of Victor as an infant. It showed a rash or abrasions around his anal area. The report stated the cause was inconclusive. Nothing major. There was supposed to have been an examination report about me too, but it wasn't there. There was nothing about any abuse, rape, or ritualistic torture.

I also found a thick packet with purple writing. It was a police guide for recognizing satanic cult activity, written to inform officers about exactly what to look for. I opened it up and began to read.

The manual contained descriptions of cult practices. It was all so familiar. Most details matched word-for-word what I had been told happened to me. It said in the manual that the cult flips everything that is Holy and good on its head and then does the opposite. The cult baptizes people in blood-filled bathtubs to reverse Holy Water baptism. I had been baptized in blood. The cult performs ritual torture on children tied to tables. I was tied to a table. Then it went on to the next thing and the next thing.

The manual wasn't about me. It was a manual of the general practices of the cult, all the stuff they do in their rituals.

Yet, it perfectly matched my experience. I could have recited my childhood stories and they would have aligned with what I was reading in that packet.

I started to ask questions I had not thought to ask before. I had been told I had been baptized in blood. If that were true, how did my mom know about it? It happened while she wasn't there. My dad surely hadn't told her he baptized me in blood while she was not home.

The more I questioned what I had been told and had believed, the more questions came up. When I took those questions one step farther, none of it aligned with my lived experience. None of it made sense. There was no evidence. All I had from these boxes and boxes was a nurse's examination of my brother and a general police manual about cult activity. There was nothing tying my father to anything except court documents and his endless letters. I took pictures of the documents and boxed everything back up. I felt empty inside, like I had been bracing for an impact that never came. I had felt strong enough to withstand the triggers, and now almost numb that none had come.

I was standing in the kitchen when my mom, G-ma, and my brother returned home. Victor went downstairs to his room while G-ma spilled the church gossip. Alan sat on the couch. I shook with nervousness but felt determined as I looked at them both.

"I looked at the evidence in the box."

They both erupted in anger immediately. "What? Why did you do that? Why were you looking at that?" someone said.

"I had to know. I need to know what really happened to me."

"You should not have looked at that," my mom said, her voice a forced calm. "You'll have flashbacks. It's so horrible. It could ruin your life. What have you done?" Her calm did not last.

I stood firm. "There's no evidence. Like, there's nothing in there. There's a manual about satanic rituals and lots of letters. But there is no evidence at all—in any of the boxes. How do you know any of it happened?" I had never questioned it before because why would I? No one would say such things if they weren't certain. I continued, speaking faster, my fists clenched. "Why would you say all those things? All those stories I heard over and over. Nobody would say that if they were guessing. Why didn't you just tell me that you thought maybe this happened, or there were suspicions of abuse? Why have you always told me that it absolutely happened?

"There's no evidence. And if there is evidence, where is it? Show me where there is evidence of all these things. Am I missing something? Because I thought it was all in those boxes like you told me, but there is nothing there. Where is it? How can you know what happened if you don't have evidence?"

"We just know."

"Like how do you know?"

"We can't tell you," one of them said.

"I can't believe you don't believe us," said the other. "We have never lied to you. And we just know that it happened."

"Yeah, but how?" I pressed. "I'm not even mad. I'm just dumbfounded. Why would... I just... I don't understand why you would say all those things. To all those people. For so long. If you didn't know what had happened. Maybe it all happened. But if there is no evidence, just tell me what motivated you to tell me with absolute surety that those things happened to me."

"Oh well," my mom spoke after a pause. "We just... we just know. And we are not going to talk about this anymore."

That's where it ended.

All the stories of my abuse, the torture and rape I had experienced, being part of the cult and them searching for us to sell us into sex slavery in China, could not be proven. I was beginning to realize all of my history was based on nothing. Absolutely nothing. There was no way they could have known what I had undergone while they were not there.

There was no way I could know either. I could not know that I had not been raped. I could not prove that I had not been baptized in blood. And I could not know whether or not my father had tried to kidnap and kill us for cult sacrifice. I had not known him. My mom had.

While she could not know what abuse I had suffered in her absence, she did know my dad, The Fly. She knew about his splits, which is why she feared I would have the same. She had told us the stories of him trying to kill us, about him hunting us down. He was the reason we had to stay in hiding, even now. I had heard how awful he had been to her and to everyone around him, to G-ma. Their experience was evidence of that. But of my experience, I had no evidence. I did not know who my father was, and I had no way of knowing what exactly I experienced in his care. My mom did not want to talk about either.

We went back to our lives, just not talking about any of the cult stuff, or the lack of evidence, or my father. I felt betrayed, somewhat by my own body. I had hurt with the remnants of the cult's abuse, but now I didn't know how to understand years of sensations and fears. I struggled to know myself. I ignored the troubled stirrings inside, placed them behind me like I had the alleged abuse and continued a prescribed, obedient life. Alan and I finished school, were planning to have our own family, and still I knew nothing about my past for sure.

Much later I tried broaching the subject again with my mom and she again shut it down. I asked her, "Mom, can we just please talk about this? I'm not going to be mad. Just tell me how do you know this stuff? What motivated you to repeat what you did? Like, can we just talk about it?"

"Absolutely not. I would much rather you blame me for everything than us to talk about it and for you to have flashbacks of all the horrible abuse and brainwashing that has happened to you. We're not going to talk about it because I'm not going to let that happen to you. You are too important to me, and that brainwashing is so deep. The Lord has blessed you to not have flashbacks so far. You don't remember all the horrible things that happened to you, and that is another blessing of the Lord. But I won't risk you splitting. You might never come back."

The conversation ended again. I knew she was never, never going to change. This was not something we can talk about. This was not something I could ever know.

心碎

Broken

Speaking to the congregation from the church pulpit, my ex-wife once said that if the mother is educated, then the entire family would be educated. In other words, the mother will influence the children and family more than anyone else. Beth will create the environment for Eleanore and Victor. They will grow up in her shadow, under her direction. They will look to her for righteousness and truth. What then if the truth is not to be found? What then if the mother spreads lies?

Angela showed Beth how to speak her lies like truths. Beth followed her mother's direction through court, lying to judges and lawyers, the attempted destruction of my life, and the successful destruction of my family. A mother's evil intentions will influence the whole family. This was an additional reason I should spend more time with my children.

Before the final verdict, Henry was able to serve as the court appointed monitor while I spent time with my children. March 25th was my day with Eleanore and Victor. We were planning on going to the park, but it was rainy. I was at Henry's home early at 9:30 to await their 10 am arrival. The court had ordered I could have my children from 10 am until 5 pm on Saturdays with the presence of a monitor. Sometimes Beth did not agree to this. She said the children were being cared for at the church, and I could come see them there, but not talk to them or touch them. This was not spending time with family. But I came. I watched them. I wanted to be close to them however I could. They were my reason for living here. Helping them was the reason behind everything.

Beth did not arrive at Henry's until nearly 11 o'clock. Eleanore jumped around full of energy. Victor wanted me to hold him. Whenever he saw something on the wall he did not recognize, he would point to it and say, "Boo. Boo." He was trying to tell me what he saw. I could have listened to him explain things all day.

Ella played with some toys on the television cabinet. She would bring me one and I would make a sound effect for the cars or stuffed bear she had. She would laugh, take the toy back to the pile and play there for a moment before bringing me something else. I could hear her talking to herself while at play. She was quiet for a moment then said, "Daddy's not mean. Daddy's nice." She repeated this to herself and continued to play.

I carried Victor around to show him more new objects. He would say "Boo" and I would repeat the object he pointed to in English and in Mandarin. A couple times Henry had to correct me on the pronunciation of the English. "We all have much to learn," I said and laughed. Victor soon fell asleep in my arms.

I sat on Henry's couch, held Victor, and watched Ella play. She had so much energy. She would stuff her toys in any drawers she could open. I apologized to Henry, but he laughed it off. Ella had hidden most of her toys. She stood in front of where she had played with them, the counter now empty. Then she walked over to me. Her face was serious. The smile of play had changed into an adult concern. She put her hand on my arm.

"Daddy, are you going to kill me?" she asked.

I fought tears back and stared her in her beautiful eyes shaped like mine.

"No. No. You should never even have to think about that, Ella. Daddy loves you. Daddy will always love you. Daddy will protect you. Daddy will always keep you safe. It is the most important thing in the world."

By the time I had finished telling her of my love, my tears poured. She must have thought I was hurt.

"Don't cry, Daddy," Ella said, still holding on to my arm. "I not scary."

I understood her love. I hoped she understood mine. She was the most perfect person I had ever known. I wanted to celebrate her life with her. It hurt me deeply to think she could ever be afraid.

My son and daughter were born physically healthy. However, I believe they were mentally damaged by my ex-wife's dirty divorce tactics. If this is true, she cannot make it up to them for the harm she has done. My children are the ones harmed most by these lies. It is their family that is broken.

Beth came to pick the children up before five. Eleanore did not want to go. She refused to put her shoes on. I told her that if she wanted to come and visit again, she would need to get her shoes on and be good for her mother. She ran to her shoes and pulled them on, then toddled over to me to tie them up. I missed her every moment until I saw her again. Victor was still asleep. I handed him to Beth.

"How can you go through with this?" I asked. "How can you throw away our love and our family?"

"I will lose much more if I don't," she replied.

Then I knew. The divorce was not about me or about not loving me. She did these things because of her mother. She walked away from her eternal marriage because she would lose her inheritance otherwise. She manipulated her children and the law because there was land somewhere in Nevada she wanted.

Did she not know I would work every day to make money for her and the children? Did she not know that we could have had our own land with the money spent in court? She has done so many things, spent so much effort, told so many lies. But it has not made her rich, and it has not given her a whole family. After all she has done, she has not gained anything of value.

Beth was raised in a Mormon family where the most important principle is the family unit. The Mormon Temple seals couples together for time and all eternity. Eternity is everlasting. So long. Our children would be with us in the afterlife in Heaven as well. This was the promise we made to one another, to them, and to God. Her family claimed to respect the family unit, but they did not follow the church's philosophy. Beth sold her Sacred Crown of Motherhood for a few pieces of silver from her mother.

Meditation

Growing up Mormon and afraid of the cult, meditation was not a familiar practice. We were taught it was something non-believers did. Meditation was for worldly people who looked inward instead of to God. My G-ma spoke of men in yellow robes who could levitate through meditation. This power, I was told, had to come from the devil. We didn't meditate. We prayed.

Good Mormons pray constantly. We're taught to keep a prayer in our heart and to pray for those around us. I would kneel by my bed each morning to pray. Sometimes we had family prayer. We always began by addressing God, then expressing what we were thankful for, then what we were seeking blessings and guidance on, then close the prayer in the name of Jesus Christ. All things must go through Him. We prayed before each meal, and again before bed. There were prayers at church meetings, and at BYU before each class. I would pray while on the bus about my day and the blessings I sought. If I had a moment by myself while I waited for Alan, I would sit and pray.

We always thanked God for keeping us safe from the cult. And we would always ask to be blessed with continual protection. I believed these prayers were the only thing that kept us from being taken and abused again—these prayers and my mom.

Decades of the surety and reliance on prayers wore thin under a new burgeoning doubt. After finding no evidence of my abuse, I began to suspect my mom and G-ma had made all this up. I could not understand why. It didn't seem rational or reasonable for someone to say such things unless they were absolutely true.

Although there was no evidence for my history of abuse, I also didn't have any evidence against it. I had spent my life fearing and running from my father and the cult. I still prayed for safety and thanked God for keeping me away from the cult. These habits took time to undo. I was no longer afraid the cult was everywhere, looking for me. Not everyone who wore red and black was signaling to other cult members. Still, I prayed. I wanted to know the truth. I had to ask this of God. All my mom would offer me was silence.

I prayed to know the truth and met the same silence. As Mormons, we're taught we can receive personal revelation from God. We are promised that if we pray with a pure heart and contrite spirit and listen to the promptings of the Holy Ghost, God will communicate with us. It was how we were supposed to know the truth of our religion, and God's will for us in our earthly lives. My mom had received all sorts of information from the Lord.

We strived to be obedient, constantly seeking His guidance. I remembered first feeling the Holy Spirit as a youth, knowing I could receive knowledge and peace through prayer. But in this case, I received no answer. Only silence. There had to be a way I could find truth if neither God nor my mom would share it with me.

In attempting meditation I learned to seek silence. I wasn't seeking answers, just the peace I felt during prayer. To me they were so similar. I started meditating regularly, and it was really a wonderful part of my life. It was not a replacement for prayer. Rather, meditation offered the silence and clarity to better hear the Holy Spirit. In that silence, I could best understand truth. If anywhere, meditation would be where my prayers found answers.

I had grown considerably. The cult and fear no longer consumed me. Alan and I had a little girl of our own and spent all our time with her. I spoke with my mom by phone and visited occasionally. She and Victor lived with G-ma still—or again. I didn't spend time thinking about the cult, and I didn't think about my father. It never occurred to me to hear his half of the story. I hadn't seen him in twenty-five years. I didn't know this person, except that he was supposedly dangerous. He was never part of my life.

One morning during meditation, I had a completely unexpected realization about my father. I wasn't searching for any answer about him or about anything in particular. I had not thought of him since Alan and I left Utah. I don't think he was really on my mind at all. I was sitting alone one morning meditating. I was focusing on my breath and being in the silence. All of a sudden, there was an almost audible voice that spoke to me, saying, "Your father is going to die and you will have never known him."

The voice shook me, breaking my meditation. I pondered who my dad might be. I did not know. I did not know anything about him for sure except that he was my father. That alone meant something. I wondered what that connection meant and what I might owe him for giving me life. I wondered what it meant to be connected by blood and what could it mean to him that I had been absent for so long. I did not know him. We were strangers to each other. The question of who he might be turned and turned inside me. I wondered if understanding him would help me understand myself—or my daughter.

Soon after that my mom called late to tell me Grandpa Tom had died. He was very close to me. He was closer to me than most anyone. I was always his favorite, and he was mine. We always got along when others found him too grumpy.

He and G-ma preferred to live in separate houses. They were happier that way. Happier in different states. When G-ma left LA, Grandpa Tom found a reason to stay. Though the house on the hill was G-ma's, Grandpa Tom lived there alone in Los Angeles for years, visiting us in Utah for holidays. G-ma said he was too stubborn to move again and that he would be grumpy in Utah. She didn't want that. They were happier apart. Though he was short with most people in his life, he was never grumpy with me.

Grandpa Tom never said that he loved anyone. Then, when I was a teenager and he was around St. George more often, I decided to tell him "I love you" regardless of the response. He didn't respond to that for quite a while. I continued to say it whenever he returned to California. It was true. I loved him and I wanted him to know. Then one day I said, "I love you, Grandpa." He just said, "Love you too." From then on, he would always say that when we'd visit the house. He would say it to me even if he never said it to anyone else.

When I wasn't close enough to visit regularly, I wrote him appreciation notes. Grandpa Tom loved them. After his funeral, I went into his office and saw he had all the notes that I'd given him in a stack. He had saved them all. He was difficult for many to understand and love, but I knew him and I loved him. Standing in his office with those saved letters, I thought again about my father, who I didn't know, who wouldn't live forever. I was grateful I'd taken time and initiative to love Grandpa Tom. Even across distance, I had gotten to know him and was able to love him. Now that he was gone, I was glad I had.

I had been told my father was quite a bit older than my mom. I did not know how old. I did not know when his birthday was, or how he liked to celebrate it. I did not know anything about him. I had heard he was evil, mean, and dangerous. But I didn't know for myself. I couldn't love what I didn't know. Nor could I hate what I didn't know. All I truly knew was that he was my father and that one day he would die.

I began wondering about who he might have been and who he was currently. The thought turned and turned. I concluded that what he was didn't matter. Maybe he was a rapist. Maybe he was a horrible, evil person. Maybe he was part of a cult, or their leader.

Maybe he had done such horrible things. Maybe all that was true. Maybe. What my realization came to, after much thought and consideration was: So what? So what if he was all those things? The worst-case scenario is that he was a horrible rapist and cult member—and he was still my dad. My only father. This was the reality I'd lived with for twenty-five years. It couldn't be worse than what I'd been told, and what I'd been raised to believe.

When I kept thinking about it, it didn't matter what he had done. I wanted to meet him. I wanted to know him. I wanted to see the person who gave me life. I wanted to see someone who looked like me. I had made up my mind.

最後一次

The Last Time

My wife took me to court as if I was a criminal. She forced me to hire attorneys to avoid a prison sentence. The allegations they falsely made about my children's abuse could not be proven. The lies of Satan worship or cult involvement were nonsense and would not persuade the judge against me. However, Beth's tears and Angela's long testimony against me did result in a restraining order.

I was ordered by the Los Angeles court that I could not contact Beth or Angela. I was not supposed to see them, interact with them, or seek them out. If I wanted to communicate with them, I could reach their attorney who would pass on a message. Angela had removed me from their lives.

I still had rights of visitation with my children. Because of the evil and sickening accusations, I could not be with my children unless in the presence of a court-appointed monitor. Henry would no longer be able to help out. We had to hire an outside party to host the children and then I could visit them.

The judgment was not fair and was influenced by cruel lies determined to break apart my family. But I could no longer argue. The decision had been made. I arranged the monitors and planned on visiting with the children. A couple times I could see them at the church house, but I could only stand in the room and watch them, not talk to them or touch them.

There was no contact from Beth or her lawyer. I could not reach her. I reached out to her lawyer again and again. He would not give me any information. He said he would contact Beth, but I could not know if that happened.

It was months before I saw my children again. I filed complaints with the court until the judge ordered Beth to allow me to visit with them.

I imagined what they would look like. I wondered how they had changed, what they had learned. I wondered if they would recognize me. I also wondered if I would be set up again, accused again, dragged to court again.

I called my church to see if I could get a chaperone volunteer. I found one, but when I called the monitor to tell them, they said that the court approved of only my visit. I hoped nothing would happen this time, and I went alone.

I brought a set of 24 tiny cars for my son and a Lite-Brite for my daughter. It was near Christmas and I did not know when I would see them again.

When I walked into the monitor's home, Eleanore was playing with toys on a small table and Victor was eating chocolate cookies. He looked so big.

"Hi, Eleanore. Hi, Victor. I'm your daddy!" Eleanore looked at me and remained silent. Victor stopped chewing. I showed them the presents they had for them and they ran over to them. Ella tore hers open. Victor was more careful, almost wary. I helped him tear a corner. He had crumbs on his cheek from one of the cookies. I brushed them off, but the monitor said I could not touch my children. She said they could approach me, but even then I could not touch them. I had not seen my children in almost a year, and now I could not hold them. I missed most of my son's babyhood. The court order was unethical. But I did not want to argue with the monitor. I did as she asked.

Within an hour my children and I became very good friends. My daughter talked to me constantly. Victor did not say too much. Eleanore told me that she wanted to go to pre-school, but her mother told her she did not have enough money. I told her I would work hard so she and her brother could go to the best schools.

Eleanore said that her mother was looking for a new daddy for them. "But that daddy isn't you," she said. She spoke so serious sometimes. Her eyes were so clear. She would grow up to be amazing, brilliant, and beautiful. She should have a good family.

Eleanore taught me how to say "I love you" in sign language. She also asked why I had not been there for her birthday. I told her I would do everything I could to be there for her birthday the next year. She was very happy to hear this.

Victor stayed silent mostly. He played with his cars but did not say anything to me. Not even when I asked.

Eleanore took my hand and led me around the room. She kept trying to pull me to other rooms, but I was afraid if I was alone with her I would be framed again. I could not lose what little contact I had with my two sweet babies.

The monitor agreed to take a picture of me when I asked. Eleanore and Victor climbed on to the couch to sit next to me. I folded my arms in front of me as proof that I was not touching them. I smiled in a real joy having my two children sit near me. It was the happiest I had been all year. I wanted more of this. I wanted to see them every day. I wanted to love them and support them and help them follow their dreams. I wanted to listen to everything Eleanore thought to say. Even if she told me the same thing three times.

I had to say goodbye to my children at two o'clock. I could not hug them, but only shook their hands. Eleanore asked if I was coming back. I promised I would spend more time with them.

When I left, my son finally spoke. "Where is he going?" he asked the monitor.

"He's going home," she told him.

"Why does he have to go?" he asked her as I left. He wanted me close. He knew I was supposed to be close to him, even if he did not share that with me. I waved to my children and left immediately because I did not want to shed tears in front of them.

I saw Beth coming to pick up the children. I said, "Hi." She stared at me. I called out, "I still love you." She kept staring. I waved my hand and left. On the way to the car I told myself that no other woman's beauty could compare with my children's mother. She would always be my first love.

I wondered if I could ever forgive my ex-wife and her family. Yes, of course. I hurt because I love my ex-wife and her family. I am upset because I see them walking away from the principles of the Gospel. My soul is deeply scarred because I can see my innocent lovely children becoming victims. I pray for the time to come when I can tell my ex-wife and children how much I truly love them.

The last time I saw my children it was a rainy day in December. It was two days before Christmas and I could not believe I was able to see my children again. Twice in the same month. I hoped it would become more frequent.

I prepared a gift for my children, for the monitor, and for Beth. I wanted to show them I cared. The last time Eleanore had told me that if I wanted her mother to be happy, I should bring her a gift. At only four she was already thinking of ways we could get back together.

I parked the car in front of the monitor's home. I saw Beth's car parked there as well. Beth sat in the backseat with a sad expression. I walked into the house to see my children.

Eleanore and Victor sat on the couch and looked up at me. They seemed sad. Neither of them spoke at first. I wanted them to recognize me as their father. I held out their gifts toward them. That only seemed to upset them more. I could not understand what child would not want a gift. I brought out a few pictures of them from when they were small so they could recognize I had been with them then. I did not have many of Victor. I offered to tell them stories of when they were little. The monitor put her hand on my shoulder and said that I could not show them these pictures.

They played slowly. Victor sat on the other side of the couch and moved his toys around. Whenever I looked at him, he would stop. He seemed about to cry. I could not figure out what had happened that morning to upset the children.

I asked my children to open their presents. I tried to make them feel comfortable. Normally children jump at the chance to open a gift. I asked Eleanore to open her present. She did not want her gift. She would not talk to me and looked away when I approached her. This was so different from the week prior when she had wanted to tell me everything.

After forty minutes of my arrival, the monitor told me the children are especially confused this holiday season and advised me to leave. Beth still sat outside in the car; I could see from the window. The short visit was probably arranged before my arrival. I had no choice but to leave. I did not have a chance to play with my children. I told them goodbye and left.

It hurt to leave. It hurt to leave the place where my children were. It hurt to see their joy not expressed at the holidays, at their father, at presents. It hurt to see them hurting and to know I could not help. Beth could not help them either. It was her and Angela's lies that kept them in this state. It hurt because I did not know when I would see my children again.

Beth sat in the car, crying. I looked at her. She looked away. I sat in my car and started the engine. Beth climbed out of hers and walked toward the monitor's house. I drove near and rolled down my window. I called Beth's name. She turned to look at me.

"After all you have done, what have you gained?" I asked. She turned away. I did not see my children again.

I joined the Mormons because they taught that God is love, and we can love God by loving His children. I love His children and my children. They are the same. The Mormons also taught family can be together for eternity. I don't want only eternity; I want family for this life as well. Family means a lot to me. To me family means love, concern, and care. Love is not a word we say when other words cannot express our emotion. Love is a care that is expressed every day in every action. You cannot claim to love someone and then continue to hurt them. This is not love. This is sickness and selfishness.

I believed Beth would love our children. Yet she hurt them. She damaged their minds and stole their childhood from them. This debt could not be repaid. There was no apology that could give our children back a childhood free from baseless fears. They were taught to fear the same being who gave them life, who only ever regarded them with love. This was destructive and selfish. Beth and Angela's ugly deceptions affected my children's childhood and adulthood.

My son and daughter are so young. They have little life experience and can only know what they are told. If they are told untruths that scare them, they will learn to be scared. If they are told things to lift their spirits, they will be lifted. Their mental health is precious and has been used as a tool to break apart our family. Beth and Angela know what they have done. They know how the dirty lies they told will haunt them. Their lies cannot stand under the light of truth. They might have won the battle in court and succeeded in breaking apart my family. But for what gain? They are not better off. Neither are my children.

Do they not know that no earthly reward can compensate for failure in the home?

I had to sell my house with the tall, wooden fence, Beth's garden, and rooms for each of my children to pay the court costs and lawyers. I sold the house that I bought with money from years of working to pay for the lies Beth and her mother told about me. They lied and I paid. I did not have anywhere else to go. Luckily, in California it was warm at night. For many nights I slept in the car with Wang Chan. We would share a couple hamburgers and then sleep with the windows rolled most the way up so too many mosquitos did not get in. They still got in.

I tried hard to live a good life and find the American dream. I did not think it would be taken away because of falsehoods told behind tears. I had lost everything I worked for, but what hurt most of all was to lose my family, my children.

I decided to take a trip. I needed a new perspective. My third sister had moved to Canada with her husband. I boarded a plane to visit them. I looked at Los Angeles from the plane window. This city had been cruel to me. I wished I could stay away from this city forever. But my two babies lived in this city. They needed their father to help them develop their minds and souls. I had to encourage myself to conquer all challenges for the sake of my children's future and happiness. I brought them to this earth. I'll would do the best to love them and take care of them. I'd always had one wish for my children: to grow up in a healthy environment. This wish could only come true if they grew up with their father. This was clear now. It was clear as the skies above the white clouds.

The high clouds were as white as my wife's wedding gown when we walked out of the LA Temple. I wished we could have spent our lives together until our hair has turned as white as that beautiful gown. But my mother-in-law took a black marker, closed her eyes, and vandalized my wife's gown without thinking about the consequences. Our love was no longer pure. It eventually tore apart, tattered and dirty.

I have tried many times to forget my past. But as long as I am living, it will continue to haunt my mind. Every time I think about the past, I feel I have irritated a wound deep in my soul that has yet to heal. Sometimes I ponder over these events in a lonely room or in a quiet park. This kind of serenity cannot mend my broken heart. What could mend it is seeing my children grow up with me, have a good education, have their own families, and have a good job they enjoy. They deserve peace and happiness. That is all that can heal this hurt.

When I returned to Los Angeles, I could not find my children. I called Beth's lawyer to set up a visit. I called the courts to get the judge to order a visit. I talked to the leaders of the church. I talked to everyone I could. Eventually Beth's lawyer called me back. He could not reach Beth either. They were not there.

I did not know where they went. I searched and searched. I could not find them. It was my duty to care for my children and I could not fulfill that because they had been taken from me first through lies and then through distance.

I will continue to look for them. I must. I love them. This will never not be true.

Meeting

I decided to find my dad. I had questions only he could answer. My mom and G-ma would not begin to discuss the situation, and I had been too young to remember all that happened. But my dad would know. I wanted to know who he truly was. If he was a rapist, I wanted to know that. If he was a cultist, I wanted to know that. I deserved to know who I came from.

Alan and I moved first to New York for his job, then to Tennessee to be near his family. In Brooklyn, we had a beautiful little girl with my eyes whom we named Violet. When she was two, just grasping her voice, we decided she should grow up close to her extended family and left New York for the South. It was then I decided to contact my dad. After all, whoever he was, he was family.

I didn't know anything about where my dad lived or what he was doing, but I had the old printout from the BYU police detective with my dad's email address. One late night, while Alan and Violet slept in our small apartment, I finally gathered the courage to send my dad an email. I wanted to believe I was safe, but I had a visceral reaction to contacting him. There was a sense of danger in even trying. I took extra measures to ensure my safety, creating a separate email address and an entirely different account that couldn't be linked to my name, location, or any other personal information whatsoever.

I wrote a very short email saying hello and that I was his daughter. And I asked if he would be willing to correspond with me and told him I had questions. I heard nothing back. The first few days I checked every day, then it became once a week. After a couple months had gone by without a response, I decided to try another approach. The printout mentioned a character reference my dad had provided to the police, a former mission companion of his, Elder Anderson. I wrote to this stranger, explained I was Jack's daughter and was trying to get in touch with him, and asked if he knew how I could reach my father.

Mr. Anderson responded a few days later. My initial excitement faded as I read his defensive message. He wrote that he would only pass along my message to Jack if I could guarantee it wasn't malicious or intended to hurt or accuse him in any way.

His response offended me. I couldn't understand why he would think I wanted to hurt my father. I had been the one who had been scared and hurt. I was the one who had been in hiding. I was angry that Anderson was being so protective about connecting me with my father. But I knew my anger wouldn't help. I needed courage and calm. I assured the former Elder Anderson that my intentions were sincere; I simply wanted to make contact.

Anderson gave my dad my alternate email address. Two days later, I had a message from him. I knew I shouldn't be afraid to read it, but I was. My entire life I had been taught he could use words to change my mind, to split my personality. I didn't know if that power could come across through email. But I had to find out what he said.

The email was loving and respectful. He wrote, "Is this true? Is this true? Is this my daughter, Eleanore, after all these years?" He didn't expect anything from me. He might have been afraid of scaring me away. I remained cautious in my responses. I did not give him any personal information. He didn't know I was married, had a daughter, or even my last name. I slowly asked him questions over email, taking my time.

He explained that he didn't respond before because he did not check that other email often, plus he'd been very busy moving from Taiwan back to the United States with his wife and daughter, my half-sister.

He told me of his life and how happy he was to be in contact. I asked questions to understand his perspective. My mom had always warned me that he would make up stories, and he would always lie, and never be truthful, so I approached our conversations with that expectation.

I asked him about the divorce to compare with the court documents I had seen in the box of evidence. He responded with a detailed spreadsheet timeline of his life. It had dates from all the important events in his life, when he had a certain job, when he didn't have a job, when he was baptized, and when I was born. He highlighted the date of the information I asked for. I was so impressed that he was so cooperative. He answered everything and was not, it seemed, hiding what had happened from me.

Through these email exchanges, I gradually lowered my guard. My dad was very respectful, never prying into my personal life. If he asked questions I did not want to answer, I simply would not answer them, and he wouldn't bring them up again. He did not have any expectations of me, expressing only gratitude for our communication. There was zero resentment of not being in contact for twenty-five years. I realized over the course of these emails that he wasn't the person I'd been told he was. I no longer felt that he was a threat.

While emailing was nice, my ultimate goal was to actually meet him in person. I could keep emailing, but if I didn't see him at some point then I would never get to truly know him. He was not going to be around forever. I wrote him a short email that merely asked, "Hey, can we meet?"

His response was enthusiastic. "Yes! Tell me when and tell me where." He let us choose a location where we'd feel comfortable and pick the time. He promised he would be there. My dad had recently moved to the United States and lived in North Carolina, about an eight-hour drive from our home in Nashville.

I wanted a neutral place. Someplace with other people where my dad wouldn't know anyone and no one would be associated with the cult. We settled on meeting at a Starbucks in Asheville,

North Carolina, about halfway between us. We set the date for a couple weeks ahead and began to prepare. Though I was determined, I felt incredibly nervous. I had gathered plenty of information about him, but he knew nothing about me. True to the habits I'd grown up with, I remained guarded about sharing personal details.

We discussed our plans with Alan's family. Initially, we thought Jim, Alan's step-dad, should go in first with a concealed weapon just in case there was cult activity. I would go in to meet my dad, while Alan patrolled the parking lot watching for any sort of satanic vans outside. Just to be safe.

When Alan's mother heard all this she raised her hand in front of me and asked, "Why? Just why, Eleanore? Why would you do all that? Do you have any actual reason at all to believe that you're in any sort of danger?"

Logically, the answer was no, though it seemed ridiculous to not take every possible precaution. After all, I was willingly going to meet the person I'd been running from my entire life. We had to make sure I would be safe no matter what might happen.

The truth was, we still didn't know who this person really was. His emails were friendly, but that didn't necessarily mean anything. The fear I felt was visceral. My body shook and my hands clammed up every time I thought about meeting him. Still, I started to question every reason for being afraid. One by one, we dropped the precautions. We weren't going to have Alan's step-dad there. No concealed weapons.

I did not know anything about him. Truly. He had answered my questions about the past, but those were all just words. Words coming from someone I'd been warned never to trust. I didn't understand what my dad wanted or why he'd agreed to meet me completely under my terms. Yet somehow, none of these facts mattered. It didn't matter who he was or what he had done. Maybe he was every bit as horrible as my mom had described. Maybe he was orchestrating a large cult operation to kidnap me, Alan, and Violet. I didn't know. He was my dad. That was pretty much everything I knew.

I also knew he deserved to meet his daughter, just as I deserved to meet him.

Alan loaded up the car. I carried Violet to her car seat, strapped her in, and sat in the passenger side. A four-hour drive separated me from finally seeing my father. Then I would know for sure—for myself—what kind of person he was. I might find my long-lost father after two and a half decades of misunderstanding, or I might never return to our home in Tennessee.

Driving to Asheville felt surreal. The trees in the Appalachian Mountains grew thick and close to the freeway. I watched them pass in wonder. The sky blazed more blue, the trees more green than ever before. Violet cooed in the backseat as we drove. Alan spoke occasionally, but his words floated past me. I watched the world fly past the windows and felt the truth that this could be my last day on Earth.

The evergreens cast shadows across the road. The drive was both the shortest and longest car ride I had ever taken. I wanted to soak everything in. Every signpost was important, every sound Violet made was precious. I did not speak for hours. I only wanted to absorb the world around me before I died. I felt like I was driving toward my death. And also toward the truth.

I envisioned no tomorrow or any years after. Yet surprisingly, I wasn't scared or nervous. Instead, a calm settled over me. There was a peaceful, solitary feeling of this being my final day. I was going to meet my father, the man who had threatened to kill me, who had tried to kidnap me, who had abused me and used me for satanic rituals. I was going to meet him, see him face to face. I would see my face in his and then it would be the end. Alan and Violet would have to live without me, knowing I couldn't live with not knowing. They would remember me as a martyr for the truth, for knowledge, and they would understand the reality of the situation. They would stay safe, hidden, and know that I died seeking truth.

I felt for their loss, and felt my own. I would not see the sun rise again. These trees would be my last memory of earth. Everything would soon be over. I would meet my makers: my father and my Lord.

This life seemed little more than a dream. I remembered my mom waking us in the depths of night because we had to move immediately. I remembered leaving town not knowing if I would ever see my friends again, unable to say goodbye. I remembered watching for anyone wearing the wrong colors or if someone looked too long at us. I remembered hearing about my abuse while G-ma talked on the phone. I remembered feeling broken for so long. I was baptized for Jesus when I was eight years old like all good Mormon children, but the devil had gotten to me first. I had been made impure before I had a choice in the matter. I remembered all the pain and fear that the abuse could happen again if I made one mistake—if I told someone my address, or we opened a gift The Fly had sent us, or I heard the wrong combination of words.

I had been afraid for so long. We never knew where the cult was, who was listening, what they were plotting against us. The fear was real. I was afraid of my father, afraid for my life, and afraid of all the destruction I would meet if I ever ever made any mistake.

This was not a mistake. Finding my father and meeting him was both intentional and dreamlike. I could die. I could live the rest of my life as a slave to Satanists. But I had to know. I had to see him for myself and make my own judgment.

We pulled into Asheville early. The first hotel we stopped at was booked full. So were the second and third. Some event must have brought crowds into town. The nervous part of me wondered if it was the cult. They all came to town to ambush us and finally capture me. This was not logical. I had to rationalize with myself. I waited in the car while Alan went in to check for vacancies. I didn't hold out much hope, but we needed a room.

We visited hotel after hotel looking for any vacancy. Some had signs advertising that they were full, while Alan checked the others. At the last hotel we could find, Alan left me and Violet in the running car and went in to ask. They had just one room left, the Presidential Suite with two bedrooms off a living room. It was 500 dollars a night. We only needed one night.

Alan looked at the concierge and said, "I know this is going to sound crazy, but my wife and daughter are in the car. The reason we're here is because my wife, Eleanore, is meeting her dad for the first time in over twenty-five years. Is there anything you can do for us?"

Touched by our story, the concierge offered us the room for half price. We had the huge suite all to ourselves. A full kitchen and living room, two bedrooms with two beds each. It was the nicest hotel room I'd ever stayed in. We unloaded our bags but couldn't rest. It was time to meet my father.

We parked in a crowded grocery store parking lot. The Starbucks was inside. I scanned the surroundings: the trees on the hillside, the carts pushed into the corral, the cars parked in their painted lines. I didn't see anyone watching for me. I looked for unmarked vans, for people wearing red and black. My eyes were trained to spot the cult, and I stayed alert.

I hugged Violet close in case I never came back out. Alan could see inside and would wait for my signal of safety or to notify authorities if anything went wrong. Alan and Violet waited outside for my signal or for danger.

I walked into the run-down grocery store, the air conditioning blasting above the automatic sliding doors. It rushed past my ears with a deafening rush before giving way to the calm of the store. I turned toward the Starbucks' seating. There weren't many people. I saw a Chinese woman sitting next to a little Chinese girl. Then I saw a man in a green baseball cap sitting across from them. I could only see the back of him. Still, I knew that was my dad.

All my fear melted away instantly. I was overcome with happiness. The woman, who I later learned was Lily, my dad's new wife, saw me first and started getting excited. My dad realized what was happening from her reaction.

He turned around and our eyes locked. He stood up as I walked toward him. We both started crying before any words were spoken, before any contact was made.

We hugged. I hadn't expected to get close to him. I didn't expect to touch him. I didn't expect any of that. But I gave him a hug, and it was so good, and it was so right.

I waved to Alan to come in. I introduced him and Violet to my dad. I called him dad. This was the first time in my life I could remember calling someone dad. "Dad," I said, the word strong and new on my tongue, "this is my husband, Alan. And this is my daughter, your granddaughter, Violet." Violet came running up to him. Until this moment, he had no idea he had a grandchild. He was ecstatic.

He didn't know what to do with himself. He spoke with his thick accent and was very much trying to take care of everyone. He wanted to make sure I was comfortable, asked if Alan needed anything, and couldn't contain his joy at meeting Violet. His daughter, my half-sister Harmony, was only four years older than Violet. Harmony immediately sat on the floor next to Violet and began playing with her toys. We all gathered around a table at the Starbucks.

Alan spoke to them in Mandarin. It amazed Lily and my dad that he could speak Mandarin. The three of them conversed while I sat there oblivious. They perhaps didn't realize I couldn't understand them. My dad and Lily kept gesturing towards me as though they were addressing me directly. I just smiled at their excitement. After a minute, my dad reached into his back pocket and pulled out a folded picture. It was very worn, folded over and over again, almost falling apart. It showed my dad sitting on the couch between me and Victor. We couldn't have been older than Harmony and Violet. My dad had his arms folded and we sat on either side of him.

My dad had tears in his eyes as he showed me the photograph. Lily spoke to me in English. "He has looked at this picture every day since I've known him. He never gave up looking for you two. Even when everyone asked him, 'Jack, what are you doing? You are never going to find your kids again. It has been twenty-five years. What are you thinking?' Still, he never gave up looking. He wanted this more than anything. Even one big reason for us moving to the United States was that maybe he could find his kids. He wanted to be here in case maybe, he could see you again. He never gave up hope for this day."

That explained why he would pop up in our lives. He was consistently looking for us. Even after decades of no information and no contact, he kept searching. He didn't have an address. He had no clue where my mom had taken us. He kept writing G-ma at her post office box and sending gifts. We never received any of them. He never got any response from us or my mom. That didn't stop him. He loved us and wanted to see us. He held persistent to the belief that one day he would find his kids again.

He showed me the folded picture then looked at me. I held the photograph, worn on the corners, and looked back. "This is the best day of my life," he told me.

I knew then my father wasn't a bad guy. He wasn't the man I had heard about. He wasn't looking to kidnap us or to enslave us. He wanted to find us because he missed us. He wanted to be with us because we were part of him and, as a loving father, he wanted to keep us safe.

We sat at the Starbucks for hours. I told my dad a history of my life, things he missed and couldn't have known. I told him all about Violet. I asked him questions and he told us stories of Taiwan, then of coming back to America. There was so much to say. It got quite late without us noticing. We lost track of time until the loudspeaker came on in the grocery store to announce they were closing. It was almost 10 o'clock and we were the only ones left. We continued talking in the dark parking lot.

Alan asked my dad where they were staying. "Oh, uh, we wanted to come straight here and see you. We will go find a hotel room now. Then we can see you tomorrow?" my dad replied.

Alan and I looked at each other. There were no hotels available. We had searched for an hour and rented the last available room in town. Alan and I didn't say anything, but continued to stare at one another.

This moment tested me. I had set out to meet my dad and his family. It was one thing to meet him; it would be a whole other thing to share a hotel suite with them. If we didn't, they would have nowhere to go.

My dad, Lily, and Harmony were walking to their car. We called them back. I couldn't muster the words, and motioned to Alan to speak. "Hey, um, this is the situation. There are no available rooms in this town and we happen to have a two-room suite. If you want, you guys could come and stay with us."

They were so grateful and followed us to the hotel. We pulled into the parking lot and they pulled in behind us. Alan looked over to me. It was obvious that this was too much for me. I wasn't saying anything, but I was internally freaking out. It was just too much. I hadn't eaten. I was emotionally overwhelmed. And now I would be staying overnight with the man I had been running from for twenty-five years.

I looked at Alan. "I gotta go," I said.

"Ok. Here are the car keys. Here's the hotel room key. We're going to be here when you get back." Alan took Violet out of the car and I got in the driver's seat. I had to go somewhere. I just had to leave.

My dad looked at us, "Is some of you driving away?" He asked Alan. His eyes filled with concern, fear, worry, care. He was talking to Alan. "Where is she going? Where is she going?"

"Oh, she's really hungry. She is going to go and get some dinner."

"Ok, I'll go with her," my dad said. He was meeting his daughter for the first time and now he was watching her drive away. "I'll go. I'll go with her."

"No," Alan said. "She needs some time, alone. She is a little overwhelmed. She'll be back. Let's go to the room and get settled."

My dad respected my wishes. "Oh, ok. Yes, yes. Whatever she needs."

I put the car in reverse, saw my family standing together in the rear-view mirror, and drove forward without any destination.

I was overwhelmed. I hadn't known what to expect, and everything weighed on me. I needed to process. I was maxed out, and I was hungry. I drove around in darkness under the towering trees of Asheville for what seemed like ages until I found a glowing neon open sign. I pulled into an O'Charley's, a place I'd never been in my entire life. I was in a daze.

I went in and stood in front of the hostess, making no eye contact, saying nothing.

"Um, do you need a table?" she asked.

"Yes," was all I could manage. She went to get a menu for me.

Everything felt surreal. The world seemed to vibrate and stand still simultaneously, clashing and yet soundless. It was all too much. Sensations flooded me that I couldn't process. While the hostess went to find a food menu for me this late at night, I desperately needed something to hold onto. Everything felt like it was slipping away—becoming too large to grasp and too small to hold. But I wanted something tangible. My brain was in a loop just looking for something. Something I could hold. Something I could make familiar and real. Something that wouldn't slip away. I searched for anything to anchor me.

I spotted the little basket of crayons they kept for kids. I grabbed a green crayon from the hostess station and held onto it. It was my green crayon now, and I just gripped it. The waiter led me to a table. I scanned the menu and found a salad I could add chicken to. I ordered, and the waiter left me at my table, alone.

In the nearly empty restaurant, I sat holding my green crayon and I started crying. I cried and cried until I couldn't cry anymore. I was sobbing uncontrollably when the waiter returned. He was a young kid with a beard and a ponytail and seemed to be concerned. He placed the salad in front of me and walked away. I continued crying. I must've eaten a few bites of my food, but I don't remember. I was too overcome with all kinds of emotion, and I just cried.

After a while, the waiter returned. "Do you want a piece of pie? No charge. I could get you, you know, a piece of pie."

I didn't eat pie at the time. It was not in my diet plan—something I could still control even if the world felt chaotic. "No, thanks." I refused the pie. I paid and left with my little green crayon.

My dad, Lily, and Harmony were already in bed when I entered the suite. Alan asked how I was doing. I started crying again, but softer now. The tears had mostly drained from my system. We got ready for bed in silence. Violet was asleep in the other bed.

Alan and I lay next to each other, both overwhelmed. I couldn't believe how the day had turned out, couldn't believe my own father was asleep in the same hotel room. Alan and I looked at each other, and I sort of nodded at him. He stood up and locked the bedroom door—just in case.

We had planned to meet at a park the next day to continue our conversation, but since we had the presidential suite, we gathered in the living room instead. Lily, my dad, Alan, and I sat on the couches between the rooms while the kids watched TV.

"Dad," I said, the word still clumsy on my tongue, "this may be difficult to understand, but I need to ask you some questions and I need you to be honest with me."

"Oh yeah. Anything you want to know. I'll be completely honest. You know, any information that you want, you know, for my daughter, you just ask. Anything. Right?"

I had prepared a list of questions I needed him to answer. I started with the hardest one: "Dad, did you ever rape me?"

He looked shocked but answered immediately, "No, I have never raped you. I have never raped anyone. No. Never. I never even thought about that."

"Ok. Have you ever killed anyone?"

"No. No. I have never. I never killed a person. I was in the army, but I never had to kill."

His sincerity was striking. He showed no judgment or anger at my questions, just a genuine desire to answer anything I might ask.

"Are you, or have you ever been, part of a cult?"

"A cult? I'm not sure what a cult means. I'm not sure. When I lost my kids, when I lost you, the Mormon church, they would not help me. I asked them. I asked the bishop and everybody. They would not help me get my kids back. And they were very unkind to me. It did feel like the Mormon church had good people in it, but they did not help me. They did not keep their promise of the family like they said. When that happened, I went to a Catholic church for a little while. Is that what you mean? A cult, like the Catholic church?"

"No, that's not what I mean. I mean a cult, a real cult."

Alan began speaking Mandarin to them. In Mandarin, the common word for cult translates to "bad church." My dad had thought the question had something to do with the Mormons and Catholics. Alan translated our conversation from English where he could for Lily, who helped relay the meaning to my dad in Mandarin. I felt incredibly grateful for having married someone who spoke Mandarin. Without Alan's help, true communication would have been nearly impossible. Once they explained what Americans mean by "cult," my dad's immediate answer was no.

Then I started asking about the sexual abuse.

"Have you ever abused children, like sexual abuse?"

"What does that mean?"

Alan was translating for Lily and she was dumbfounded. She had no idea that my dad had ever been accused of any of this. She was shocked. "Is this how American people do things? Do they accuse each other of these things? In China, we never even talk about these things, much less accuse somebody of them." She was visibly upset about the stories I'd been told as foundational truths. "This is not the Chinese way. This is not what we do."

My dad answered every question. He had no idea he'd been accused of such terrible acts. He explained that the divorce court had claimed he had hurt the children to justify taking away custody. He'd been furious about not being allowed in the courtroom during those discussions. But everything about a satanic cult and brainwashing was completely new to him. He had never heard of it and did not know anyone who had. He found this all out for the first time while we talked. He was not angry, but so confused.

"When would I have brainwashed my children? I did not see my children. I did not even know about Victor's birth until after. Don't you have to be close to someone to wash their brain? Can you brainwash them when you don't even know where they are, and you are not close, and you are not allowed to see them?"

We worked through all my questions. He wanted to ensure I had answers, and we both wanted everything exposed. His approach was much different than my mom's. He wanted to talk. He wanted to share. He did not want to hide anything.

As we talked through these difficult questions, I experienced a unique physical sensation I'd never felt before. I was overcome with an unmistakable sensation of relief. It felt like I was trapped inside a stone sculpture of myself. With each question I asked, I could feel pieces of stone falling off of my body. As my dad talked, reassuring each doubt and suspicion, more and more pieces fell. They fell off my head and shoulders, off of my legs and back. I could physically feel the stone falling off of me. I had never felt this before. I began to feel so light and free.

When one piece of stone fell off, it opened a place in my mind where I could hear myself speak internally. It said out loud but still in my head, "I've never been raped. I've never been raped." Growing up that fact had defined so much of my identity. It was who I was. I was a victim of the cult. I was a rape victim. It had shaped what I knew and what I ran from. I had all the symptoms of rape, the trauma, the fear. I had been dealing with all these, and I realized none of it was true. I had never been raped. The cult never abused me. There were no trigger words. Nobody was trying to find and kill us, kidnap us, or sell us as slaves. None of that had ever happened. I had never been split.

The stones fell from every pore. I could feel them crack open and fall away. I was almost surprised no one else could hear them breaking apart.

We talked until we had to check out of the hotel. Then we went to a Dairy Queen and talked more. I brought out my laptop with pictures of me when I was little. I showed my dad how I grew up. I showed him pictures of high school and prom, friends, and college graduation. I showed him pictures of my wedding day and Violet's birth. I wanted him to see what he had missed, so it could fill the empty space in his mind. I wanted him to see my childhood, my growing up, my journey to adulthood. I wanted him to know who I had been so he could take part, some part, in who I was now.

He was so interested to see everything, to hear anything. He was so grateful. When there were pictures of Victor, he repeatedly pointed them out to Lily, saying proudly, "My son."

When it was time to leave for our drive back to Nashville, we gathered together next to our car to say goodbye.

My dad stood beside me, unashamed of the tears in his eyes. He looked right at me, and he said, "I met my daughter today. That is so important. I met my daughter. I don't know if I am going to meet my son. I would want to see him, but I am so happy I met you."

He wanted to know when we'd see each other again. He assured me I could call him anytime for any reason. He wanted to establish a connection, and when I told him I would stay in touch, he believed me.

We shared a deep hug before driving our separate ways. I watched him leave, then Alan, Violet, and I began our five-hour journey back home, five hours in the opposite direction, a decade back to Nashville.

At home, I understood myself more clearly than ever before. Moreso, I could get to know who I was with integrity, pulling from an actual history—one based on a love too long denied. Released from the phantoms I had shrunk from for twenty-five years, I could now rise unafraid and begin to piece together who I had always been.

I finally knew the truth. I had answers to questions I'd barely known how to ask in areas I had been told to never question. I reached out and made contact with my biggest fear. I had seen what I was running from, and who I could now hold dear. I had met my dad.

The End

Behind The Panic

Throughout the 1980s, a wave of fear gripped North America in what is known now as the Satanic Panic. This moral hysteria was defined by the belief that a vast underground network of satanic cults was ritually abusing children, brainwashing adherents, and torturing any who threatened their power. It sounds extremist and surreal now. But at the time, it was accepted as truth and a present danger by therapists, pastors, law enforcement, and courts.

It began, in large part, with a book. Michelle Remembers, published in 1980, was marketed as a true account of satanic ritual abuse "recovered" through therapy. In it, Canadian psychiatrist Dr. Lawrence Pazder helped his patient and future wife, Michelle Smith, unearth what they claimed were repressed memories of childhood trauma at the hands of a satanic cult. The book was filled with grisly, cinematic details: demonic ceremonies, sacrifices, and torture, all hidden behind suburban respectability. Though it has since been thoroughly debunked, the book gave a narrative shape to a growing cultural anxiety.

Because of this and the widely televised McMartin Preschool trial, by the mid-1980s, fear of "ritual abuse" had become a national obsession. High-profile trials dominated headlines and sermons, with daycare workers and teachers being accused of unthinkable crimes. Children—many just toddlers—were subjected to extensive interviews and therapy sessions, often led by adults already convinced that satanic abuse had occurred. Under guidance, children produced details that substantiated adult fears. The more shocking the story, the more it was believed.

Los Angeles became one of the epicenters of the panic. The city's multiculturalism was twisted into suspicion. Immigrant families, especially Asian households and Buddhist practitioners, were faced with baseless accusations stemming from xenophobia and cultural ignorance. Any practices unfamiliar to the dominant Christian narrative were seen as suspect and sinister. To the fearful, emboldened by moral authority, difference became danger.

These biases shaped who was accused and who was believed. Communities actively lobbied for charges not based on evidence, but on the emotional certainty that something "evil" must be behind their discomfort. The courts, too, were often unequipped to question the emerging therapy techniques and how malleable a child's memory could be under repeated, suggestive questioning.

It is also true that abuse of children did occur. But for many, the idea that their own trusted men—fathers, brothers, pastors, and priests—could be responsible was unthinkable. Rather than confront real abuse stemming too close to home, they turned to the myth of organized satanic cults to protect reputations while still expressing outrage. In this collective misdirection, genuine harm was obscured by fantastical claims, preventing accountability and compounding the trauma of survivors.

Families were torn apart. Careers were ruined. Scores of people—many entirely innocent—were imprisoned based on inconsistent, coerced, and spurious testimony. Some remain behind bars today. In later years, many children who had testified recanted, saying they were scared, confused, or told what to say.

The Satanic Panic was deeper and more convoluted than a hyperbolic moment of cultural overreaction. It became an entrenched belief system that shaped religious practice and prayers, media coverage, law enforcement practices, and sparked nationwide social anxiety contemporaneous with the "Stranger Danger" that flooded after-school Public Service Announcements.

This panic has not gone away. The tendency to blame shadowy groups for the world's ills lives on in today's conspiracy theories. The language has shifted, but the pattern is familiar. When communities can't face the harm within, they reach for the comfort of a distant villain.

All these fears, under the guise of protection, masqueraded as truth. The baseless Satanic Panic weaponized fear and dictated protocol for peace officers, all the while cloaking itself in righteousness. This mass hysteria, justified by "good intentions," had enough power to upend lives, and reminds us how easily fear becomes dogma, and how nefarious that dogma can be when disguised as moral certainty.

Afterword

What follows is a transcript of the last recording James (Fan Yung-Chi) made for this memoir. It is transcribed here exactly as told to represent his language, cadence, and philosophy.

This is my last tape, I guess. Because I almost tell you all of the things that I know.

I have so many appreciations. Even though I was born when the second war ended. After the second world war, many country's people become very poor. Most of them work very financially poor because of the war and some family lose their members. But no matter what, I am lucky I am survived. My family members they all survived. Now I live in a peaceful time, no war. Everybody focus on how to live a better life.

Even though my life has been many difficulties has happened to me. Basically because I don't have much life experience. If I have more life experience, I know many things that will avoid me to involve something that is not right. Even though I am survive. I feel I am lucky.

I also want to let you know that I very appreciate our universe. Our universe is so huge, so big. There is no boundary. There are billions of galaxies. Our solar system, our Milky Way, has one sun called our solar system. And they have eight planets. They have one, number third, they call Earth. And it's beautiful planet. And I was born here. I appreciate the Earth provide me water, the fresh air, the mountains. This is a beautiful planet. Also the sun. And it provide me the air so I can breathe. And the sun also give me the warm, the heat so I won't feel cold.

I have all these good things in front of me every day. So I should know how to enjoy this life.

Also, I appreciate that I live in the country that has freedom. This country can provide me my free religion, whatever I like to believe. I have the freedom to move around. I have freedom to do whatever good business I want to. I have the freedom to vote. Compare other countries. This country is the best suitable for human being. Also, they have lots of environments for me to live. If I like to live in the desert, I move to the west of this country. If I like to see lots of greens, trees, rain, whatever, I can move to the east. If I want very cold, I move to Alaska. This country has many different weather for whatever people like to live.

I also know there is no such perfect countries. But if there is something happened that we would like to change we can use our vote to change policy. Every individual people has the right.

Right now I am very satisfied with my life. First, I want to let you know I have very good family. I have three children. Lydia is my oldest daughter.

I feel she know lots about life. I feel she knows how to enjoy her life, she already enjoy her life pretty much. She's very smart. She's very soft-hearted person. She cares about her loved ones, her family, and the people around her. And she has one beautiful, smart daughter. She is my first grandchildren. I love her so much. Every time I think about her I feel how beautiful life can be in the future. Also, my daughter has one man that really love her. They respect each other. I can tell they are such a lucky couple. I wish this love can stand for their entire life.

Regarding my son I don't know that much. But as far as I know he's fine. As his father, I will always love him. He's my only son. There is not anything that can compare my love to him. I always love him.

My youngest daughter, Melody, is very kind person actually. Is very nice kid. In school study she's very good. She study very very good. She's so smart. In the future when she grow up she like to be like her mother a doctor, she says she wants to be a doctor. Her college she choose Harvard. Well, it's a beautiful dream, but time can tell. If she is study good, at least no matter what she know life pretty much. I taught her a lot.

You know. Safety is important. Enjoy life is important. No matter what kind of job she like to be, once she know how to enjoy life, how to do the right things, that is all enough.

My wife work every day. And she already know how to enjoy herself, how to take care of herself. She's a nutrition doctor. She know how to eat properly. My home, we eat almost everything is organic. If we can buy. Our milk, our apples, egg, meat, fish. All of these, of course, organic. And other things too, whatever we can buy. Even it is more expensive, but she feel that health is worth it. So we eat very good healthy food every day.

Of course she can make lots of money to do whatever she need. But because we come to rich country, she become a regular worker. Even though the money is not a lot. At least we have enough money to pay bills, that's all we need.

My wife and me we all join the gym. I want to play basketball about five days a week, every time about two to three hours. Melody join the gym too. She went to the gym at least five times or six times a week. Every time is about two to three hours. And Melody has her swimming class. And Thursday she has piano class. Our family so far everybody live healthy lifestyle.

My wife and me don't fight often, of course argue sometimes. But I remember she put piece of paper on the wall, has two regulations for me to follow. Number A say wife always right. Number two is if wife has do something wrong, please refer number A. (Laughs). We have these regulations so we don't have to fight. It's useless to fight.

Our house is not a big house, but we pay for it. We own house. Our car is not new car, it is not fancy car, but it runs good. That's all we need. I don't want any brand name, you know. Anything that is suitable for me to wear I wear. My wife buy some brand name stuff, but I don't. I prefer everybody is healthy.

I also know every family has their story, has their difficulties. But if you know, you know the universe, you know enjoy life, everything can overlook. Once you are alive you have chance to solve your problems. People who are still alive have to know safety and how to know take care themselves. That why I feel every day is peaceful life. That's all I need. All my family need. All my members of my family need.

If I have more things to tell you I will let you know OK. Buh-bye.

James Fan, 2019

About the Author

Lydia Knight

Lydia Knight is an author, professional speaker, executive coach, expert on neurological thought patterns, and recipient of the *Sacred Service Award*. Her innovative approach has earned recognition from major outlets like *The Wall Street Journal*, CBS, NBC, Fox News, Yahoo!, and beyond. Knight is the founder and CEO of **The She Center**, a top 2% woman-owned business globally. Knight has taught leadership and communication trainings for the U.S. Army, for those in Forbes 50 Over 50, and for team members at National Geographic, Disney, and Adobe, among others.

Lydia Knight lives in Santa Fe, New Mexico with her partner, daughter, cat, chickens, and a pure-white ball python.

For inquiries on Knight's availability for speaking and coaching, contact info@theshecenter.org.

About the Author

James Fan

James Fan is a hard-working man of business now retired. Born and raised in southeastern Taiwan, where his family has lived for twelve generations, he was the first in his lineage to immigrate abroad. In the United States, he founded several businesses before returning to the Far East to prioritize his health and to document his story.

James Fan shaped his memories into narrative and, with the help of his doctor who later became his wife, translated his journals into English. Together they have one daughter. He is also the father of two children from his first marriage, as detailed in this book.

Fan enjoys cooking and playing basketball at the YMCA where they know him as "Sky Hook" for his signature shot. A proponent of "Safety First," he will share his life philosophies to any willing to listen. He lives with his wife and daughter in Las Vegas, Nevada.

GOOD MEDICINE PRESS
Where Stories are Sacred

Good Medicine Press publishes bold, soul-stirring works that challenge the status quo, honor ancestral knowledge, and open space for healing, truth, and transformation. We amplify underrepresented voices—particularly those of women, people of color, Indigenous storytellers, and historically marginalized communities—to uplift narratives that inspire a more just, connected, and equitable world.

We believe that reading words written in courage and authenticity is an act of liberation—one that helps deprogram internalized oppression and reclaim voice, power, and self. Every book we publish is an offering: a disruption of systems that harm and a celebration of resilience, community, healing, growth, and radical hope.

At **Good Medicine Press**, we publish books for a world where stories redefine what is possible, where diverse voices are centered, and where literature becomes a sacred force for restorative change.

Discover more at goodmedicinepress.com

GOOD
MEDICINE
PRESS